W9-ASQ-553

19.50

NUMBER FIFTEEN

The Walter Prescott Webb Memorial Lectures

Essays on Culture and Society
in Modern Germany

[THE WALTER PRESCOTT WEBB MEMORIAL LECTURES]

Essays on Culture and Society in Modern Germany

BY DAVID B. KING, CHARLES E. McCLELLAND
DAVID L. GROSS, GORDON A. CRAIG
GARY D. STARK, VERNON L. LIDTKE

Introduction by LEONARD KRIEGER
Edited by GARY D. STARK *and*
BEDE KARL LACKNER

Published for the University of Texas at Arlington by
Texas A&M University Press: College Station

Wingate College Library

Copyright © 1982 by the University of Texas at Arlington
All rights reserved

Library of Congress Cataloging in Publication Data
Main entry under title:

Essays on culture and society in modern Germany.

(The Walter Prescott Webb memorial lectures; no. 15)
Includes bibliographical references and index.
Contents: Culture and society in modern Germany /
David B. King—The wise man's burden / Charles E. McClel-
land—Kultur and its discontents / David L. Gross—[etc.]
    1. Germany—Civilization—19th century—Addresses,
essays, lectures. 2. Germany—Civilization—20th century—
Addresses, essays, lectures. I. King, David B. II. Stark, Gary
D., 1948– . III. Lackner, Bede K. IV. Series: Walter Prescott
Webb memorial lectures; 15.
DD66.E7   1982   943.08   82-40315
ISBN 0-89096-137-9

Printed in the United States of America
FIRST EDITION

092636

Contents

Preface   ix

    Gary D. Stark and Bede Karl Lackner

Introduction   3

    Leonard Krieger

Culture and Society in Modern Germany: A Summary View   15

    David B. King

The Wise Man's Burden: The Role of Academicians in
Imperial German Culture   45

    Charles E. McClelland

Kultur and Its Discontents: The Origins of a "Critique
of Everyday Life" in Germany, 1880–1925   70

    David L. Gross

Irony and Rage in the German Social Novel: Theodore
Fontane and Heinrich Mann   98

    Gordon A. Craig

Cinema, Society, and the State: Policing the Film
Industry in Imperial Germany   122

    Gary D. Stark

Songs and Nazis: Political Music and Social Change in
Twentieth-Century Germany   167

    Vernon L. Lidtke

Preface

ON March 27, 1980, the University of Texas at Arlington sponsored the fifteenth annual Walter Prescott Webb Memorial Lectures. The four lectures delivered that year, as well as the two winning entries in the Webb-Smith essay competition that are also reprinted here, explore the interaction between culture and society in modern Germany.

Professor David B. King of Oregon State University, winner of the 1980 essay competition, examines German resistance to the modern cultural values and social institutions that have emanated from western Europe since the sixteenth century. Germany's historic divergence from the Western experience culminated, in our own century, in nazism. While King argues that the catastrophe of the Third Reich finally discredited Germany's long-standing refusal to join the modern Western core, he also questions whether Germany may now have swung too far in the other direction, embracing Western models more uncritically than is healthy, either for Germans or for the West.

In his contribution, Professor Charles E. McClelland of the University of New Mexico illuminates the values and the subculture of imperial Germany's academic elite and explores the role of cultural leadership that fell to these academicians. As McClelland makes clear, it became increasingly difficult for the embattled German professoriate to uphold its rigid cultural traditions in a society that was undergoing rapid modernization.

Several German academicians sought to develop a sophisticated methodology for analyzing the modern mass culture that emerged in the late nineteenth and early twentieth centuries. Their efforts are detailed in Professor David L. Gross's essay, runner-up in the Webb-Smith competition. Gross, who teaches at the University of Colorado, demonstrates how, in conceptualizing the problems of everyday cultural life and in devising a suitable form of cultural criticism, these theorists moved steadily from a conservative, rightist to a socially radical, leftist orientation.

Another vehicle of social criticism, the German novel, is examined by Gordon A. Craig. Craig, Professor Emeritus at Stanford University and featured speaker at the 1980 Webb Lectures, asks why penetrating social analysis so rarely appears in works of German literature and why when it does, as in the novels of Theodor Fontane and Heinrich Mann, it has failed to have much of an impact upon German society. The answer, Craig concludes, lies in the tastes of the German reading public and in the peculiar German view of the proper function of literature.

Professor Gary D. Stark, of the host institution for the Webb Memorial Lectures, analyzes the rise of the popular cinema in imperial Germany and the response of the political and cultural elite to this new form of popular culture. Because German leaders initially regarded the cinema as a threat to both the social order and high culture, the state sought to censor and otherwise to limit the influence of the film industry. Only during the First World War, Stark finds, did the elites in imperial Germany begin to realize the political potential of the popular cinema and use it to mobilize and manipulate mass opinion.

German music and song, another form of popular culture, were used even more effectively in the 1920s and 1930s for political ends. As Professor Vernon L. Lidtke of the Johns Hopkins University demonstrates, the Nazis' political music mirrored the eclectic origins, broad social appeal, and emotional dynamism of their early movement and served an important propagandistic function in their rise to power. After the establishment of the Third Reich, music and participatory singing were used by the regime to mobilize and socialize the masses and to help create an aura of legitimacy for the new Nazi order.

Collectively, then, these essays address several broad and significant problems of modern German history: Germany's responses (especially by that nation's social and cultural elite) to the emergence of modern social relationships and modern mass culture; the relationship between elite "high" culture and "low" or popular culture; and the reciprocity of the cultural and sociopolitical domains.

We and the Webb Lectures Committee wish to express our gratitude to all those who have made this undertaking possible—the contributors to this volume, the audience and other participants in the lecture series, the faculty of the University of Texas at Arlington, and above all Mr. C. B. Smith, whose esteem for Walter Prescott Webb originally inspired this lecture series and whose generous support makes it all possible.

GARY D. STARK
BEDE KARL LACKNER

Essays on Culture and Society
in Modern Germany

LEONARD KRIEGER

Introduction

THE essays that compose this volume finesse the much-debated problem of the continuity or discontinuity of German history by focusing upon those sectors of the German past that, in contrast to most political history, have to do with middle- or even long-range structural issues: the sectors of culture and of society and the relations between the two. Three major issues are confronted in these essays: the high-cultural vogue of neo-humanism; the integration into this high culture of popular-cultural motifs, which are inseparable from mass democracy; and the growing convergence of high and popular culture, concurrent with the growing democratization of life in the twentieth century.

Clearly, these are universal issues that take an inescapable form in Germany because of that country's decidedly authoritarian social structure (attested by the longevity of its viable aristocracy) and because of its tradition of cultural indifference toward the affairs of this world, especially its political deeds and its social arrangements. These issues—the neo-humanistic authoritarianism of a stratified social structure and the problem of the social and cultural integration of the masses—reached their apogee during the latter part of the nineteenth century and the first part of the twentieth century, when the hierarchical social structure appropriate to Germany's industrial civilization was challenged both from within and from without: from within by an academic elite that at once upheld an aristocratic principle against the triumphant economic bourgeoisie and made its peace with it, and from without by the newly conscious masses who were playing a larger role in industry and the state. The fact that the academic elite and the masses possessed a common opponent—the society and culture of industrial capitalism—shows the connection between the two issues. For, during the industrial period, the emphasis on nonutilitarian neo-humanism was clearly an exercise of the preindustrial upper crust. This was true both outside of Germany and within the country distinguished as the special land of "poets and thinkers." This neo-humanist stance was embraced by a preindustrial social and cultural elite that was deemed compatible with the industrial sector, yet it was directed against the industrial society and culture and its utilitarian proponents. At the same time, and particularly during its mature industrial period, this utilitarian bourgeois society and culture was being denounced for its hypocrisy by the democratic masses it had spawned. Mass culture, in other words, emerged in Germany when both the established culture that was its main target and the neo-humanist tradition that helped to attack it were still strong. It is on this crucial period—roughly the imperial, Weimar, and Nazi eras—that these essays are focused.

In the essays that follow, the stress is upon the alternatives that Germans envisaged to the established culture and the established society for which it spoke: the reactionary alternatives of the neo-humanist tradition or its National Socialist projection and the progressive alternatives of a newfangled popular culture that contravened the hypocritical religiosity and hollow secularism of the established culture of the burghers and their aristocratic henchmen. Thus, Charles E. McClelland describes both the neo-humanist orientation of the German academic elite and its championship of purposeless knowledge vis-à-vis the utilitarian and technical emphases first of the economic bourgeoisie and then of the masses. McClelland shows that despite support from the political elite of the imperial era, the cultural mission of the conservative academic elite by and large failed in this period. This failure was partly because the values of this elite, grounded as they were in the language and conditions of classical antiquity, were more appropriate to the earlier period of the nineteenth century than to the decades that followed, when its clientele underwent important changes, especially democratization. It was also partly because the two bases of neo-humanism—classicism in education and scientific (*wissenschaftliche*) specialization in practice—proved to be mutually inconsistent under the changing circumstances of the late nineteenth and early twentieth centuries.

David L. Gross concentrates on the criticism of the established culture that was emerging along with the new industrial society, and he shows the twofold movement of this criticism as one moves from the cultural and social conservatism of the imperial age to the experimentalism of the Weimar period; that is, he demonstrates both the movement of cultural criticism from the Right to the Left during this era and the movement from an abstract rejection of mass culture (which the early critics on the Right considered to be merely an extension of the established culture) to the leftist critics' acceptance of this culture and their attempts to emend it in a popular direction. Gross demonstrates this dual shift in German cultural criticism through detailed analyses of the theories of Georg Simmel, Georg Lukács, and Walter Benjamin; he shows the development from a starting point in the concrete phenomenon, universally and formally interpreted, through a holistic Marxism, to the particularistic cultural Marxism of Benjamin and, later, of the Frankfurt School. In so doing, Gross demonstrates how this movement eventually transcended its German origins and came to fulfill a generic integrative function in the modern cultural life of the West.

Gordon A. Craig analyzes an analogous process in the field of imaginative literature. One can perhaps see in Craig's intellectual portrait of the novelist Theodor Fontane, that "gentle critic," a parallel to that misunderstood and despised academic pessimist, Georg Simmel, and in his discussion of Heinrich Mann a parallel to Gross's selection of Lukács, who like Mann received his training during the imperial era but attained his fame during the years of the Weimar Republic. Two points about these novelists (both of whom wrote at a time when traditional values were being challenged by the arrival of the masses at the level of moral, social, and political accountability) become clear from Craig's treatment: first, that the use of irony is a social weapon against those who formerly transmitted and applied values; second, as attested in Heinrich Mann's obsession with the idea of power, that the turn of the century is a period when social and political rights meet. In Craig's mind, German literature has been atypical of western Europe's in its relative indifference to social and political themes. Fontane and Mann, then, are German literary critics who have been influential instead of representative in their function.

The union of society and politics in the context of mass participation in culture, society, and the state becomes explicit in the essays by Gary D. Stark and Vernon L. Lidtke. Stark's paper stresses the repressive stance adopted by upper-class administrators toward the new medium of the cinema, for in the perception of these administrators the cinema fostered in the masses immorality and religious, social, and political irreverence. This new popular medium, Stark argues, actually did involve the lower social strata, especially the urban working class. The upper-class social prejudices of Germany's civil and military administrators obviously affected their political judgments of the dangers and usefulness of the cinema as a popular medium. Thus, Stark shows the shift that occurred in the attitude of the authorities toward the cinema during the last, war-torn years of the Wilhelminian Empire: they abandoned their negative policy of mass repression and adopted instead a positive policy of mass integration, equally in the service of the established order. This shift toward an appreciation of the more positive functions of mass culture presaged the future manipulation of mass culture by the Nazis, who, as Lidtke shows, relied heavily on popular songwriting and singing as a means of controlling the German masses.

Although Lidtke's focus is on the peculiarly German and the particularly political relationship between song and National Socialism, his essay serves also as an object lesson in the pattern of mass integration by the extreme Right of Europe, of the union between the state and society in the treatment of the masses, and of the growing identification of elite and mass culture in the social movements characteristic of our century. This pattern is especially evident in the years before the Nazi takeover, when existing songs were adapted by ordinary Nazis, but can also be detected in the final, "songless" years of the Nazi wartime regime. For the middle period of 1933–39, Lidtke adopts the newer trend in interpreting nazism that argues for the authenticity of the Nazi appeal to the working masses; for it was during these halcyon years of the Third Reich that song became an "instrument for indoctrination and socialization" by the Nazi regime.

The opening essay by David B. King is maverick in that it does not dwell upon the period or the phenomena of popular culture in the late nineteenth and the early twentieth centuries, but it does concentrate upon the kindred general problem of the historical relations between Germany and the rest of Europe. King assumes an early convergence of social structure and politics in both the German and the generic Western cases, and he assumes, too, a modern age lasting from around 1500 to around 1880—that is, until the start of democratization in politics, equality in society, and the cultural counterparts of these changes associated with the names of Einstein, Planck, Freud, Kandinsky, and Schönberg. He then posits the parallel expressions of society and culture and argues for Germany's critical participation in the generic West's modern age. According to King, developments in Germany bore a considerable resemblance to those in western Europe through the time of the West's generic crisis of the seventeenth century; only in the heyday of modernism, characterized by the rise of a strong bourgeoisie and the recurrent spells of Enlightenment in the West during the eighteenth and nineteenth centuries, did the Germans adopt a critical stance toward the modernity in which they shared, and only then did they increase their social and cultural distance from the core areas of the West. King concludes that Germany, like the generic West, graduated from the modernism of the nineteenth century, evolved its own brand of antimodernism in the twentieth century in the form of the Nazi movement, and has grown back toward generic modernity since 1945—at a time, ironically, when the culture of the generic West has become postmodernist and when Western society threatens to become so as well.

These essays thus provoke reflection on three of the main themes in modern Western history: First, what has been the relationship of Germany to the generic West, of which it both has been and has not been a part socially and culturally? Second, what is politically conservative about the neo-humanist tradition? Third, what has been the pattern—or, if there is more than one pattern, what have been the options—of integration of the democratic masses into the political, social, and cultural scene so long dominated by elites?

First, then, what has been the relationship of Germany to the generic West? Those who see Germany as an integral part of the West can hardly avoid the comparative view that judges things German by things English and French, while those who see Germany as a sector of central Europe independent of the West and existing in its own right view things German as *sui generis*. The answer is that of course Germany forms and has always, at least since medieval times, formed an essential part of the Western political system, of Western society, and of Western culture, but that it has always expressed Western tendencies in an exaggerated manner. As King indicates, Germany's participation in the West has most obviously emerged during the romantic "subepochs" of Western culture, when great names like Kant, Goethe, Schiller, Hegel, Schelling, Heine, Nietzsche, Rilke, Freud, Einstein, Planck, Heisenberg, Tillich, and Küng testify to German leadership, even German dominance, within a shared culture. But what is not so obvious is the exaggerated German participation in the pan-Western motifs of humanism, Enlightenment, industrial capitalism, and scientism. The relationship between Italian and French humanism on the one side and the German Reformation on the other is clear for the sixteenth century. It should be pointed out too that the German vogue of enlightened absolutism, personified in Frederick the Great of Prussia, in the Hapsburgs Joseph II and Leopold II, and in the Grand Duke Karl August of Sachsen-Weimar, simply carried the work of enlightened ministers in the West, like Pitt the Younger and Turgot, one step farther along the road to increased royal power. Additionally, there was in the nineteenth century not only the post-1850 German rush to match and surpass the British in establishing an industrial economy (a tendency King sees as a main element in Germany's modern economic and social convergence with the Western core), but also the German scientific community, peopled by such luminaries as the Du Bois-Reymond brothers (Emil and Paul) and Hermann von Helmholtz, who were influential on the European scene as well as authoritative at home. Even during the Weimar period of the twentieth century the classical Marxism of the West was carried beyond its standard base by German theorists like Karl Korsch, Ernst Bloch, and the Frankfurt School, while artists amplified Parisian avant-gardism into Berlin experimentalism, which in its boldness outdid the twentieth-century culture of the generic West. The pattern of German-Western relations seems clear: the German case can be seen as an exaggeration of the generic Western tendencies, with Britain and France constituting the core societies and cultures of the West during the eighteenth and nineteenth centuries.

The second theme on which these essays provoke reflection is the relationship in the West between neo-humanism and political conservatism. The elite of German academic mandarins, who are the protagonists of McClelland's essay and the targets of the cultural critics Gross analyzes, were considerably more closely associated with nationalist and establishmentarian causes than were neo-humanists in the rest of the West. The perspective of these essays gives the definitive lie to the idea of the unpolitical German and places the emphasis where it belongs—on the conservative political consequences of the putatively unpolitical stance of neo-humanism. It is well known that both Wilhelm von Humboldt and Goethe were, despite their administrative posts, relatively unpolitical as well as classical in their interests; if they helped to set the tone for the association of neo-humanism with indifference to politics in the German cultural tradition, they also set the tone for the implicit conservative political consequences that stem from a nominally unpolitical emphasis on neo-humanistic educational values and a life-style consisting of seemingly selfless scholarly pursuits.

The political consequences of the proverbial German indifference to politics were made clear by the extreme Right at the end of the nineteenth century, when Lagarde and Langbehn, as Gross points out, wrote an unacademic critique of contemporary culture in which they associated political commitment with liberalism and rejected both of these in the name of national German *Kultur.* Although, as Gross shows, these extremist nonacademic critics included the culture of German academics among their targets, actually this academic culture represented the neo-humanist sector of the National Liberal portion of Germany's dominant political and social elite. Throughout the nineteenth century, from Humboldt to Heinrich von Sybel, neo-humanism was the cultural value system best suited to an elitist intellectual estate that sought somehow to reconcile a liberal state with an established hierarchical society. In this sense German neo-humanism was representative of the more advanced industrial societies to the west. When Germany was unified under politically conservative auspices in 1870, this neo-humanist intellectual elite tended to side with the aristocratically dominated national state; and if the preindustrial aristocratic core of Germany's newly unified state and society was atypical of the rest of the West, the politically conservative slant of the German academic elite was not.

As McClelland and Gross equally demonstrate in their different approaches to the same phenomenon, by the end of the nineteenth century German academic culture had become not only socially but politically establishmentarian. This occurred partly in response to the conservative reunion of state and society and partly because of the new challenge posed by the recently enfranchised masses, including the reinforced economic bourgeoisie. What they do not say, in the absence of comparative studies of British and French societies of the same vintage, is that this "mandarin" culture of Germany was representative, in an exaggerated way, of the generic West. When the Liberal William Harcourt, an earl's son who was exposed to the British neo-humanist educational track, said around 1870 that "we must educate our masters," he was undoubtedly thinking in terms of the establishmentarian integration of the mass electorate, created in 1867, into the existing state and social structure in Britain, an integration that was to occur under neo-humanist auspices. The movement of wildcat strikes by industrial laborers, women, and Irishmen against the progressive Liberal regime in Britain after 1910 shows both the success and the failure of this endeavor: success insofar as the oppositional movement, except for its radical Irish sector, merged into the defense of the national state after 1914, and failure insofar as the movement occurred in Britain at all. But in any case this sociopolitical protest movement, arising from the depths of British society and mirrored in the theoretical vogue of socialism, shows the representative character of the superficially opposed German development; it shows, that is, the politically conservative character of the dominant elitist culture in the West, when it was forced into political assertion by the continuing conservative administrative and military sinews of the state and by the new threat from below in both society and politics.

This brings us to the third theme of our reflections, which indeed overlaps the second just as the second overlaps the first. The problem of the pattern by which the democratic masses of the late nineteenth and early twentieth centuries were integrated into the political, social, and cultural scene so long dominated by elites overlaps the theme of the politically conservative character of the elitist culture that did the integrating, just as the theme of the politically conservative consequences of the dominant neo-humanist culture raised the question of the relationship between this German culture and the rest of the West. For, whatever the objective situation, the political and social equalization of the masses with the elite was perceived as a single movement (as made clear by the German-educated Spanish philosopher Ortega y Gasset in his *Revolt of the Masses* [1930]). This perception of a combined political and social threat from the working class and lower middle class succeeded in synthesizing the sociopolitical prejudices of the academic bourgeoisie throughout the West in a way the utilitarian challenge from the economic bourgeoisie never could. Indeed, the utilitarian aspects of capitalism, embodied in the economic bourgeoisie, were seen by the working and lower middle classes as integral parts of the established society. The stress by the masses on practical, vocational education and on their coming liberation from the bonds of bourgeois domination was considered different in kind from both the neo-humanism and the utilitarianism of the bourgeois establishment. The masses correctly viewed the long-standing struggle between the academic and the economic bourgeoisie as an internal struggle within the establishment, for they and their theoretical representatives saw neo-humanism as simply the cultural expression of the social feudalization of the bourgeoisie.

As the essays by Gross, Craig, Stark, and Lidtke demonstrate— Gross and Craig indirectly, through the critics of integration by the establishment; Stark and Lidtke directly, through their descriptions of the policies of the imperial and Nazi integrators—the masses have been integrated into the institutionalized society. At least five means were employed for their integration.

First, there was old-style repression by the elites of the moral, social, and political claims made by the working and lower middle classes. As Stark makes very clear in his essay, and as Craig demonstrates indirectly in his, the objective of the repression was moral and social as well as political. The fact that the repressors enjoyed both an authoritative social position as well as political power no doubt alerted them to the menacing analogous amalgamation among the masses of political convulsiveness with moral and social claims. As Craig in particular shows, the taste of the masses was one of the elements in the repression; so too was the taste of those like Fontane and Heinrich Mann who spoke for the masses in social and political terms, as against the nonsocial and nonpolitical posture of the neo-humanistic repressors.

Second, there was the establishment's positive, propagandistic use of the mass media as a means of integrating the masses. This is evinced by Stark in the cinema policies of the military authorities during World War I and by Lidtke in his portrayal of the Nazis' employment of song. The National Socialists' combination of conservative instincts and revolutionary reason appears in their deliberate appeal to the working masses for reverence and obedience. Although, as King maintains, there was no necessity for nazism to be adopted in Germany when it was, nazism was the logical conclusion of the attempts to integrate the masses into the existing economic and social system through authoritarian political means that acknowledged the role of new men in the state as well as in society. In the final analysis, the Nazis applied revolutionary means to a socially and politically conservative end. Although nazism once more makes clear the German pattern of exaggeration, it was a way of integrating the newly risen masses into the Western scheme of society and culture.

A third means of integrating the masses, with their claim to social and political equality, was institutional. Craig notes that one of the chief differences between the sociopolitical messages of Heinrich Mann and Theodor Fontane was the inclusion by Mann of socialist leaders among the targets of his wrath. If we generalize from this apparent idiosyncrasy and add to it both Robert Michels's theory of the oligarchic tendency within German social democracy (drawn from Michels's own socialist experience) and the establishmentarian policies of German social democracy during the Weimar period, then we get the pattern whereby the preexisting social hierarchy and political authoritarianism invaded the trade unions and the party that was ostensibly created by the working masses themselves to realize their claims and champion their interests. Despite the apparent hostility between the court and respectable society on the one hand and the socialists on the other—a hostility that mirrored the French experience and the attitude of Britons toward the Labour party—the form eventually assumed by working-class institutions was but an extension of the form of the established social associations and political parties of the West. They thus became means of integrating the masses into the existing society and the established state.

The cultural analog of this social pattern, and the fourth variety of integration, was the convergence of high and popular culture. As Gross shows for academic life and Craig for literary culture, the critics of late-nineteenth-century and early-twentieth-century culture posited an ideal in which popular culture was merged with traditional, ideal, elite culture. Whether in the detached expository analyses favored by Simmel, Lukács, and Benjamin or in the more judgmental novelistic form adopted by Fontane and Heinrich Mann, the approaches to this ideal endeavored to integrate popular culture into traditional values. In the first instance, Marxism furnished the means of advancing from a contemporary, alienated bourgeois culture to one in which the synthesis of particularity and totality would coincide with the merger of popular or mass culture with humanity—that is, the integration of mass culture with the subjective tradition of humanitarianism. In the second instance, whether we talk in terms of the detached social and political irony of a Fontane or the intense social and political criticism of a Heinrich Mann, we should note the hidden democratic implications of the practical criticism of both novelists: both would use their art to reform society, and the reformation could be only in a more populist direction. (One might add here that the absence of discussion of the masses in Fontane as against its inclusion in Heinrich Mann indicates the progressive populism from Fontane to Mann, a development that can be compared to that from Simmel to Lukács and Benjamin in academic circles.) Moreover, whatever the critics said—and often they spoke in the vague terms of an undefined mass utopia—what they actually did, when they were concrete about the future, was to integrate popular culture into tradition rather than to work the other way around or attain an independent new cultural stage. This kind of integration was the function of Marxism in the Frankfurt School (which included Benjamin as a marginal participant) and the function of the morality in the social and political criticism by the novelists. Unlike the counterculture of the 1960s, then, but on the way to it, the convergence of mass and elitist culture in the early decades of the twentieth century was a means of integrating the masses into traditional culture by using popular culture to revitalize a tradition that had grown old and calcified with partial secularization.

The fifth and final means of integrating the masses that is revealed in these essays was the promise of a future realization of the good society—that is, of a society that is good for the masses. According to Gross, the gap between the rejection of the existing culture by the extreme Right in the imperial era and the improvement of the existing culture that was the message of the extreme Left in the Weimar years was one of the main differences between the intellectual life of the Second Empire and the intellectual life of the Weimar period. The difference is explicable both by the change in political and social conditions between the two regimes and by the course of intellectual evolution from Simmel's timeless doctrine of the tragedy of culture to Benjamin's historical doctrine of the potential value of contemporary mass particularity. The future junction of popular and traditional humanitarian values was the promise held out to a mass society by leftist

Wingate College Library

intellectuals, who adopted a Marxist framework precisely to ensure the realization of such a prospect. The desperate promise of the good society and the union of popular and elite culture lay behind the sophisticated Marxism of the Frankfurt School, into which both Lukács and Benjamin afford insights, and behind the adoption of Marxist politics by a Bertolt Brecht, after his contradictory commitment to an elitist new objectivity and to the desirability of a popular culture. The presentist orientation of Nazi songs in the 1920s and 1930s, as revealed in Lidtke's analysis, stands in contrast to the future-oriented posture of theoretical Marxism in both the pre- and the post-Nazi eras.

These three subjects, then—the relationship between Germany and the generic West, the political consequences of the unpolitical (that is, the neo-humanistic) Germans, and the mode of integrating the masses into the social and cultural structure during the last part of the nineteenth century and the early decades of the twentieth century—are the issues that the papers comprising this volume raise in the mind of one historian and for the resolution of which they supply useful information. For each reader the issues that are raised may be other, or may be more. Certainly, the essays here presented are provocative and informative enough.

DAVID B. KING

Culture and Society in Modern Germany:
A Summary View

THIS essay will offer an interpretive summary view of Germany's modern culture and society, suggesting that both have been shaped in large part by the circumstances of their confrontation with the institutions, systems, and cultural styles that emanated from the Western core during the Modern Age. Modernity arrived late in Germany and was received ambivalently. Germany had been accustomed to a role of political leadership and cultural eminence in the Middle Ages; yet after 1500 she found herself rather suddenly victimized by the various shifts that accompanied the phasing out of medieval patterns and the introduction of their modern counterparts. And she reacted with a not unreasonable mixture of fear, envy, and disdain. Germany joined the new age, since there was little choice—as others more geographically remote would eventually discover. For as the lines of modern advance spread outward, first the Western peripheries and then the rest of the world were forced to face the same predicament: to preserve a distinct culture it was absolutely necessary to stand apart, but standing apart meant renouncing the West's technology and the military power that flowed from it. There were only two options: to remain unique and vulnerable or to become Westernized and viable.

Thus Germany's commitment to modernism was from the outset more defensive than enthusiastic. And even when modernization came on with a rush and was being, at least on a selective basis, intensely cultivated, its effects were still viewed suspiciously. The initial stance had become habitual, a national style. Modern German culture and society would be modern, but critically modern. Germany became early on and for a long time remained the great modern dissenter, offering from time to time everything from mild objection to moderate heresy to, finally, the thoroughly vicious opposition of the Hitler years. Only after 1945, chastened and repulsed by the apparent results of her resistance, would she make an unconditional and willing peace with the Modern Age.

I

Before moving on to a more specific commentary on Germany's modern culture and society, an explanation is due regarding several assumptions made here. With respect to the core area of the West in the Modern Age—that is, the area within which the basic modern forms were developed and from which they were disseminated first to the remainder of Europe and then to much of the world—it should be noted that its boundaries have never been entirely fixed. Its earliest center was Italy, but Italy was also the first to slip beyond the pale. Spain was part of the core during the sixteenth century, but not after that. Its most consistent nation-states have been England and France, which presided over Western developments when the Modern Age was at its zenith. More recently, the United States—and, some would add, the Soviet Union—have joined the core. Finally, as will be argued below, West Germany must now be included.

Concerning culture and society, it should be said that by *culture* is meant both intellectual production and the *milieu*, or climate of opinion, in which it takes place and that *society* refers to the entire social fabric, encompassing the full variety of orders and classes and manifested most obviously in its political history. As for the causal interplay between culture and society, the essay's position is agnostic. The two are taken to be roughly contemporaneous expressions of broader civilizational movements. They thus would seem to move as a unit, usually following together, in more or less parallel fashion, the path set by the civilization of which they form a part. And when they deviate from that path, as with German culture and society in the Modern Age, they do that also together—or at least often enough so that when they do not, as indeed occasionally happens, we are right in searching for unique explanations. This essay will be for the most part the story, then, not of a culture in opposition to a society but rather of a culture and society united in opposition to their encompassing civilization.

It is also necessary, given the intention of juxtaposing the German experience to that of the Western mainstream, to say something about what is meant by the Modern Age. While it is one of those labels that is used often, considerable disagreement exists with regard to elemental matters, among them the point of origin, nature, inner periodization, and, particularly, current status.

As for the point of origin, despite the arguments for moving the beginning of the Modern Age back to one of the medieval renaissances or ahead to the coming of the scientific revolution,[1] it seems reasonable to keep the traditional date of about 1500 for Europe as a whole, with the acknowledgment that the changes arrived somewhat earlier in Italy. Much that is considered essentially modern had already been foreshadowed and much was still to come, but 1500 continues to offer an adequate compromise.

Concerning the nature of the Modern Age, this essay will again adhere to convention. In politics, it meant, first, the centralization of power, at least relative to what had gone before, and that in the context of the national state; second, the gradual rise of the bourgeoisie. In economics, it meant the joining of an already partly formed capitalism to the new state, within which the new entrepreneurial class would provide the impulse to the creation of a Western-based world economy. And in the realm of ideas—as expressed not merely in art and written works, but in the full range of human activity—it meant the swing to secular concentration, with that *saecula* conceived as intrinsically good. Moreover the benefits of the *saecula* were now seen as obtainable, available to mankind as a whole, but especially to the individual, who was raised to a position formerly reserved for the semidivine and given the free will to prosper and ascend—or, as Pico noted without seeming much to worry about it, to sink to the depths.[2] And, indeed, the modern mind was not given to worrying, at least for long, for it was an age marked by a self-confident optimism with respect to life in this world and a growing indifference to what, if anything, might occur in the next.

Regarding inner periodization—that is, the division of the Modern Age into particular epochs or phases—there has been a recent modification of the older practice. Formerly the only units referred to were the early modern and modern periods. With the emergence of the conception of a general civilizational crisis in and around the seven-

[1]See especially Herbert Butterfield, *The Origins of Modern Science* (London, 1951).

[2]The reference is to Pico della Mirandola's *Oration on the Dignity of Man*.

teenth century,[3] however, a tripartite division has appeared: the early modern, the crisis, and what might be called the high modern.[4] This high modern age, in turn, can be divided into a series of subepochs or phases, each punctuated by additional crises. Thus the first high modern phase was interrupted in the late eighteenth century by a romantic interlude, which was in turn followed around the middle of the nineteenth century by a second high modern phase (named by Franklin L. Baumer, with a view to its intellectual content, the New Enlightenment). This second high modern phase was then also interrupted by a romantic reaction beginning in the 1880s.

At this point, a problem arises within any study that wishes to pursue into the twentieth century the evolution of the Modern Age or, as is the intent here, Germany's relationship to it. For this interruption of the late nineteenth century, the second romantic reaction, was more than merely an interruption. The break is so sharp that many have been led to suspect that the Modern Age has come to an end or that, at the very least, that end is imminent.[5] The evidence is both impressive and confusing, for culture and society would seem for the moment to point in different directions. With regard to culture, it is now well understood that modern forms—the old modern forms generated by the Renaissance and the Enlightenment—were between roughly 1880 and 1930 overturned and all but abandoned in art, architecture, music, and literature. During the same decades, in philosophy, social theory, theology, and, perhaps most strikingly, physics, new ideas and systems were expounded that either returned to premodern assumptions or

[3] See especially *Crisis in Europe 1560–1660*, ed. Trevor Aston (Garden City, N.Y., 1967); Theodore K. Rabb, *The Struggle for Stability in Early Modern Europe* (New York, 1975); and Geoffrey Parker and Lesley M. Smith, eds., *The General Crisis of the Seventeenth Century* (London, 1978).

[4] A sensible effort at periodizing the modern period is to be found in W. Warren Wagar, *World Views: A Study in Comparative History* (Hinsdale, Ill., 1977); see especially app. II, "Comparative Chronologies," pp. 207–208; also Franklin L. Baumer, *Modern European Thought: Continuity and Change in Ideas, 1600–1950* (New York, 1977).

[5] See, for example, John Lukacs, *The Passing of the Modern Age* (New York, 1970). Some of the earlier speculations on the meaning of the cultural revolution are remarkably insightful. See especially Nicholas Berdyaev, *The End of Our Time* (London, 1935); José Ortega y Gasset, *The Dehumanization of Art* (Garden City, N.Y., 1956); and the brilliant essay by Thomas Ernest Hulme, "Modern Art and Its Philosophy," in *Speculations: Essays on Humanism and the Philosophy of Art*, ed. Herbert Read (London, 1936), pp. 75–109.

moved beyond modern thought to positions that can best be described as postmodern (although these are often referred to, misleadingly, as modern).[6] There can be no doubt that the turn of the century brought a profound cultural revolution.

But if modern culture has gone through fundamental changes that would seem to have converted it into something new, nevertheless much of contemporary economic, political, and social life remains relatively untouched and still essentially modern. Certainly it is premature to insist that the Modern Age has entirely disappeared from the stage. Capitalism looks unhealthy to many, but it survives. The national state also has problems, but in some respects it is stronger than ever. The bourgeois family, possibly modernity's crucial societal institution, manages to hang on. Modern ethics are being challenged, too, but they have yet to be swept aside. And modern individualism, at least at the popular level, is still vital, as are the several emancipation movements. Yet no Western society has ever survived a cultural revolution without having experienced, sooner or later (and usually sooner), a revolution of its own. Roman society and its culture proved inseparable; so too medieval institutions and medieval culture. If cultural change remains an adequate index of societal change, then the most probable conclusion is that the Modern Age is well into another of its occasional periods of epochal transition, much like those that marked the West's transformation first from classical antiquity to the Middle Ages and again from the Middle Ages to the Modern Age. If that is so, it gives irony to Germany's present relationship to the Modern Age, for it would mean that, just as German culture and society have finally succumbed, the West may have taken off in a new direction.

II

At the time of Europe's emergence from the Dark Ages, Germany had been at the very center of things. She was the first to unify, and her

[6] In this essay, *modern* refers only to the naturalistic style and associated world view that became dominant during the Renaissance and continued until the late nineteenth century; *postmodern*, to their rejection. There is more to the matter than the problem of superficial confusion. Using "modern" to denote a cultural upheaval that clearly rejected the canons of the Modern Age obscures the significance of what has happened and encourages the assumption that these "modernist" styles and pronouncements are some-

early start permitted her to dominate Italy and Burgundy. The prosperous Rhineland served as a link between the northern and southern European economies. Germany also made important contributions to the development of the high medieval cultural structures. But then, in the later Middle Ages, she entered a period of confusion. The German monarchy, strong in the tenth and eleventh centuries, was powerless by the thirteenth; the economy suffered a lengthy and debilitating depression; and intellectual production reflected fully the stresses brought on by plague, war, and famine. It might appear that it was these upheavals that marked the beginning of Germany's divergence from the Western core. This period saw confusion everywhere, however. As the West's medieval period was drawing to a close, Germany was obviously experiencing difficulties, but her situation was not yet unique. Only as the West recovered and entered upon its transition to modern ways did Germany begin to differ.

Yet at first, at the very beginning of the Modern Age, there was reason to think that Germany would also recover. Renaissance humanism had been drifting northward gradually and was now beginning to emerge as an important strain within the intellectual life of France and England, and much the same could be said of Germany, where Reuchlin, Erasmus, and others were at work. Germany was also participating in a general Western urban revival. If she was not contributing much to the movement of overseas exploration, Gutenberg's press at Mainz served as a symbol both of her cultural vitality and of her technical accomplishment. The new monarchies of Europe's western flank were more distinctly beyond their late medieval problems, but only recently. The French victory over the Burgundians had come in 1477, the end of the English civil war in 1485, and the fall of Granada to the new Spanish kingdom in 1492. It would have seemed to a contemporary that Hapsburg efforts might well produce some sort of German variation on the common theme, as they were indeed intended to do and almost did.[7]

The German nation-state, however, did not gel, nor did any other major aspect of German culture or society from this juncture on quite

how a final expression of that modern age, a dubious proposition. For a discussion of the terms, see Malcolm Bradbury and James McFarlane, "The Name and Nature of Modernism," in their anthology of essays, *Modernism, 1890–1930* (New York, 1976), pp. 19–55.

[7] See G. Barraclough, *The Origins of Modern Germany* (Oxford, 1952), pp. 339–73.

conform to the models being worked out in the Western core area. What made Germany different? Just as it is hard to avoid tautologies in explaining what caused the Middle Ages to become the Modern Age, so it is also in trying to account for the German divergence. The failure to unify politically is often made responsible for much that followed, but it is just as likely a result as a cause. The same can be said of the religious division, which reinforced late medieval particularism but was itself certainly in part a result of already-existing fissures. Luther, after all, did not have to invent Elector Frederick's suspicion of the Hapsburgs.

When we turn to the gradual removal of Europe's economic locus westward in the early modern period, a development of obvious significance for Germany, it is again hard to know how much it should be stressed as a cause. The main trade routes did gradually shift from the Mediterranean-Adriatic-Rhine axis to the Atlantic. But the Hanseatic League continued to flourish. Moreover, there is no reason that Germany could not have joined in the modern push into the Atlantic and beyond. The Dutch did, and so did individual Germans. Still, it is a fact that the balance of economic activity swung to the west, and Germany was, for whatever reasons, left behind.

Germany's geographic position is sometimes seen to have contributed to her modern history in another respect: because Germany is in the middle of Europe, she has been constantly vulnerable to foreign intervention, which continually served to frustrate efforts at unification, which in turn hindered the growth of modern institutions and attitudes. This central position, however, was not an insuperable hurdle to unification in either the tenth century or the nineteenth, and, as with the other suggested causes, it is impossible to unravel the skein of priority. The only thing that is clear is that once Germany's modern path began to diverge its continued divergence was more to be expected. History tends to accumulate. Yet Germany was hardly alone, for most of the West was still outside the core area. For the better part of the Modern Age, vast areas remained more medieval than modern. In fact, some of Europe's more remote enclaves by 1800 had not yet become fully medieval. Thus Germany was idiosyncratic only in that her size, potential power, and proximity to the core combined to ensure that her quarrel with the modern themes would be heard.

If Germany's retention of particularism was her first departure from orthodox modernism, the second was her Reformation. The Western core was of course also to experience Reformations. But in England reform was an import, held in check and subordinated to politics, with the radicals emigrating. In France, Calvinism would seem initally to have had reasonable prospects, but it was finally suppressed. Only in the Netherlands, where it was helped along by the revolt against Spain, was there a full Protestant Reformation. It was not that the Western core was too Catholic for the Reformation in its purer forms, it would seem, but rather too secular, too modern.

But was the German Reformation indeed heretical with respect to modernism? It has been also interpreted as just the opposite, an attempt to breathe the modern spirit into a worn-out medieval religion. Part of the problem is that evaluations have been made with regard to what only later became modern. Luther has, for example, been both praised as democratic for having defied the princes of the Roman church and condemned as reactionary for having turned against the German peasants. But he acted in each instance for other reasons and, like his contemporaries, was not much conscious of democratic effects, one way or the other.

Another difficulty in determining the German Reformation's relationship to the Modern Age lies in the matter of deciding what its essential works in fact were. The creation of a German national church and Luther's translation of the Bible into German were certainly contributions to modernism. If, however, the essence of the German Reformation was Luther's religious dogma, as it would seem to have been,[8] then an estimate rests on one's evaluation of that dogma and especially of its theological centerpiece, the insistence on justification by faith alone. And when the focus is put on the crucial point of Luther's argument, that the individual, without free will and unable to avoid sin, could not effect his or her salvation, the implications are inescapably hostile to modernist assumptions. The modern world has, from its beginnings in the Renaissance through the Enlightenment and on into the nineteenth century, postulated and used as a starting point for so many of its systems a vitally efficacious individual. Luther could not accept such an assumption without withdrawing from his insistence on grace as God's freely given, unearned and unearnable gift. On

[8] See Roland Bainton, *Here I Stand: A Life of Martin Luther* (Nashville, 1950).

this crucial point, Luther would align himself with the early medieval tradition. He may have been forced further into his antimodern corner than he wanted to go by the compulsion of his own logic, especially in his debates with Erasmus, but it is easy enough to see on which side he wished to be counted.[9]

Luther revealed his antagonism to modernism in other ways as well. Not only did he reject the growing secularism of the age, but he also condemned reason's challenge to faith, preferring a theology that returned to its patristic fundamentals. Nor was Luther any more fond of modern science, art, architecture, or economics. The Renaissance was changing the world that he knew, and he found the changes corrupting. The fact that several of the West's Protestant areas later came to play leading roles in the modernization process and in the course of it found their Protestantism modernized as well has tended to lend credence to the view that Luther was a precursor of modernism. But, except unintentionally and peripherally, that was not the case.

The German Reformation in retrospect, then, seems to have given a representative cultural expression to the developing societal circumstances of Germany's early modern history. Already passed by in the rush to modern national unification and empire, and with an orientation toward the Rhine, Baltic, and trans-Elbian East lending also to her exclusion from modern economic and social development, Germany through Luther announced her disapproval of the new ways. Like the Land of Oz, she would not be civilized, if that was what it meant to accept fully the Modern Age, preferring to retain her mysteries. The Modern Age opened with both German culture and German society set upon an independent course: Germany was in the process of dropping out of the new Western economy and had accepted neither the modern state, the modern overseas movement, nor the modern mellowing of traditional Augustinian Christianity. The degree of difference can be overdrawn, but from the very start Germany was clearly renouncing medieval habits more slowly and, when and where she did, opting for alternatives other than those suggested by the Western core.

[9]See Stephen E. Ozment, ed., *The Reformation in Medieval Perspective* (Chicago, 1971), especially the contribution by Bernd Moeller, "German Piety Around 1500," pp. 50–75.

III

Beginning around the middle of the sixteenth century a long period of European growth came to an end and the entire West experienced a general crisis, one that would last until about the middle of the seventeenth (later, if one looks beyond the core). It can be observed, like the great crisis of the fourteenth century, in almost every area of life. A century of economic expansion was once more being followed by a time of disorder, depression, and shifting fortunes. Revolution and war, never absent, were again ever more frequent. France suffered her wars of religion; England, after the stable reign of Elizabeth, soon found herself under the Stuarts on the path to civil war; and the Dutch embarked upon their long fight for independence. In and around all this swirled the great dynastic struggles. Crime increased, too, and in the countryside the highwayman operated freely. Clearly, the authority of the early modern state, challenged at all levels, was in danger of breaking down. And in art, architecture, and music there was change as well, as the mannerist and baroque styles, complex, sensuous, ornate, and emotional, considerably modified those of the classical Renaissance. It should also be noted that this was the century of the great witch craze. Supernaturalism, recently on the wane, returned with a vengeance, and at all levels of society.[10]

The causes of the crisis are again obscure. There are, of course, abundant individual and local ones, but a "wholesale coincidence of special causes,"[11] as Trevor-Roper has pointed out, does not make for much of an explanation; yet it is hard to find a general cause, one that somehow links them all. One possibility that emerges as we gather more information on the history of climate is that European temperatures declined by several degrees, eliminating certain crucial areas from agricultural production and thus delivering a solid blow to fragile early modern society. Still, it would seem that the colder climate only precipitated a collapse already imminent. The Renaissance had come on with a rush, raising many questions and creating much unease. After more than a century of pushing forward, Europe was being seized by doubts.

[10] See Hugh Trevor-Roper, *The European Witch-Craze of the Sixteenth and Seventeenth Centuries and Other Essays* (New York, 1968), pp. 90–97.
[11] Ibid., p. 3.

Whatever the cause or causes, it adds little to our understanding of what was happening in Germany at this time to pursue explanations that have to do only with German history. The reaction was European, not exclusively German, although Germany participated fully. And with both creative and destructive results. With regard to the world of ideas and the cultural milieu, the most articulate German contribution to the general effort at revision and reform of the initial modern positions came from the line of theologians that runs from Jakob Boehme through Philipp Jakob Spener and his Pietist followers. Mystical, inward-looking, much intent on personal authentic experience and disdainful of the orthodoxy and institutional rigidity that had even before Luther's death begun to settle in on German Protestantism, these men provided German counterparts to both the mood of rejection and the search for renewed supernatural contact peculiar to the period. In art, a parallel, if not entirely contemporary, expression is to be found in the German baroque, especially in the Austrian and Bavarian churches and palaces designed by Johann von Hildebrandt, Johann Bernhard Fischer von Erlach, and Balthasar Neumann. Although as it disintegrated into rococo it became increasingly frivolous, this earlier baroque, a sort of modern Gothic, was able to provide religious monuments for an age of revived religious enthusiasm—that was as well, of course, an age of revived persecution and superstition.[12]

In economics, Germany felt acutely the effects of the wider depression of the early seventeenth century, especially after 1620, as a general decline of prices made even worse the chaos produced by constant warfare. The results were to eliminate the network of commerce that had heretofore been sustained, destroy the remaining enclave of prosperity along the upper Rhine, and sink central Europe to levels of hardship that had not been experienced since the initial ravages of the Black Death. And, with regard to politics, Germany, without an effective national monarchy against which to rebel, might be said to have

[12] It should be noted that the baroque was not a rejection of the Renaissance style but a distortion of and elaboration upon it. In this it resembled the general crisis in so many of its manifestations: the early modern themes were bent, but not broken, and were left in a condition that permitted them to spring back into something like their original shapes when the crisis was over. For a survey treatment, see R. Furneaux Jordan, *A Concise History of Western Architecture* (1969; reprint ed., London, 1976), chs. VIII ("Renaissance, Mannerism, and Baroque Outside Italy"), IX ("The Return to Classicism"), pp. 213–82.

created a semblance of one just for the occasion—and then proceeded, with the assistance of the Swedes and the French, to tear it apart with the ferocity for which the Thirty Years' War remains rightly infamous. The results were desolation, depopulation, impoverishment, and, finally, the confirmation of particularism, for the Peace of Westphalia's guarantee of *Landeshoheit*, which in effect granted sovereignty to the individual princes, ensured that no new efforts at national reconstruction would be forthcoming in the foreseeable future.[13]

Still, until this point, the middle of the seventeenth century, Germany continued to bear a considerable resemblance to the Europe of the core, for the general crisis had had its effects there, too. The German pattern had remained more typical than not. If Germany was in disarray, so was most of Europe, or had been until recently. In the second half of the seventeenth century, however, England and France would surmount their difficulties, just as they had done at the end of the late medieval crisis, and return to the business of modernization. Germany either would not recover or, in recovering, would turn eastward to find different solutions. Thus the disparity that would characterize the relationship between Germany and the Western mainstream was increasing as Europe passed into the high modern period.

IV

Europe's Western core not only recaptured the momentum that had been dissipated during the long crisis of the seventeenth century but also went on in the course of somewhat more than a century nearly to complete the constructions that characterize the Modern Age. If the Renaissance had laid the foundations of the modern edifice, then the period of Enlightenment was able to put up the interior skeleton and the exterior walls before the romantics performed their various acts of imaginative vandalism. The restructuring of society in accordance with the requirements of entrepreneurial capitalism; the development of a centralized government, operated in a practical, if stormy, collaboration with both the old aristocracy and the new bourgeoisie; and the ascendance of reason and science to cultural dominance: these were

---

[13] See Theodore K. Raab, ed., *The Thirty Years' War*, 2d ed. (Lexington, Mass., 1972).

the works of the years from approximately 1660 to 1780 in the Western heartland.

Germany's experience was again essentially different, although it took place, as always, within the modern Western context—and with an acute perception of the differences, noted with the now traditional ambivalence. During the general crisis, it had been, in a sense, an excess of bad fortune that had set Germany apart. Now, oddly enough, it was two good turns of the wheel that increased the distance. The first was the acquisition of large eastern territories by Brandenburg in the course of the seventeenth century, with the result that the Hohenzollerns were now tied more firmly to Eastern Europe, where a very unmodern aristocracy was reducing the peasantry to serfdom to facilitate large-scale, single-crop commercial farming. It is interesting to speculate about what might have happened had the whole of the Rhineland rather than Pomerania and East Prussia been joined to Brandenburg at this point; but, as it happened, the new Brandenburg-Prussia was given a push to the northeast.[14]

The second piece of good fortune with dubious consequences came in the form of Hapsburg victories over the Turks in the last decade of the seventeenth century, resulting in the addition of Croatia, Slavonia, the central part of Hungary, and the vast Transylvanian area, giving Austria a corresponding southeastern expansion. Thus, within a half century of Austria's final failure to impose a unification, one that might have guided Germany back into Western and modern paths, both Austria and Prussia set out in new directions. They did not yet have the influence over the rest of Germany they would acquire after 1815, but the fact was that the two largest German states were becoming thoroughly involved in Eastern Europe just as Eastern and Western Europe were drifting further apart. In the early seventeenth century Germany had been at something of a crossroads. Weakened, with the faith in older traditions badly shaken, she might conceivably have pulled closer to the Western core. But Austria and Prussia found it to their advantage to face eastward and thus inevitably influenced German society as a whole to reconstitute itself along eastern lines, and this at the moment at which in the two halves of Europe the bulk of the popula-

[14] See F. L. Carsten, "The Rise of the Junker," in *The Origins of Prussia* (Oxford, 1954), pp. 89–178.

tion was undergoing very different experiences. In the West, the peasant was beginning the long (and uneven) ascent to citizenship and relative prosperity; in the East, he was beginning the rather swift descent
into serfdom. The ramifications for German history were to be tremendous, beginning immediately. The very first effects were felt as Germany attempted to come to terms with the Enlightenment.

The Enlightenment was of course a product of the Western core.
From its beginnings with Locke and his contemporaries through its
late period with Rousseau and his, the movement was led primarily by
the English and French, with the former providing the original innovations and the latter presiding during the decades of its greatest pro-
ductivity. German culture—like the cultures of others on the outskirts
of the Western core—was a recipient, distinctly affected but also ac-
tively contributing. Yet the Enlightenment was never entirely accepted. And it is hard to see how it could have been, arriving as it did
in the early stages of this renewal of the German move to the East,
where Western ideas, whether with regard to art, religion, government, or social relationships, remained foreign and threatening.
Where the Enlightenment did show itself in Germany, it was accepted
critically and had few lasting successes. When Joseph II and his reformers attempted to change aspects of Austrian society to conform to
Western models, they could build only in the temporary vacuum created by royal authority, with the innovations destined to disappear
with the innovators. In Prussia, Frederick the Great was genuinely
committed to the Enlightenment, but he preferred to use its principles
to strengthen the administration of the state, not to share his authority.
Nor did he try to alter the paternalistic-authoritarian bond that linked
the Junkers with the peasantry. If he thought like Voltaire, he continued to govern much like his father.

The *Aufklärer* themselves gave a certain reflection to Western
themes, but the more prominent of them, notably Leibniz and Kant,
espoused philosophies that were recognizably off-center. Leibniz,
whose thought has been described as "proto-romantic organicism,"[15]
directed his arguments against Locke's more typically modern mechanistic empiricism and offered a relativist and immaterial conception of
the universe that turned out to be more similar to that of Einstein and

[15] Wagar, *World Views*, p. 43.

Heisenberg than that of Newton. Leibniz saw order, but for the hard-and-fast, machinelike, commonsensical creation of the *philosophes* he substituted a brilliantly complicated, eccentric world of insular animated units, his monads, each set from the beginning on its preordained course in such a way that an insistence upon cause and effect, the *conditio sine qua non* of most Enlightenment propositions, was entirely obviated. And, while Leibniz defended rationalism, it was a spiritualized variety that reinforced the ultimate harmony of this best of all possible worlds that God might have created. One comes away from Leibniz's thought with an impression similar to that produced when confronted by Western scenes depicted by an artist from another civilization: the view is familiar, but the assumptions underlying the portrayal are essentially foreign.

Kant was equally resistant to the predominant Enlightenment positions, although in part his purpose was to prevent their complete demolition at the hands of David Hume. By this time, the Enlightenment was already fading and in the process of being succeeded by the Romantic movement. Kant's ideas were an interesting combination of both. He retained reason as a tool with which to obtain knowledge, but only of appearances, of the "phenomenal" world, not of the world of true reality. This latter was essentially beyond the reach of rational methodology and could be approached only occasionally by intuition. Thus Hume according to Kant was wrong about the ultimate unreliability of natural laws. The phenomenological world was indeed orderly enough. Still, it was correct to conclude that all was not right with the optimistic claims of the Enlightenment. It was possible to know, and with certainty, but only about that which does not matter. Kant, then, like Leibniz, gave a very German response to the major intellectual problems with which the Enlightenment was concerned. Neither rejected entirely the Western core positions, and, in certain ways, they even strengthened them. In an age of optimists, Leibniz was, for example, a superoptimist,[16] and Kant salvaged what he could of rationalism from its attack on itself. Both, however, were appropriate intellectual representatives of a German society that stood, as it still did, partly in and partly out of the Western mainstream.

[16] Bertrand Russell has pointed out that Leibniz in his private works was not quite the optimist that he was in those that he permitted to be published. See Russell's chapter on Leibniz in his *A History of Western Philosophy* (New York, 1945), pp. 581–95.

For most Germans, the full impact of the Enlightenment was felt just as its vitality was waning, when the French armies carried it across the Rhine during the wars of the Revolution and Napoleon. It then was welcomed with instant enthusiasm, which changed almost as quickly to disillusionment as liberation disintegrated into mere occupation. Nor did the Enlightenment-inspired reform efforts in Prussia of Baron vom Stein and his colleagues have the sort of success that might have rescued the Enlightenment's reputation.[17] With the disappearance of the French model (and menace) that had done so much to inspire them, they withered rapidly. In any case, the mood had already changed. Goethe had written *Götz von Berlichingen* in 1773 and *The Sorrows of Young Werther* the next year. Sentiment was in, rationalism out. In some parts of the West (for example, in North America), the Enlightenment arrived late but stayed a long time.[18] In Germany, however, it arrived late (Leibniz excepted) and left early, without having won a major victory. The Romantic movement that replaced it, on the other hand, was treated much more hospitably.

V

The West's Romantic age began to become visible after 1760 (Rousseau's *La Nouvelle Héloïse* and *Émile* appeared in 1761–62), reached its years of greatest intensity between 1790 and 1830, and then in the course of the 1830s and 1840s was gradually superseded by a revival of Enlightenment themes, which had never lost all their adherents. A consensual definition of romanticism has been hard to produce, for at one time or another it embraced almost every conceivable position, so that one might even at times suspect that there was no such thing. All things considered, it would seem to have been another of those fundamental convulsions experienced by the Modern Age.[19] As the baroque convulsion followed the Renaissance, so the romantic convulsion followed the Enlightenment. And, like the baroque, it was essentially an objection to modernism. Perceptively, the romantic poet Novalis crit-

---

[17] See Walter M. Simon, *The Failure of the Prussian Reform Movement, 1807–1819* (Ithaca, 1955).

[18] Wagar, *World Views*, p. 207.

[19] See the comments in Roland N. Stromberg, *An Intellectual History of Modern Europe* (New York, 1966), p. 210.

icized in just these terms Goethe's *Wilhelm Meister's Apprenticeship*: it was too classical, too modern, not enough romantic.[20] There were, of course, modern elements within romanticism—for example, the concern with the individual. But even these were given new turns.

As one would expect, Germany's tradition of dissent from the modern suited her well during the Romantic age, and her contribution was impressive. The catalogue runs from E. M. Arndt to the Viennese *Zauberpossen* and includes the best, and perhaps also the worst, that romanticism inspired.[21] What is remarkable is not, however, the quality and depth of the German production but that German criticism remained in the aggregate during these years as moderate in its objection to modernism as it did. Goethe, certainly the most prominent German intellectual figure of these years, indeed shared many of the romantic outlook's fundamental positions: rejecting Newton, he preferred an organic and teleological to a static and mechanistic view of nature;[22] he insisted on limits to knowledge:

> Mysterious even in the light of day
> Nature will never let her veil be stolen;[23]

he praised intuition; and, most tellingly, he complained that his efforts at philosophy only ruined him for poetry, his true calling. Yet he never renounced the Enlightenment. In fact, he seems to have viewed it as his mission to join it to romanticism, preserving the best of both.[24] Much the same can be said of the only German of the early nineteenth

[20] See Robert Anchor, *Germany Confronts Modernization: German Culture and Society, 1790–1890* (Lexington, Mass., 1972), pp. 28–29.

[21] For a summary treatment, see Ludwig Pesch, *Die romantische Rebellion in der modernen Literatur und Kunst* (Munich, 1962).

[22] That Darwinian evolution came to resemble Goethe's theories somewhat is perhaps more a comment on the romantic heritage to mid-nineteenth-century science than on Goethe's ability to contribute to a scientific biology. Arnulf Zweig has cautioned that Goethe's doctrine of the *Urpflanze* is "more Platonic and, perhaps, mythical than Darwinian." See Zweig, "Goethe," *The Encyclopedia of Philosophy* (New York, 1967), III, 363.

[23] C. F. MacIntyre, trans., *Goethe's Faust: A New American Version* (New York, 1957), p. 18. Goethe declared that "the highest happiness of man as a thinking man is to have probed what is knowable and quietly to revere what is unknowable." Goethe, *Maxims and Reflections*, ed. Hermann Wiegand (New York, 1949), p. 94.

[24] Certainly the German bourgeoisie was convinced for the remainder of the century that he had succeeded. See Ernest K. Bramsted, *Aristocracy and the Middle-Classes in Germany: Social Types in German Literature, 1830–1900*, rev. ed. (Chicago and London, 1964), pp. 278–79.

century whose stature is comparable to that of Goethe, the philosopher Hegel, who brought enlightening reason and romantic faith together into a new and dynamic synthesis—and then enlisted it, very practically, in the service of the Prussian state.

In these compromises, Goethe and Hegel seem again to have provided a cultural statement that accurately mirrored the contemporary status of German society. After the nearly simultaneous acceptance and rejection of the Enlightenment, Germany was having to deal with a modern residue that would not go away but would become, despite the efforts of Metternich (who, after all, had his own considerable modern residue),[25] the nucleus of an indigenous German growth. For the nineteenth century in Germany was a time not only of romantic dissent but also of industrialization, bourgeois expansion, rapid urbanization, political unification, and, finally, spectacular national power.

VI

By the time Europe was plunged into the upheavals that began in the spring of 1848, the Romantic age had come to an end and been succeeded by the New Enlightenment, what Warren Wagar termed the Age of Improvement.[26] Romantic doubts and sentiments had been put aside. As the Enlightenment had taken up the theses of the Renaissance and made them explicit, this New Enlightenment took up those of the old and made them more explicit still. The result was an intense secular humanism, reinforced by a complete confidence that the rule of science (which had edged reason from its former center spot) meant progress. Liberty had evolved into liberalism, meaning that government should get out of the way of the individual and let the future happen. This buoyant optimism was confirmed by remarkable economic accomplishments, especially in Great Britain.

And in Germany? The history of German culture and society since the middle decades of the nineteenth century can be seen from several

[25] Metternich, like Frederick the Great, would use rationalism to give order to a conservative society, feeding it its modernist remedies only in small doses.

[26] Wagar, *World Views*, p. 95. Wagar's dates are 1840–90. The label was first used by Asa Briggs with a broader period in mind, although the point is the same. See Briggs, *The Age of Improvement, 1783–1867* (London, 1959).

vantage points, and the view is very different from each. The prevailing one in the West outside of Germany, although shared with reservations by some German historians as well, is that Germany failed in her nineteenth-century confrontation with modernism—failed to become truly modern and also failed to find a workable alternative: in 1819, 1848, 1867 (when the Indemnity Bill sanctioned *Scheinkonstitutionalismus*), 1897 (when the Kaiser quietly gave up his experiment with popular government), and in 1918 (when Germany failed to give the Augean stables a thorough sweeping). These failures, then, set the stage for 1933 (when the German Right in effect chose Hitler rather than make concessions to modernism), which brought on Hitler's war and the Holocaust. One might mention one other failure, one that ran throughout: that of Germany's intellectuals, who by their reluctance to embrace modernism and more than occasional attacks upon it encouraged Germany in her long march toward catastrophe.

There is much to be said for this line of argument.[27] Hitler was indeed a product of German history, and it is certainly reasonable to seek his origins in the German past. Further, Hitler was in many ways a product of just those parts of the German past that are unique. Yet this approach, although it is usually not meant to, can easily obscure the fact that the failure of German culture and society to conform fully in the nineteenth century to the modern models was only that, and not a moral failure. Nor is it obvious that Germany's dissent from the modern need have resulted in Hitler. Certainly it is not true that Hitler was in any significant way foreseeable at the times that Germany approached her several turning points, the last, 1933, obviously excepted, although all that Hitler was to do was not foreseeable then, either—if it is true that he had said early on that he would do what he later did do, he had also said that he would not. There is a continuing predicament, no less difficult for being obvious, that dogs efforts to come to grips with recent German history: how is it possible to balance the knowledge that the path led to Hitler, with all that that implies, without becoming a victim of the assumption that the path could have

[27] Perhaps the two best accounts that employ this approach are A. J. P. Taylor, *The Course of German History: A Survey of the Development of Germany since 1815* (New York, 1946), and Gordon Craig, *Germany, 1866–1945* (Oxford, 1978). Both are excellent histories.

led only to Hitler? Surely it is necessary to exercise appropriate restraint in the attempt to identify those instances that would seem to
have committed the German future to National Socialism.

Returning to the mid-nineteenth century and the question of the
relationship of German culture and society to the Western mainstream, several remarks can be made. The first inevitably have to do
with the revolution of 1848 and its outcome, which, however it is as-
sessed, continued to dictate the events of the next several decades. If
1848 was a failure, and it certainly was if measured by the intentions of
the revolutionaries of Berlin, Vienna, and Frankfurt, then that was
hardly remarkable, given Germany's contemporary social development. The middle-class liberals were not strong enough to impose
their constitutional forms on any of the monarchies, to say nothing of
creating a liberal national unified state, be it *kleindeutsch* or
großdeutsch, republican or otherwise. The commercial and industrial
growth that would later create a powerful German bourgeoisie was in
1848 only beginning. Nor did the allies of the liberals, the peasants and
the artisans, offer much in the way of usable revolutionary power. That
this was so is clearly due to the liberals' neglect of peasant and artisan
grievances,[28] but there was very little that could have been done to
bring the two sides together, for their goals were diametrically opposed. Briefly put, the liberals wanted to press forward to a laissez-
faire economy, the peasants and artisans to abolish it or, at the very
least, to contain it in such a way that their traditional enclaves would
not be affected. Had the liberals somehow won out under these circumstances, they could have maintained their position only by em-
ploying a very unliberal authoritarianism. As it happened, during the
reaction that followed the peasants and artisans, still the vast majority
of Germans, were granted concessions that the liberals had been
barred by their ideology from considering.[29]

In the last analysis, 1848 failed for the same reasons that the Prussian reform movement had failed, and before that the efforts of Joseph
II: these were modern reforms, inspired by the historical experience of
the Western core, especially designed to accommodate a strong bour-

---

[28] See Theodore S. Hamerow, *Restoration, Revolution, Reaction: Economics and
Politics in Germany, 1815–1871* (Princeton, 1958), pp. 137–72.

[29] Ibid., pp. 219–37.

geoisie. Not having undergone a comparable experience, and that partly by choice and partly as the result of historical circumstance, Germany would resist. The forces of modernism in Germany may have been more vigorous than the romantics would have preferred, but they were not strong enough in 1848 to re-create Germany in the liberal image. Before the liberals could expect to achieve any of their goals, they would have to accommodate themselves to the facts of both Germany's social history and her distribution of power, which is what was to happen.

German cultural expression during the period of the New Enlightenment seems, puzzlingly, to be divisible into two distinct and antithetical parts. On the one hand, there were the intellectuals of the Frankfurt Parliament. They had clearly opted for modernism and would, consistently, applaud Bismarck's unification and subsequent concessions and follow him enthusiastically as he led them in the 1870s into the *Kulturkampf*, the German contribution to the warfare between science and theology.[30] On the other hand, we have the cultural elite, the creating figures, such as Schopenhauer, Marx, Wagner, and Nietzsche, whose works were explicitly hostile to modernism. Marx and Wagner shared its evolutionary, progressive heritage,[31] and Marx even praised the Modern Age for having disposed of feudal Europe, thereby rescuing the West from its "banal" agrarian condition. But the thrust of most of Marx's and Wagner's thought was consciously antimodern. Schopenhauer conceded nothing at all to modernism, rejecting indeed history itself as meaningless. And Nietzsche, who began with the entirely modern assertion that God is dead, then passed directly to a thorough condemnation of those substitutes, a law-giving nature and an inherently rational and good humankind, that the Modern Age had put in God's place. Nature, for Nietzsche, provided no guide, and man he likened to "a rope, fastened between animal and Superman—a rope over an abyss."[32] To cross that abyss, he must over-

---

[30]"Thus the March revolution, by the hopes that it awoke and the reality it could not produce, was likewise a preparatory stage for 1871." Rudolf Stadelmann, *Social and Political History of the German 1848 Revolution*, trans. James G. Chastain (Athens, Ohio, 1975), p. 199.

[31]See Jacques Barzun, *Darwin, Marx, Wagner: Critique of a Heritage*, 2d rev. ed. (Garden City, N.Y., 1958).

[32]Nietzsche, *Thus Spoke Zarathustra: A Book for Everyone and No One*, trans. R. J.

come himself: not fulfill his nature, as in the modern version, but reject it. Nietzsche also scrapped the modern concept of progress in favor of the doctrine of eternal recurrence, in which perfection remained a possibility, but not via progressive development. Further, Nietzsche's very style was a rejection of modernism: obscure, hostile, religious, epigrammatic, and elitist, his works would become the primers of the antimodern movement.

One can only guess at what caused this dichotomy. Certainly the intellectuals of the professional classes—the physicians, lawyers, professors, schoolteachers, and occasional representatives of the business community—felt themselves to be a new element within German society, one that could only benefit from the arrival of modernism. Its national state would give them an identity, help fulfill liberal dreams, and bring economic growth and military power. The creating intellectuals, those who undertook to provide theoretical, symbolic, and artistic commentary, would seem, however, to have remained more remote from the present, with its modernist stirrings, and closer to the traditions of German dissent. If what had been partial aversion to the modern now devolved into an almost full revulsion, it was no doubt because the modernization of German society finally had begun to take on the appearance of an inevitable process.

Certainly Bismarck thought that he saw the handwriting on the wall. And he took care to fulfill the prophecy in such a way that his authority, the Prussian monarchy, and Junker privilege would all be preserved.[33] In Austria steps were likewise taken to insure the old order against the coming storms, although there the nationalities problem would make a shambles of every experiment. In neither case, however, were the attempts to find a means of borrowing from the modern without being overwhelmed by it necessarily ill conceived, although selfishness, arrogance, and a refusal on all sides to accept compromise often made it look otherwise. After the late 1870s, consistent

---

Hollingdale (Baltimore, 1961), p. 43. For a general treatment of Nietzsche, see Walter Kaufmann, *Nietzsche: Philosopher, Psychologist, Antichrist* (Princeton, 1950).

[33] A. J. P. Taylor has commented that Bismarck "claimed to serve sometimes the king of Prussia, sometimes Germany, sometimes God. All three were cloaks for his own will; and he turned against them ruthlessly when they did not serve his purpose." See his *Bismarck: The Man and the Statesman* (New York, 1955), p. 13. If, however, Bismarck did what he wanted, it is also true that what he wanted corresponded nicely to the long-term class, state, and national interests that he attempted to reconcile.

cooperation with the liberals came to an end in both Berlin and Vienna, but it should be noted that classical liberalism was on the way
out just at this time throughout the West. All in all, the German attempts at finding in these years a middle path between traditional and
modern ways were again appropriate to the circumstances of central
Europe, where a large agrarian segment made the construction of a
homogeneous modern polity impossible. Toward the end of the nineteenth century, of course, rapid industrialization would dramatically
alter the social balance and make the prospects for political and indeed
for all forms of modernization much more favorable—for a time. But in
the period that stretches from the revolution of 1848 to the fall of
Bismarck German society was in a condition of transition, partly modern and industrial, partly premodern and agrarian. The government
adequately, if not to everyone's satisfaction, reflected that circumstance. Despite the often bitter criticisms of the cultural elite, German
history seemed to be proceeding along a reasonable course at a reasonable pace.

VII

By 1900, the German economy (much more so in the German than in
the Austro-Hungarian Empire, but in part there as well) had become a
flourishing part of Western industrial capitalism. No longer was there a
significant gap; in fact, German production in key items was threatening British leadership.[34] With corresponding changes occurring in social relationships, Germany was modernizing at a rapid rate, taking on
the look of a more or less typical Western industrial state. That there
were conflicts arising from such swift changes is clear, and they are apparent in the art and literature of the prewar years. Yet the remarkable
evolution of the Social Democrats, the one party that could honestly
claim to represent the masses, from revolution to reform to war credits
would seem to indicate that the underpinnings of the German social
structure were reasonably sound. German society by the eve of the
First World War had finally joined the Western core in a final swift
transition that had been, all things considered, remarkably smooth.

[34] See the tables in Michael Balfour, *The Kaiser and His Times* (New York, 1972), pp.
437–47.

German culture was also moving toward the mainstream again, but, ironically, the mainstream since the late nineteenth century had been veering yet once again toward renewed dissent, toward a rejuvenated romanticism—the "second flood of the same tide," in the words of Edmund Wilson.[35] As twice before, German dissent to the modern met and reinforced a mood indigenous to the Western core. This time, however, the disaffection on all sides was much more profound and produced the great cultural revolution in which modern—that is, the old Renaissance-Enlightenment modern—thought and style were renounced in favor of a postmodern set of conventions—although to call them conventions is not quite right. In fact, there was a mad scramble of experimentation, with only a rejection of the modern canons providing the common theme.

From the start, Germans were instrumental. Nietzsche, hardly read while he was writing, now was accepted as the mad scramble's mad prophet (although to be fair he had not been mad when a prophet and not a prophet when mad), and the major German cities became centers of innovation. First Vienna and Munich before the Great War and then, after it, Berlin and the northern provincial capitals played leading roles.[36] From the last decades of the nineteenth century until the coming of Hitler, the German outpouring was astonishing. With Freud, Einstein, Wittgenstein, Gropius, Kafka, Brecht, the brothers Mann, Hesse, Planck, Kandinsky, Schönberg, and many others, it was a golden age for Germany. And although they differed widely in their intentions, many resisting or noting with regret the implications of their work, common to all of them was a questioning—and often flat rejection—of modern models.[37] Thus, German culture, just at the mo-

---

[35] Quoted in the insightful chapter on the cultural revolution in Richard Pipes, *Europe since 1815* (New York, 1968), p. 367. A discussion of the problems of definition is to be found in H. Stuart Hughes, *Consciousness and Society: The Reorientation of European Social Thought, 1890–1930* (New York, 1958), pp. 31–37.

[36] Both Peter Gay and Walter Laqueur stress that the culture of the several decades before World War I and Weimar culture are two parts of the same thing. See Gay, *Weimar Culture: The Outsider as Insider* (New York, 1968), pp. 5–6; and Laqueur, *Weimar: A Cultural History* (New York, 1965), p. ix. For a highly interesting overview of Weimar, see Alex de Jonge, *Weimar Chronicle: Prelude to Hitler* (New York, 1978). On prewar Vienna, see Allen Janik and Stephen Toulmin, *Wittgenstein's Vienna* (New York, 1973); and the handsomely illustrated work by Carl F. Schorske, *Fin-de-Siècle Vienna: Politics and Culture* (New York, 1980).

[37] For a comment on the German contribution to the novel and for general remarks

ment when German society was becoming at last fundamentally modern, either declared itself indifferent to or turned decisively against the accomplishment.

In Austria, the early rise to power of an authoritarian antimodern clericofascism blunted and confused the issue, but in Weimar Germany there was a clear division, with the moderate, modern parties in the middle and the critical forces attacking from both extremities. Here the cultural revolt was given a rare opportunity to confront its opponent directly. In the Western core, cultural antimodernism in the twenties and thirties also took on more than occasionally political forms. One need only remember the original attraction of fascism for T. S. Eliot, to say nothing of lesser Western opponents of liberal democracy, right and left. But there the benefits of the modern life remained fundamentally attractive to the broad masses of the population, and when the system was tested with the arrival of the Great Depression, there occurred a crisis, but not a general loss of faith. Where, however, the lack of a strong modern tradition was accompanied by other significant difficulties, the outcome was different. The combination in Germany of the effects of the centuries of dissent, neoromantic revival, military defeat, and massive economic dislocation proved too potent, and the result was Hitler. Although it is true that at the last he might have been kept out of office, it would have taken a coup against what remained of Weimar democracy. Hitler was by 1929–33 the leader of the party with the most popular support. Political logic plus the growing fear of communism made his selection obvious if a way could not be found to split the Nazi party, and one could not.

Part of the reason for Hitler's popularity was that he offered a cure for unemployment (in fact, this was Gregor Strasser's doing, but Hitler got the credit). But another was the rapport with both the masses and the intellectuals created by his artful use of the current antimodern *Zeitgeist*.[38] That this spirit emanated from diverse elements, some mad at the West for having ruined Germany's bid for a prominent place in the modern world, others for threatening the integrity of German culture and society with continued modernization, did not matter. Hitler

---

on the period, see William Barrett, *Time of Need: Forms of Imagination in the Twentieth Century* (New York, 1972).

[38] See the section on the intellectuals and Hitler in Craig, *Germany*, pp. 639–45.

was able to bring Germany together in support of his rejection of modern values and institutions.

It can be asked whether or not Hitler was sincere in his antimodern stance. Did he in fact believe in anything? It would seem that he did, that nihilism describes his thought poorly. He was truly antimodern, if also unbalanced, petty, and vicious. To be sure, Hitler was not unaffected by the modern tradition. He admired science, technology, and even rationalism. He believed in progress. His taste in art and architecture was essentially modern, and he vehemently rejected the production of the Weimar avant-garde anti- or postmodernists. Also, he had nothing but ridicule for the mystical meanderings of Himmler and Rosenberg. Yet for all of that he was in his basic attitudes a true expression of the cultural revolution against the Modern Age. If he managed to modernize Germany in several respects, that was for the most part an accidental by-product,[39] for his ideal society was static and agrarian, not dynamic and industrial; his politics demagogic and authoritarian, not democratic and liberal; and his approach to problems intuitive and sporadic, not logical and methodical. The various emancipations that modernism encouraged he held in contempt. And he readily accepted the proposition that all values should be transvalued, that Germany must be stripped of her Western accretions and led forward to a new primitivism, complete, to be sure, with Viennese pastries and other select holdovers.[40] That he was antimodern did not, it should be added, make him criminal, although it influenced the forms that the crimes took.

[39] On his modernizing effects, see, for example, David Schoenbaum, *Hitler's Social Revolution: Class and Status in Nazi Germany 1933–1939* (Garden City, N.Y., 1966); the critical review of Schoenbaum in Heinz Lubasz, "Hitler's Welfare State," *New York Review of Books*, December 19, 1968, pp. 33–34; and Ralf Dahrendorf, "National Socialist Germany and the Social Revolution," in *Society and Democracy in Germany* (Garden City, N.Y., 1967), pp. 381–96.

[40] On Hitler's world view, see Hugh Trevor-Roper, "The Mind of Adolf Hitler," in *Hitler's Secret Conversations, 1941–1944* (New York, 1961), pp. vii-xxxii; Percy Ernst Schramm, *Hitler: The Man and the Military Leader*, trans. Donald S. Detwiler (Chicago, 1971); Eberhard Jäckel, *Hitlers Weltanschauung: Entwurf einer Herrschaft* (Tübingen, 1969); my comments thereupon in "The Making of Hitler's Outlook," *Review of Politics* 34 (July, 1972): 441–45; J. P. Stern, *Hitler: The Führer and the People* (Berkeley, 1975); Sebastian Haffner, *Anmerkungen zu Hitler* (Munich, 1978); and Leonard Krieger, "Nazism: Highway or Byway?" *Central European History* 11 (March, 1978): 3–22. Krieger's remarks on the agreement in essentials between the new culture of the twentieth century and Nazi ideology are especially trenchant. See ibid., pp. 18–19.

VIII

That Hitler was antimodern also came to influence necessarily the reputation of antimodernism throughout the West, but especially in Germany. The destruction, the defeat, and, perhaps most, the full revelation of the Holocaust turned German culture and society away from the tradition of dissent to modernism. What Hitler had so brutally caricatured could not be revived. Thus, because the culmination of the long German quarrel with the modern turned out to be what it was, Germany—meaning here West Germany, the only Germany, for better or worse, with a valid claim to the German past—was shocked out of her dissenting role. The fact that the Bundesrepublik witnessed a rapid economic revival and became by the 1970s the showcase of Western capitalism did nothing to encourage a return to dissent once the initial feelings of repugnance and guilt had been dulled by time.[41] The venerable critic of modernism has been silenced, apparently for good. Caught between a real Nazi past and an imagined communist future, Germany, again as much a part of the Western mainstream as in the medieval centuries, has become a leader and defender of the Modern Age. As Joachim Fest has noted, "We rarely meet any more those romanticized, aggressive ideas of flight into imaginary realms of the more distant past or future, which for so long left their disastrous mark on the German political consciousness. The dream of the 'Third Reich' . . . has perished along with the horrifying reality of its final form."[42] Present-day Germany lives very much in the present.

This is not to say that there is no contemporary German dissent. There is, and some of it extremely radical, even murderous, and in its fanaticism hardly in keeping with the modern mean. Violence, however, is now employed not to prevent modernization but to further it, unlikely as are the prospects of creating more liberty by experiments with assassination. It is consistent, too, that it is Germany that has contributed the theology of liberation to the attack on conservative Ca-

[41] As important as the return of prosperity was the Germans' acute consciousness of it: when polled in 1957, by far the largest segment designated the Federal Republic as the European country with the highest standard of living. See Elisabeth Noelle and Erich Peter Neumann, eds., *The Germans: Public Opinion Polls 1947–1966*, trans. Gerald Finan (Allensbach and Bonn, 1967), p. 370.

[42] Fest, *The Face of the Third Reich: Portraits of the Nazi Leadership*, trans. Michael Bullock (New York, 1970), p. 306.

tholicism.[43] That there is an abundance of postmodern cultural production is only another demonstration of how thoroughly neoromanticism has been co-opted by the entire late modern West—much as the Church once put to use Renaissance art and architecture in support of medieval theology. Also, of course, Hitler's lack of acuity and consequent condemnation of postmodern art (and, again, it is the art that is often called "modern" that is meant) has contributed a great deal to its postwar revival in Germany.[44]

The West would seem to have profited during most of the modern centuries from having a source of criticism close at hand. Now, with modern culture in disarray and the modern economy and its dependent society seemingly approaching some sort of reckoning,[45] it is perhaps unfortunate that Germany is no longer pointed toward the search for alternatives. Thomas Mann, in commenting a few months before the opening of the Second World War on *The Magic Mountain*, suggested that finally Hans Castorp had been able to experience the darker, mysterious side of life without being consumed by it, "ohne sich geistig von ihr beherrschen zu lassen."[46] Clearly, Mann had hoped that Germany would do the same: acknowledge the wisdom of the antimodern heritage without falling victim to its demonic charms. But in 1933 Germany did fall victim. And the ultimate result has been a rush to the opposite pole. As it turned out, it was not too thorough a success of the antimodern that finally prevented the achievement in Germany of the balance that Mann sought, but of the modern. Alfred Grosser concluded his comprehensive study of Germany 1945–70 with the admonition that West Germans "should ask themselves how soon and in what way Germany, instead of being merely absorbed into the contem-

[43] On Karl Rahner, for example, see Eugene Kennedy, "Quiet Mover of the Catholic Church," *New York Times Magazine*, September 23, 1979, pp. 22–23, 67–75; on Hans Küng, see Michael Novak, "Behind the Küng Case," ibid., March 23, 1980, pp. 34–38, 76–82.

[44] Krieger argues effectively that "Nazism articulated on its own destructive level a mental structure homologous with the period's constructive lords of the high culture. . . ." "Nazism: Highway or Byway?" p. 19. For a different opinion, see John Willett, "Art of a Nasty Time," review of *Art in the Third Reich* by Berthold Hinz (New York, 1979), *New York Review of Books*, June 26, 1980, pp. 9–12.

[45] The best summary of these difficulties remains Robert L. Heilbronner, *An Inquiry into the Human Prospect* (New York, 1974).

[46] Thomas Mann, "Einführung in den Zauberberg für Studenten der Universität Princeton," May, 1939, reprinted in *Der Zauberberg, Roman* (Berlin, 1956), p. xii.

porary world, can begin to make a fully creative contribution to it."[47] The dissenting tradition could only respond that the best contribution would be not to become absorbed into it. Given Hitler, that may be too much to ask.

IX

The history of the relationship of Germany to the Modern Age has been, then, far from simple. At first suspicious and even contemptuous of the innovations that were producing to the west a new and dynamic world, she looked on with a mixture of indifference and hostility, participating at times, but never with much enthusiasm. Toward the end of the nineteenth century, however, modernism began to overtake her, as it was bound to if Germany chose, as she did, to participate fully in the industrial revolution. But this belated conversion was to be followed almost immediately by two portentous developments. First, the West's culture rather suddenly deserted the modern forms to which it had adhered for approximately half a millennium and began putting together a totally new set. It is difficult to say why, but perhaps Western civilization, which has been distinguished chiefly by its insistence on change, had run through the modern idea by about 1880 and was attempting a fresh start. Whatever the reasons, the culture of the Modern Age began to undergo a transformation into something very different just as German society got around to accepting modernism. To make the problem for Germany worse, it was the German intelligentsia, long ardent practitioners of antimodernism, who took the lead both in attacking the old and in seeking the new.

And then, as Germany began to accustom herself to the oddity of a modern society that was arriving as rapidly as its modern culture was departing, a second thing happened: the newly modern German society was subjected within a decade and a half to a series of profound shocks—military defeat, a dictated peace, inflation, and, finally, severe economic depression—that quickly destroyed the newly acquired allegiance to modernism. The result was a plunge back into the German past, with a frantic search to identify premodern and antimodern Ger-

[47] *Germany in Our Time: A Political History of the Postwar Years*, trans. Paul Stephenson (New York, 1971), p. 330.

man traditions. Hitler of course was both a participant in the new wave of anti-Western feeling and also its chief benefactor. Had he only restored the economy, he would have been popular, but in a limited sense; that he could pose as the great purifier, the restorer of the virtues that modernism had insidiously corrupted, permitted him to become the true leader. Although he refused to see the affinities between his world view and that of the cultural revolution, that should not prevent their being acknowledged. Hitler was essentially an anti- and postmodern figure (that he was in fact authentically premodern is less obvious).

Germany since 1945 has reacted as one might expect she would: turning away from the destructive association with extremist anti-modernism, she has taken to modernism with a zeal for orthodoxy that would be entirely reassuring were it not for the fact that the West's present dilemmas suggest that contemporary society must somehow follow in the wake of the cultural experimentation and devise new, postmodern solutions. If that proves to be the case, it will not necessarily mean that Germany will continue myopically in her modern commitment. But one thinks back to Konrad Adenauer's old campaign slogan, *Keine Experimente*, and recalls why it was so popular. It may be some time yet, regardless of coming pressures, before Germany again feels the need to contribute to radical reconstruction. Some will still see that as good news, although it may be doubted that it is. In many regards Germany (that is, West Germany) is at present the healthiest major member of Western society. If, however, that society itself is in trouble, with growth-inhibiting shortages of almost every material item and an excess only of cultural despair, then German cooperation in the quest for alternatives should be welcome.

CHARLES E. McCLELLAND

The Wise Man's Burden:
The Role of Academicians in
Imperial German Culture

IN virtually all advanced societies, teachers in institutions of higher learning can automatically be regarded as members of the educational elite, and therefore of the cultural elite as well. In our own age of mass culture, however, one cannot assume a very strong influence of academicians upon the general culture. Nor would most academicians regard themselves as guardians of a specific cultural heritage, even if one could define such a thing in the tangle of specialized, largely autonomous disciplines that comprise the academic world of today. In our age of unprecedented proliferation of information, an academic instructor can barely keep abreast of what he or she must know as a specialist or even subspecialist. The bewildering heterogeneity of cultural values and the rapid rate at which they change have rendered arbitrary any statement about "what every educated person should know."

This situation, however, is rather new. Nineteenth-century Europeans and Americans had much clearer ideas of what every educated or cultivated person should know. This consensus was particularly strong in Germany, where *Kultur* served as an important focal point of national consciousness well before the economic and political unification of the German lands. By *Kultur* German intellectuals meant essentially the spiritual and intellectual *cultura animi* of Renaissance humanism, a set of skills and values designed to produce the best possible human being. But Germany had also institutionalized *Kultur* while modernizing its school system in the early nineteenth century. Ever since the establishment of the classical secondary school system (*Gymnasium*) and the reform of the university system at the beginning of the nineteenth century, *Kultur* was thus tied to formal education.

The German academic elite quite naturally, then, came to regard itself as a vital element in the process of German culture and, by implication, as a crucial pillar of the German nation. Although this attitude predated the creation of the empire, academicians' identification with the national state was stronger after 1870 than ever before. For the widespread satisfaction with which the German academic elite greeted Prussia's unification of the country tended to align professors firmly behind the new Reich. As the rector of the University of Berlin, Emil Du Bois-Reymond, put it in an address to the university in 1870, "The University, billeted across from the royal palace, is . . . the intellectual bodyguard of the House of Hohenzollern."[1]

In fact, under the empire, the academic elite had to work harder than ever to maintain its role of cultural leadership. Fears about inroads that modern life was making on intellectual culture and concern over competition from a host of new cultural trends made their position less secure than in the halcyon days of the early nineteenth century. Maintaining the kind of cultural values that had come to be shared among the academic elite was an increasingly burdensome and conscious responsibility. Just as German missionaries, soldiers, and traders went out into the colonial world to bring the benefits of German *Kultur* to benighted savages (a justification often invoked by professors who supported Germany's colonial adventures), many academicians felt obliged to take on the "wise man's burden" of internal missions within Germany itself, attempting to maintain their vision of cultural standards in a rapidly changing world.

Sociology of Culture in Imperial Germany

In order better to understand why the academic elite played such a visible role in German culture, one must first understand the peculiarities of German society in the nineteenth century. Germany, unlike such countries as France and Britain, lacked a large, strong, and self-confident bourgeoisie capable of shouldering the burden of cultural leadership. Not until the rapid industrialization of Germany in the last third of the nineteenth century were large fortunes available to many members of the German bourgeoisie. The relative economic weakness of Germany during the first half of the century reduced the capacity of

---

[1] Emil Du Bois-Reymond, *Reden*, ed. Estelle Du Bois-Reymond, 2 vols. (Leipzig, 1912), I, 418.

its bourgeoisie to act as patron of the arts and sciences. This is not to say that countries such as France and Britain did not contain among their middle classes large numbers of "philistines" uninterested in culture, just as Germany did; but they also had larger numbers of the bourgeoisie who took an interest in culture.

The cultural and political fragmentation of Germany throughout most of its modern history also played a role in weakening the cultural engagement of the propertied middle class, the *Besitzbürgertum*. Particularism based on regions and states did not encourage the creation of a national culture, and rivalry among regional centers such as Munich and Berlin hindered the development of a national cultural center on the order of London or Paris. But even when these regional centers were carefully nurtured by patrons, they did not necessarily create a cultural life shared by the local bourgeoisie. Late-nineteenth-century Munich is a case in point. In order to add cultural vitality to his basically sleepy capital in the early nineteenth century, King Ludwig I of Bavaria began patronizing a handful of painters, the so-called colony; later King Maximilian II invited poets and other writers as well. The "colony," even in name an alien group, did draw a certain amount of attention to Munich and helped attract other artists and writers. But the *Kulturschaffende* (the culturally productive) of Munich were never wholly accepted by the natives, who resented their lack of regard for Catholicism and Bavarian ways. As Moritz Bonn depicted Munich in about 1910, the Munich citizenry "saw no reason why good Bavarian money should be put into the pockets of mere Prussians whose only contribution to Munich life was the cash they paid for their houses and their bills to tradesmen. . . . Bavarian jobs should go to Bavarians. Moreover, most of the newly appointed North Germans were Protestants and as such worse than infidels; they should not be allowed to corrupt the minds of the young."[2] Munich may have been an extreme case, but widespread indifference toward cultural life by the workaday bourgeoisie was not limited to the Bavarian capital alone.

In the absence of a strong, wealthy middle class interested in supporting culture, this task was taken up, like so many others, by the state. Within the limits of their financial capacity, many German princes, like their brethren elsewhere in Europe, had served as patrons

[2] Moritz Bonn, *Wandering Scholar* (New York, 1948), p. 159.

and had even, like Frederick the Great, been culturally productive themselves. The German states did much to create a solid educational system in the nineteenth century, to encourage the arts and sciences, and to foster libraries and other cultural collections. But they were also culturally conservative, usually giving strong support to the values of traditional religion. When new cultural values came into open conflict with old ones, the German states before 1870 usually chose to support the old. Their fear of change frequently led to cultural repression, sometimes of a very ugly sort.

What the German states did foster, however, was a small cultural patronage group of its own: its officialdom. To be sure, the great cultural revival of eighteenth-century Germany was only here and there, as in Weimar, encouraged directly by governments. But the social stratum carrying that revival derived in large part from the ranks of the civil and ecclesiastical services. These men were highly educated as a condition of their office. Higher education in Germany had long served as a mark of distinction, even for graduates who came from humble backgrounds. Thanks to the movements of neo-humanism and philosophical idealism that arose in the late eighteenth century, the value of a specific kind of education—*Bildung*—rose even higher.[3] *Bildung* was not mere education, not just the successful acquisition of certain skills requisite for a profession. Instead, it was regarded as the highest possible aspiration of man, at least by such influential thinkers as Fichte or the Humboldt brothers. Such neo-humanist reformers were able to translate at least some of their ideas into practice, perhaps most successfully in the establishment of a secondary school system with a strong emphasis on studying classical antiquity.

Other countries at this time also stressed a classical curriculum. The difference in Germany, however, was the almost mystical expectation that such a curriculum, as taught in the *Gymnasium* and possibly rounded out by university education in the techniques of *Wissenschaft*, would produce an elite of wisdom and philosophical depth. Although a sizable percentage of those who enjoyed this *Bildung* were nobles by birth, the vast majority of this educationally produced elite were members of the bourgeoisie. They felt a keen sense of their supe-

[3] For a recent survey of the German concept of *Bildung*, see W. H. Bruford, *The German Tradition of Self-Cultivation: "Bildung" from Humboldt to Thomas Mann* (Cambridge, 1975).

riority to the mere traders and businessmen of the *Besitzbürgertum*, or propertied bourgeoisie, and they found a name for themselves to stress the difference: the *Bildungsbürgertum*. Although originally spawned from the ranks of the bourgeois civil service, and still performing many roles in it, this stratum of the bourgeoisie, small as it was, gained a high degree of self-awareness and cultural influence by the middle of the nineteenth century.

In order to illuminate the peculiarities of the *Bildungsbürgertum*, its self-understanding and values must be compared to those of the educated elite in the nineteenth-century Anglo-Saxon world, where education was also an important distinction. The ultimate purpose of education differed in significant ways. In Britain, the goal was to produce a *gentleman*—that is, a man of refined manners and ethical character. The American variant was similar, though with more emphasis upon ethics and practical knowledge. The German idea of the "cultivated man" was sufficiently different that the Germans persisted in using the English word "gentleman" untranslated: it was simply not the same as a *gebildeter Mensch* (cultivated man). Refined manners and one of the unspoken prerequisites for being a "gentleman"—not having to do much work for a living—were not significant components of the German ideal. Instead, the emphasis fell much more heavily on knowledge and the technique of knowing—that is, on *Wissenschaft*. This almost untranslatable word implied not "science" or "scientific method," but perhaps most approximately "the systematic pursuit of knowledge." *Wissenschaft* was held by German educational and cultural theorists to be a difficult and exclusive enterprise requiring years of formal preparation and dedicated hard work by the individual. Just as *Bildung* was on a different plane from mere "training" (for example, practical preparation for a trade), *Wissenschaft* was on a different plane from mere experimentation or empirical reasoning.

Given the conditions obtaining in German society in the early nineteenth century, it is perhaps understandable that the "cultivated" (that is to say, the *Gymnasium*- and university-educated) minority developed a strong sense of its obligation and capacity to lead the German people. This leadership sometimes took the form of criticism and even outright opposition to the policies of the patriarchal, conservative German princes. To cite but one familiar example, the Frankfurt National Assembly during the 1848 revolution was dubbed by subsequent critics as "the parliament of professors." This appellation is of course not accurate, for professors constituted only a minority of the delegates. It would, however, be wholly accurate to characterize it as "the parliament of cultivated men." Whether radical or conservative, northern or southern, Protestant or Catholic, the vast majority of the delegates in Frankfurt shared a similar educational background and a sense of responsibility for the nation's fate. And if the deputies failed to overturn the basic structure of German political life, it may have been chiefly because they did not wish to. Instead, they wanted to infuse it with their own values and to shape what the philosopher Fichte had called a *Kulturstaat*,[4] a "cultural state."

It is unnecessary to explore here what a "cultural state" meant in terms of political theory. What is significant is the propensity of German idealism to begin most discussions about a desirable society with attention to culture. *Kultur* was the ethical goal of the state and its servants, including the educational establishment. Individual *Bildung* was the means; *Wissenschaft*, the method; educational and scientific institutions, the structure; and the educational establishment of *Gymnasien* and universities provided the personnel for the achievement of ever-higher levels of *Kultur*.[5] Certainly the educational establishment overestimated its capacities in this regard, but we cannot understand the attitudes of the academic elite of Germany before World War I if we overlook its high sense of mission and obligation.

In German sociological terminology, "academicians" were not merely professors or scientists. The term *Akademiker* applied to all graduates of *Gymnasien*, including that portion which went on to study at universities and the even smaller portion that went on to teach at them. The professional cadres of the universities formed the pinnacle of this hierarchy of *Akademiker*. They were not only at a pinnacle because of their high status among the graduates whom they taught; they

---

[4] See Fritz K. Ringer, *The Decline of the German Mandarins: The German Academic Community, 1890–1933* (Cambridge, Mass., 1969), pp. 114–15; and Franz Schnabel, *Deutsche Geschichte im neunzehnten Jahrhundert*, 8 vols. (Freiburg, 1964), II, 28–37.

[5] It is interesting to note that a recent German work on the history of "cultural policy" still defines "culture" as science (*Wissenschaft*), education (*Bildung*), art, and the representation of these components to the outside world. See Manfred Abelein, *Die Kulturpolitik des Deutschen Reiches und der Bundesrepublik Deutschland* (Cologne, 1968).

were also the leaders in important fields of research and discovery. Even for mere *Gymnasium* graduates who did not go on to the university, the professoriate had an indirect but strong influence, for it trained teachers of these classical high schools. Any child wishing to enter the higher civil service or the old-line professions such as medicine or the clergy had to go through the route of the *Gymnasium* and, usually, the university. Many middle-level careers required at least attendance at a *Gymnasium*. Thus even mundane aspirations to a career of high social standing were channeled through a required respect for the "academic" system of secondary and higher education at whose pinnacle stood the professoriate. Its members were not only the transmitters but also the masters of knowledge and the very embodiment of the German idea of cultivated humanity.

The leadership role of the academic elite, particularly of the professoriate, was, it must be stressed, so strong only because of the weakness and disorganization of other groups in German society and, perhaps in part, because the professoriate was also a part of the state apparatus. But after the unification of Germany in 1871 this role was challenged by new and vociferous social groups. The swift onset of the Industrial Revolution transformed Germany between 1871 and 1914, fostering numerous changes that weakened the academic elite's leadership role. The despised *Besitzbürgertum*, men of property rather than cultivation, grew in number, wealth, and influence. An urban proletariat and, beginning around 1900, a new class of white-collar employees grew along with the burgeoning German economy. None of these groups shared the academic elite's high degree of education and dedication to *Bildung*. To be sure, the propertied bourgeoisie did begin to send its sons through the university in greater numbers, and lower-middle-class children began appearing there in force after the turn of the century. But the professoriate tended to look with suspicion on these students, regarding them as careerists bent solely on a professional career rather than on the pursuit of self-cultivation.

These "new classes" had their own subcultures, developed in large part without the aid of universities and classical high schools. A mass culture "market" grew up to serve the new proletariat and lower middle class with reading matter and entertainment. The members of the propertied middle class, while not so indifferent to the classical values of the academic elite, nevertheless tended to behave as conspicuous consumers of cultural products rather than as creators and critics of culture. The new German middle class, it seemed to many horrified professors, was characterized by the pursuit of wealth, power, comfort, and recognition.

It is thus not surprising that a certain amount of cultural pessimism weighed upon the academic elite, especially in the first two decades of the German Empire. The celebration of military power, the naked pursuit of profit, and a sense that even art and poetry were in the hands of epigones exercised a depressing influence on the self-appointed guardians of German cultural values. The savage criticisms of Friedrich Nietzsche and Paul de Lagarde are an extreme example of this mood among the German academic elite, although most of their fellow academics rejected their vehemence. This sense of pessimism may have abated somewhat after the 1890s, but a certain nervousness about the future of German culture remained. It led many academics to speak out and attempt to reassert the cultural role they now felt was under attack. Although largely in agreement with the political direction of the Reich, the professoriate did not think the imperial government could provide strong leadership in the defense of German *Kultur*. So professors attempted to provide this leadership themselves. Perhaps the most stunning example of their campaign comes from the First World War, when hundreds of German academicians took it upon themselves to rally the public behind the war effort by setting out and explaining what made German *Kultur* different from and better than the mere "civilization" of Germany's enemies. Many of these writings were of course embarrassing rubbish, but they did demonstrate the academic elite's self-understanding as the guardian of what it perceived to be Germany's noble cultural heritage.

The professoriate did not have to look very far to find evidence of a certain decline in the cultural niveau during the course of the German Empire. It was a time of wrenching change, not only in economy and society but in the academic world itself. Many professors felt that they were losing control over the education of the nation's elites. The universities expanded in size at a breathtaking rate, with a fourfold increase in students between 1871 and 1914.

Professors complained that many of these new students were ill prepared or, even if intelligent enough, not fully committed to the ideal of self-cultivation. The term *halbgebildet* ("semicultivated") recurs again and again in their comments on the new student body. Complaints were even more pronounced after the turn of the century, by which time the monopoly of the classical high schools' graduates on university admission had been broken. After 1900, graduates of such schools as the *Realgymnasium* and the *Oberrealschule* were allowed to matriculate at universities, provided they could pass Latin and Greek examinations. These schools taught some parts of the classical *Gymnasium* curriculum, but they had originally been designed to prepare their pupils for the practical demands of workaday life. Professors accepted Humboldt's view that the mark of a cultivated man was the "purposelessness" of his study—it should not be mere training for a job. Thus practical-minded students flocking into the professors' lecture halls symbolized danger to the neo-humanist concept of university education. So, at least, it seemed to many professors, who sneeringly referred to such people as *Brotstudenten*—"bread-students," young men in a hurry to obtain the external qualifications for a comfortable career and the "bread" that came with it.

The monopoly of the professoriate over the educated elite had also been gradually eroded by the rise of technical colleges, which came to rival the universities in attracting large numbers of college-level students. The idea that graduates of these institutions, for example engineers, could also be cultivated men was difficult to accept for the university professoriate. Even though the technical colleges were allowed to award higher degrees after 1900, the university professoriate pretended that these degrees were not entitlements to enter the world of the cultivated elite. A man who built bridges or designed electric dynamos could not possibly understand the true sense of culture. The professoriate stubbornly held to the distinction between *Wissenschaft* and *Technik*: the first, while obviously producing useful knowledge, was justified chiefly because it ennobled the mind; the second was merely useful.

The Problem of Cultural Tradition

Members of the professorial elite in the German Empire necessarily arrived at both their career positions and their cultural values by passing through the classical secondary system. The spirit of this system, if the memoir literature is any guide, was that of classical antiquity and the philosophical idealism of the early nineteenth century. There was general concern that the secondary educational system was declining in quality by the late nineteenth century and that the teaching staff was not as deeply grounded in *Geist* as previous generations; but the values taught in the schools did not differ much from those introduced by such reformers as Humboldt and Altenstein, the creators of the model Prussian *Gymnasium* system, in the first decades of the century. What were these values?

Classical antiquity can be studied for three general reasons. First, it is a subject of intrinsic interest, much as any other subject such as chemistry or music. Second, the revival of interest in the classical world since the Renaissance could be justified on the ground that thorough exposure to the Greek and Latin classics of literature, art, philosophy, rhetoric, and natural science provided a superior discipline for the mind. These reasons were found everywhere in Europe in the nineteenth century. In Germany a third and strongly perceived reason was the reification of classical antiquity into the font of all culture, science, and cultivation. As Ernst Curtius, the great nineteenth-century classicist, put it:

> No people has absorbed this blessing [the rediscovery of the classical world] like the Germans. Their most significant deeds in the field of spiritual development, the Reformation as well as the creation of their national literature, rest upon the fertilization that the German spirit has gained from antiquity. The spirit of antiquity is a power in the present, one which is pervasively near and influential. We are hardly conscious of how the modes in which we think and write, how the images of the language we use, how our judgment of spiritual achievements, how the form of our buildings and vessels, how our art and artisanship stand under the influence of that spirit. Thus no part of human history is closer and inwardly more related to us than classical antiquity.[6]

Curtius spent a lifetime tirelessly restoring and studying classical sites in Greece, notably Olympia, frequently with the support of his former pupil Crown Prince Frederick of Prussia, the future Emperor Frederick III. Curtius proudly noted that "the first great peace project of emperor and Reich after the glorious unification of Germany . . . was to clear Olympia of rubble."[7] The state-supported museums that

[6] Ernst Curtius, *Antike und Gegenwart*, 4th ed., 3 vols. (Berlin, 1892–95), I, 9.

[7] Ernst Curtius, *Ein Lebensbild in Briefen*, ed. Friedrich Curtius (Berlin, 1903), speech of January 27, 1889, p. 683.

Curtius helped organize were, in his opinion, more than mere store-houses of the dead past: "The museums should keep us bound to the past, preventing us from becoming one-sidedly modern. As once in Antioch and Alexandria, in Rome and Byzantium, so today they should point to the foundations on which our present culture rests. Thus understood, public collections become places of historical observation; they become, . . . in the Hellenic sense, museums—that is, places serving the muses, dedicated to quiet recollection and to fruitful reflection about the goals of the spirit and the laws of its development."[8]

To be sure, Curtius's enthusiastic assessment of the centrality of classical antiquity to German culture was not shared by all members of the professorial elite; some of these perceived a certain cultural decline setting in during the very decades Curtius was working to save the central place of classical antiquity in the enculturation of the educated classes. Curtius himself acknowledged such widespread sentiments, but even at the end of his life he perhaps willfully misread the evidence and continued to feel optimistic about the abiding importance of the classical world for German culture.

This sense of decline in one of the central institutions of cultural transmission, the *Gymnasium*, is a recurring theme in the memoirs and other writings of German university professors who grew to maturity in the generations after Curtius. As Friedrich Meinecke recalled:

> And were our humanistic teachers the same as in the time of Wilhelm von Humboldt and Friedrich August Wolf? A few, probably, but not the majority. Raabe's *Horacker* sketches very well the types of teachers in the higher schools after the great Napoleonic wars, the somewhat absentminded but warmhearted teacher in whom humanist and human being were fused, and the energetic young teacher, drilled in philology, with his recipe of "Always strict, strict, strict, everything uniform!" The great philologist, Hermann Diels, to whom I talked about this once, confirmed that just about 1870 the generations of teachers had changed dramatically. But I think it is not because of the curriculum that the humanistic *Gymnasium* began to decline; rather, the teachers who were supposed to make us pupils enthusiastic, as well as the student body which was supposed to be inspired, no longer stood on the same level as in the early nineteenth century.[9]

Quite apart from the question of whether the schools were really declining during the German Empire, the important point is that the

[8] E. Curtius, *Antike und Gegenwart*, I, 114.
[9] Friedrich Meinecke, *Erlebtes, 1862–1901* (Leipzig, 1941), p. 66.

professorial elite perceived such a decline. If one looks beyond the
professoriate, however, one finds critics who viewed the classical *Gymnasium* as an anachronistic tradition. The classical world, they argued,
might have a place in the curriculum, but Germany's elites must also
have some knowledge of the modern world and how to run it. Some
professors even agreed with this criticism; but even these would not
contemplate in their wildest dreams giving up Greek and Latin as the
main stem of school curriculum for the German elites. They were serious about the study of ancient languages, history, and philology—
plus some mathematics—as the only thinkable core of elite education.

Consequently the professorial elite could accept only a limited
amount of cultural innovation, and much of what it could accept had to
be measured against the immortal values derived from the past,
Greek, Roman, or German. Classical values were always the best,
even if they were often difficult to apply in the realm of modern
culture.

Having accepted the worth of the classical age and of German philosophical idealism as essential guides to timeless cultural values, the
professorial elite tended also to accept the methods most appropriate
to studying these values. The habit of thinking in philological, philosophical, and historical terms, acquired in school and university,
tended to persist on one level of thought even when individual professors worked and did research using more empirical methods. Thus
even professors who ordinarily used such methods in their research
could also openly express doubts about the usefulness of "empiricism"
when they discussed deeper cultural values. When they spoke of
Geist, they did not usually mean the mind as a tool for making empirical discoveries but rather as a vessel of the soul that must be filled with
the richness of the past. Indeed, the active mind could hardly pursue
true *Wissenschaft* until it was moulded by classical values first. The
fact that these values and this preforming of the mind in a restricted
sense might also limit the scope of *Wissenschaft* was not seriously
questioned by most of the professorial elite.

Another serious dilemma posed by the acceptance of a classical cultural tradition as the only way to cultivation and to involvement in
Wissenschaft lay in the fact that access to true culture was restricted to
the few. The education necessary for *Bildung* was too costly for most

citizens to enjoy it. The pursuit of *Wissenschaft*, which in the view of the professoriate was the highest calling for a cultivated man, was itself restricted to only a small portion of the educated. The leisure necessary for the pursuit of *Wissenschaft* was ordinarily not available to the professional classes outside the professoriate, and even the professors felt they had to wrest time for their research from their burdensome teaching duties, closely as these were allied with their research under the German university system. How could a mere civil servant, although also a product of the classical *Gymnasium* and a graduate of the university system, be expected to find the time to pursue the lifelong assignment of cultural enrichment through continuing study? As one professor, Max Dessoir, put it, the civil servants were more concerned with duty than with cultivation, although they had title to being *gebildet:* "They piously believed in God; the high and mighty emperor stood, by God's grace, as a link between the Almighty and themselves. They fulfilled their exactly prescribed duties correctly and servilely, but beyond that they did not think a great deal. Their world rested on trust, and whoever shook it was hateful to them."[10]

If even the professors could keep up their cultural mission and their "exactly prescribed duties" (for they were also civil servants of a special kind) only by working sixteen-hour days, it is difficult to see how normal mortals could be expected to do likewise.

The professoriate persisted in making sharp distinctions between the real world and the world of culture. As the Nobel Prize–winning neo-idealist philosopher, Rudolf Eucken, described the situation in the German Empire, there existed a culture of work and a culture of the spirit, with the former gaining the upper hand:

> The main tendency of the times was an unconditional affirmation of life; there was an unmistakable untruthfulness in the external claim of the age to believe in a spiritual world and in a religion of Christian coloration. All this produced a mere culture of work which achieved much in itself but tended to forget the human soul in its achievements. It could be seen as a contradiction that this people continued to call itself a nation of poets and thinkers, since no inner necessity was working for art, religion, or philosophy. . . . The average intellectual offering was a mixture of intellectualism and naturalism, hence the spiritual nadir which could not be overlooked.

[10] Max Dessoir, *Buch der Erinnerungen* (Stuttgart, 1946), p. 32.

Later ages will wonder how a people that produced men like Leibniz, Kant, and Hegel could have been so abandoned by the muses and yet have taken pride in its cultural poverty. Its culture had all the advantages and limitations of a mere culture of work; we were good workers, but we were shallow men.[11]

Eucken's almost Nietzschean condemnation of this culture of work included, by implication, his own colleagues, the professors. Here was another hindrance to the efforts of the professional men of high culture to maintain and transmit their values. For the demands of *Wissenschaft* drove them, as researchers and innovators, into an ever-greater isolation from each other. Specialization was the characteristic tendency in research and teaching in the German universities after about 1860. In order to succeed in research, the individual scholar was forced to limit his investigations to ever-narrower questions and problems. The rapidly growing size of the academic world meant a loss of contact with students and other professors, a trend toward the impersonalization of social and intellectual dialogue, and a withering away of a sense of common cultural endeavor. As Ludwig Curtius put it:

There were occasional contacts with the members of the medical faculties, for instance, through musical or artistic interests, in which overworked surgeons and internists liked to seek recreation, . . . but there were no intellectual contacts. The scientists and mathematicians of our faculty went their own ways; the professors of law were seldom inclined to regard the philosophy of law as anything more than an empty mental game. . . . The majority of the professors were so taken up with the demands of their individual disciplines that few felt a need to glance across their boundaries. . . . With the growth of increasingly more specialized disciplines and the creation of ever more chairs for them, as demanded by the growth of modern *Wissenschaft*, it was natural that even at middle-sized universities like Freiburg and Heidelberg the full professors no longer knew each other personally in every instance. They met only a few times a year to elect a rector and to attend formal events.[12]

Under such conditions, as Curtius complained, the prewar German university sytem could still create effective scholars (Eucken's "good

---

[11]Rudolf Eucken, *Lebenserinnerungen* (Leipzig, 1921), pp. 65–66. For a more recent exploration of the German perception of antithesis between the "ideal of culture" and the "mechanistic" values of the culture of work, see Theodor Litt, *Das Bildungsideal der deutschen Klassik und die moderne Bildungswelt* (Bonn, 1957).

[12]Ludwig Curtius, *Deutsche und antike Welt* (Stuttgart, 1930), p. 330.

workers"), but it was failing in its mission of furthering the spiritual education of the nation's youth. If this gloomy evaluation was correct, then one must wonder how the professoriate expected to combine faith in *Wissenschaft* as the means with faith in the classical cultural tradition as the end of their efforts. If the pursuit of *Wissenschaft* in its specialized form precluded even the enculturation of the next generation of students, then there was a glaring inconsistency in the professors' theories of *Bildung*. The difficulty arose from their clinging to an idea of a fixed cultural tradition while they accepted the dynamics of a growing and changing society that invaded the halls of academia. This paradox is of course not unknown to professors today in advanced societies; it is indeed a central area of concern. But in imperial Germany it arose for the first time in a most dramatic form, thanks, on the one hand, to the particularly insistent attachment of the professoriate to a fixed cultural heritage and, on the other, to the stunning rapidity with which German society was changing under the impact of industrialization.

The Problem of Cultural Innovation

In a recent exploration of the role of Jews in the cultural life of the German Empire, Peter Gay analyzed and basically repudiated the old charge that they were quick to become modernists, to join the European-wide artistic and cultural revolution against old forms and styles at the end of the nineteenth century.[13] Gay points anew to the particular conjunction of anti-Semitism and abhorrence of modernism in the minds of many of imperial Germany's cultural critics, both distinguished (including university professors) and vulgar. A good deal of cultural anti-Semitism in cultivated non-Jewish circles of imperial Germany may have been motivated by a certain nervousness in the face of the perceived decline of cultural tradition discussed earlier. Modernism thrived in late imperial Germany despite great odds. But it did not thrive at all among the majority of the professoriate (including even many Jewish professors).

The "Jewish spirit" in this nineteenth-century version of anti-Semi-

[13] Peter Gay, "Encounter with Modernism: German Jews in Wilhelminian Culture," in *Freud, Jews, and Other Germans* (Oxford, 1978), pp. 93–168.

tism was associated with a restless, rootless, and materialistic approach to life and culture. Since this was also perceived by many professors to be the fundamental malaise of the "culture of work," it was not very hard for anti-Semites to blame everything on the influence of Jews. Yet the fundamental point is that most German professors, as "bearers of culture," were more antimodernist than anti-Semitic. Some, undoubtedly, were both. But even great thinkers such as Max Weber, who looked unflinchingly into the visage of the modern world and described the unstoppable process of modernization, could not do so without an occasional gloomy word of disapproval.

It is ironic that German professors eagerly looked forward to every new discovery and work of scholarship in their professional fields, accepting the dynamic of scientific innovation, while at the same time they remained at best ambivalent toward innovations in culture outside their spheres. For example, it is rather striking to find in the memoir literature repeated and sincere avowals of interest in music, art, literature, and theater, which sometimes went as far as helping organize music festivals, translating and mounting stage performances, and playing musical instruments, at times with great skill. Yet the festivals would involve Bach or other musical classics; the theater pieces, Greek tragedies; and the literary readings, the classics, or even second-rate older works. Even as unconventional a professor as Max Dessoir, whose memoirs betray a refreshing wit and lively interest in the arts, admitted that in the 1890s, as a young academic, he attended mostly concerts that "did not go beyond Schumann" and that the most daring music he heard was that of Berlioz, Liszt, and Wagner.[14]

No doubt many of the German professors shared to some degree the highly limited tastes of the official setters of cultural policy, from the emperor on down. The authorities exercised very effective control over what could be staged in the many theaters, opera houses, and concert halls of Germany. Thus modernist experiments had to be carried out more or less privately, outside the realm of official culture and often against the hostility of officials. A number of professors disapproved of the sometimes clumsy manipulations of the authorities and occasionally resisted them in the name of intellectual freedom; but that

[14] Dessoir, *Buch der Erinnerungen*, p. 33.

does not mean they were particularly effective, nor that they had any sympathy for the art produced under such freedom of thought.

A good example of this ambivalent attitude toward cultural innovation can be found in the comments of Ulrich von Wilamowitz-Moellendorff, an influential Berlin professor. Wilamowitz-Moellendorff described his activities in the Prussian Schiller Commission and the Chapter of the Order for Merit, Peace Class (*Ordre pour le mérite, Friedensklasse*), an award occasionally given to scientists and artists. He was upset that William II and his cultural bureaucracy tried to ignore the statutes and make the committees' recommendations merely advisory, instead of binding as before. Thus Wilamowitz-Moellendorff voted to give the naturalist playwright Gerhart Hauptmann a prize from the Schiller Commission, even though he "couldn't stand" Hauptmann's more recent work. Nevertheless, to make a point about who should really award the prize—the king or the committee— Wilamowitz-Moellendorff voted for Hauptmann and reminded himself that *The Weavers* and *The Beaver Pelt* (two classics of the naturalistic theater) were not so bad. When it came to awarding Hauptmann a *pour le mérite*, however, Wilamowitz-Moellendorff rebelled. That a majority of the chapter members voted for Hauptmann was, to Wilamowitz-Moellendorff, "a proof that the courage which had no fear before the king failed in the face of the tyranny of the masses."[15] Hauptmann had become, in Wilamowitz-Moellendorff's view, a cultural symbol of the socialistic mob and was therefore "unworthy" to wear the *pour le mérite*.

Similarly Wilamowitz-Moellendorff considered it just to award the realistic-impressionist painter Max Liebermann a *pour le mérite*, but only after Liebermann had become a member of the Prussian Academy and had begun to criticize the more radical artistic styles before World War I.[16] Typically, this prominent professor was perhaps more tolerant than the official cultural bureaucracy and William II, to whom "modern art was the art of the gutter."[17] But he showed little taste for defending truly innovative or avant-garde art and literature.

[15] Ulrich von Wilamowitz-Moellendorff, *Erinnerungen 1848–1914* (Leipzig, 1929), p. 255.
[16] Ibid.
[17] Gay, "Encounter with Modernism," p. 100

Even for the younger generation of German professors who had been more open to experimentation in the arts, the old and trusted forms were usually more appealing. Friedrich Meinecke, for example, admitted to an interest in Ibsen and Hauptmann in the 1890s. But he also spoke very warmly of the contemporary revival of the Biedermeier age, which in his view provided aesthetics and values for the German youth movement at the beginning of the twentieth century. Wilhelm Raabe and Theodor Storm, whom he read in his youth (he had thought of becoming a novelist himself), remained sentimental favorites into late age. Among composers, he greatly admired the neoromantic Hugo Wolf, another reviver of past cultural forms.[18] "It was as if," Meinecke wrote, "a great German tradition of the most profound art, which people believed had ended with Möricke and Brahms, suddenly blossomed again in all areas. And my own inclinations were very similar."[19]

If German professors were hardly in the avant-garde of cultural innovation, neither were their counterparts in other countries. In several important respects, however, the German professoriate appears to have played a relatively more prominent role in evaluating, criticising, and setting standards by which cultural innovations could be judged.

It was, for example, quite common for the professoriate to form a part of the audience for theatrical and musical productions, art exhibitions, the unveiling of public monuments, and the like. Most German professors' memoirs from the imperial era mention an ongoing interest in performances of this kind. Their judgments and tastes, while perhaps not original and profound, must have had some impact upon the next generation that they taught. Professors also shared in the domestic cultivation of aesthetic pursuits common to the educated middle class: poetry readings (and in many cases the writing of poetry), play readings, musical evenings, book discussion groups, and similar forms of extraprofessional sociability were common experiences. Backed by its professional authority, the professoriate was in a strong position to transmit to its student audience and even to the general public the cultural values it had acquired through such activities.

As mediators, critics, and standard setters, the German professors

[18] Meinecke, *Erlebtes*, pp. 72, 167, 174, 189.
[19] Ibid., p. 217.

enjoyed additional opportunities for influencing the public through writing for and editing national and regional journals. One of the most prestigious of these, the *Preußische Jahrbücher*, was edited until the end of World War I by such professors as Heinrich von Treitschke and Hans Delbrück. High-quality journals were all too glad to solicit the contributions of the professoriate, a tradition established as far back as the eighteenth century, when many national periodicals designed for the educated elite were founded by professors and frequently published in university towns. The subscribers to such journals were of course usually limited in number, but they appear to have encompassed the university graduates at least.

German professors also willingly served as cultural ambassadors of the empire abroad. Particularly after 1900, the Prussian Ministry of Education took a strong interest in such missions and recruited heavily among the professoriate. Trips as far afield as America and Japan were no longer rarities. But their impact was debatable. As one delegate to the 1904 World Exposition in St. Louis wrote after his journey: "Unfortunately, political decisions are not affected by foreign trips and lectures by great scholars, nor by the proliferation of cultural institutes or international journals. A mediating and slowly working effect can not be denied, however, especially in times of peace. But as soon as the politicians raise their droning voices, it completely disappears. We should therefore consider the international contacts of scholars as a matter of furthering scholarship, not as an instrument of foreign policy."[20] Nevertheless, German universities still enjoyed enormous prestige abroad before World War I, and it was perhaps natural for the German government to hope that the professoriate, by traveling to international congresses and by pursuing cultural exchanges, could bolster the crumbling national image as a land of poets and thinkers.

Academic Culture as a Subculture: Style and Mores

The German academic elite in the empire was recruited preponderantly from the German bourgeoisie, and it naturally tended to share many of the traits of its subculture. Hard work, orderliness, thrift, sobriety, and responsibility were just a few of the values com-

---

[20] Dessoir, *Buch der Erinnerungen*, p. 209.

monly found among the academic elite. The professoriate was furthermore largely recruited from the stratum of professional and civil service families that ultimately owed its sense of superiority over the
other members of the middle class to a high degree of education and
cultivation. Even professors whose childhood included great economic
privation had somehow obtained the necessary exposure to the values
of the *Bildungsbürgertum* to break away from their uncultivated milieu.[21] It is thus not surprising to read in most of the professorial
memoir literature reflections on a childhood spent immersed in music
and literature, not only by attending family musicales and reading
aloud in groups but also by performing music and even composing it;
writing poetry, dramas, and stories; and moving in a small circle of
other cultivated families in the town. These habits usually continued
into mature life, although lifelong involvement in *active* cultural production (such as writing poetry) was not common to the majority. But
in this way the professoriate shared in and transmitted the canons of
cultivation common to the stratum of the *Bildungsbürgertum*.

Increasingly under the German Empire, however, the professoriate rarely had the leisure or, in many cases, the money to carry its pursuit of cultivation as far as it would have liked. The increasingly burdensome demands of research, teaching, and administrative work left
the professoriate with little free time. Even if the professors did not
follow the great Theodor Mommsen's dictum that a real scholar had to
restrict himself to four hours of sleep a night,[22] the professoriate no
longer enjoyed the sort of leisure that Wilhelm von Humboldt had
thought of when he helped establish the University of Berlin in 1810.
His demand that the German professor must live in *Einsamkeit und
Freiheit* (solitude and freedom) came to be less realistic as far as freedom from obligations was concerned. The solitude, however, remained a part of the professor's life, and many members of the professoriate in imperial Germany complained about it.

Ludwig Curtius, for example, attributed a decline in communica-

---

[21] Perhaps no memoirs from this era reflect the full absorption of the values of the
Bildungsbürgertum by one not born into it more than Dietrich Schäfer's *Mein Leben*
(Berlin, 1926). Schäfer, a dockworker's son, was one of the few German professors of the
time to climb out of the working class through hard work (and a patron) and end his life as
a professor at the University of Berlin.

[22] Meinecke, *Erlebtes*, p. 216.

tion to the growth in size and number of German universities during the empire. As noted earlier, specialization, preoccupation, and the alleged German vice of unsociability added to the physical and intellectual difficulties of maintaining a common cultural basis among the professoriate.[23] Another professor reported his astonishment that during a visit to the United States he had to introduce two of his colleagues from Berlin University not only to some American hosts but to each other as well.[24]

If the nature of the professorial career left little time for the pursuit of cultivation, the economic and social forms of the times interfered, too. Professors were much better off financially than they had been earlier in the nineteenth century; but they were hardly on the level of top civil servants, factory owners, or physicians. A few professors had private wealth or a lucrative practice on the side, but most did not. Yet it was considered obligatory for professors to maintain a certain level of comfort in their domestic arrangements and to engage in a certain amount of rather formal, and often empty, entertaining—not necessarily dinner parties, as was common among the wealthier middle-class families, but at least receptions. Much of the socializing was also *de rigueur,* formal, and stuffy: formal clothes and gestures, calling on officials as an obligatory courtesy, and attending various public functions (for professors were also civil servants) consumed leisure time. As Meinecke observed, it was somehow an "era of plush furniture and parlors, an age of cramped convention."[25]

Much of the social life of the professors went on without the intellectual assistance of their wives, who were usually not as well educated and cultivated as the professors or the society in which they moved. "A good many of them [professors' wives] did not shine in the drawing room," one academician wrote.[26]

Such social contacts were of course not frequent: a well-to-do professorial household might have two or three large social events such as receptions or, more rarely because of the expense, dinners in the course of a year. Having one evening a week set aside for an open house was perhaps a common, but by no means universal, custom, and

[23] L. Curtius, *Deutsche und antike Welt,* p. 335.

[24] Dessoir, *Buch der Erinnerungen,* p. 203.

[25] Meinecke, *Erlebtes,* p. 187.

[26] Bonn, *Wandering Scholar,* p. 161.

it was probably restricted to the more senior and influential professors. Otherwise, the professoriate spent much of its time in its institutes, laboratories, and lecture halls and in all likelihood much of its evening locked away in a study after dinner. Professorial memoirs rarely dwell on the joys of being a parent, and one can assume that looking after children was the duty of the *Frau Professor*.

Contacts with students outside the classroom were evidently not a normal part of the professorial style, except for the handful of disciples nearing the end of their training to become professors themselves. Even so, these academic adoptive children would more often than not have a social relationship only with their *Doktorvater* and not with many other professors. Intermarriages between such students and professors' daughters seem to have taken place at a high rate. The sisters of professors were also prime candidates for marriage to the professors' colleagues, which perhaps is understandable considering the small social circle in which professors moved and the tendency of academics to marry rather late in life. Under these circumstances, it is not surprising to discover that distinguished Berlin professors were actually brothers-in-law: for instance, Wilamowitz-Moellendorff and Theodor Mommsen, and Adolf von Harnack and Hans Delbrück.

Despite the fact that German professors had many opportunities to broaden themselves by travel and to mix with the upper levels of German society, which included occasional contact with royal families, one does not receive the impression that they developed complete ease in such situations. As one professor remarked, his brethren were "not very good at small talk" but tended to remain rather limited by their scholarly expertise. Another implied that German professors seemed to be less able than their French or British counterparts to discuss their work or cultural matters in general with laymen without feeling that they were somehow demeaning themselves as scholars.[27] Memoirs of German students thus do not surprise us by often depicting professors as aloof, somewhat unapproachable, and turned inward toward themselves—in contrast to the image of, for example, an English don. Thus, even in personal style and manner, the professors paid a price for their immersion in *Wissenschaft*.

One may legitimately ask what kind of subculture the professors experienced while they had been students. From the memoir literature,

---

[27] Ibid.; L. Curtius, *Deutsche und antike Welt*, p. 335.

it would appear that the self-preparation of future professors bypassed to a large extent the mainstream of general student subculture. They appear to have brought with them from their homes and families a certain aloofness from that subculture, a serious continuation of the ideal of self-cultivation that shaded off into the ideal of the pursuit of specialized *Wissenschaft*. It is rare to discover in the memoirs of professors a serious and lasting attachment, when they were at a university, to the drinking and dueling traditions of the German student organizations; and even most of those who joined the more serious-minded student organizations (often those in which dueling was frowned upon) did not take a very active part in them. Nor did most professors apparently mix with or appreciate the large number of students, the so-called *Brotstudenten*, who attended the university for the main purpose of achieving professional qualifications as rapidly as possible. When they were students German professors tended to despise their classmates who were bent on a purely utilitarian purpose in attending the university; and their attitudes did not change in later life, as we have seen.

It is a popular misconception that the majority of German students in the imperial period participated in the romantically tinged subculture of the student *Korps* (dueling fraternities). Indeed, it would be too much to say that the type of student who joined a student fraternity and played an active role in it was likely to be a "careerist" student himself but financially and socially better off than the majority of *Brotstudenten*. As Gustav Schmoller complained about his law students at Berlin, they clung "to the privilege of devoting four or five semesters of the best studying years to the bars, dueling, a thoughtless *carpe diem*, or the vain pleasure of society."[28] Law students traditionally came from the higher levels of German society, and many were destined for civil service. And, as one civil servant wrote in his memoirs, "for the future civil servant, the university years meant, for the most part, socialization in a certain life-style and, through the fraternities and the military service (which was usually done during the university years), making acquaintances and friendships for one's future life and career."[29]

As university enrollment expanded rapidly in the imperial era, the proportion of students bent on a quick and inexpensive entrée into the

[28] Gustav Schmoller, review of *De l'enseignement du droit dans les universités allemandes* by Georges Blondel, *Schmollers Jahrbuch* 10 (1886): 613.

[29] Wilhelm Deist, *Aus dem Leben eines Glücklichen: Erinnerungen eines alten*

professions also grew. Especially after 1900, academicians complained about the poor academic preparation and narrow utilitarianism of these students. They, too, had their own variant of a student subculture, but it was hardly as colorful as that of the fraternities. Frequently having to take odd jobs to finance university study, such students had little time, let alone money, to indulge in organized social life. According to many contemporaries, such students were found in large numbers in the philosophical faculties, where many of them were hastily preparing for a career in schoolteaching. The cultural life of such students is difficult to study, since they tended to function as isolated individuals and left few records of their subculture. But one may assume they shared many of the cultural traits of the lower-middle-class families from which most of them came. Their professors, in any case, accused them of bringing the "semicultivated" values of these crass, upwardly mobile social strata with them to the university.

For their part, the student fraternities, which attempted to set a certain tone and arrogate to themselves the role of representing the student subculture, tended to become more socially exclusive, politically and socially conformist, and culturally conservative during the German Empire. To be sure, some new student fraternities were more socially open and less wedded to the rigid habits of the inherited codes of behavior; and even nonfraternity students founded a national organization around the beginning of the twentieth century.

Yet all these organized expressions of student subculture had apparently one thing in common: they were designed primarily to provide some form of bonding to make up for the growing anomie of student life. Just as the communication among the academic elite of professors was breaking down under the strain of sheer size and specialization, so the impact of the professoriate on the acculturation of the students was also diminishing.

Conclusion

It is difficult to escape the conclusion that the role of cultural leadership that the academic elite enjoyed under the German Empire was

---

Beamten (Berlin, 1904), p. 116. University students were entitled to serve as "one-year volunteers" in the armed forces instead of being drafted for longer service, and they normally served this year while being students.

more modest than it had been earlier in the nineteenth century and was less than these academicians would have liked. In attempting to uphold a set of cultural values that had been produced not only in a preindustrial society but also at a peculiar juncture of that society's development, the professoriate was faced with a battle against the cultural effects of modernization. Although not completely hostile to cultural innovation, the professoriate tended to opt for the preservation of traditional cultural values and thereby to cast itself increasingly into the role of an embattled rear guard.

This role was still credible in the imperial era, since the political elites tended to support it. Under the altered conditions of the post–World War I period, however, the professoriate no longer enjoyed such support from those who made cultural policy for the Weimar Republic. Even those professors who mistook National Socialist rhetoric about a "national uprising" for a promise to restore traditional German cultural values were to be bitterly disappointed after 1933.

It would not be quite fair to accuse the German academic elite of total failure, however. For it did have some impact on German society and helped to shape a certain mistrust of modern cultural values, a mistrust that lingered on well into the twentieth century. It is also difficult to see how the professoriate could have escaped the contradictions of its tasks: it wished to provide cultural leadership, a role it assumed under the peculiar conditions of the early nineteenth century, but it had to struggle against the constraints of changing and increasingly burdensome professional and scholarly obligations by the century's end. Under the impact of rapid change in German society and in the educational environment in which the professors functioned, cultural leadership proved a burden too heavy to bear.

DAVID L. GROSS

Kultur and Its Discontents:
The Origins of a "Critique of Everyday Life"
in Germany, 1880–1925

I

JUST as culture itself has a history, so, too, does the concept of a "critique of culture." Since the beginning of the modern era some rudimentary forms of cultural criticism have existed, but their scope has always been partial and limited. The French *philosophes* of the eighteenth century, for example, attacked aristocratic values and peasant customs, and the romantics of the early nineteenth century opposed philistine tastes, but neither waged a frontal assault on culture as such—that is, on modern culture as "a whole way of life," material, intellectual, and spiritual.[1] This total critique of what became known as "mass culture" occurred only after the Industrial Revolution took hold and initiated a complete transformation in the modalities of everyday life and experience.[2] Such a transformation produced a double reaction: in some it induced a tremendous sense of loss for all that had been destroyed, while in others it sparked expectations of higher, unfulfilled possibilities which were yet to be realized. In both cases, the immediate result was a critique of the social reality and culture of what appeared to be a prosaic status quo. But each critique was nonetheless shaped from an opposing point of view, the first that of the political Right, the second that of the political Left.

Though the solutions offered by these two camps were very different, they were in general agreement about what was wrong with the state of culture in the nineteenth century. For instance, to both groups

---

[1] For a brief definition of the term "culture" in this context see Raymond Williams, *Culture and Society: 1780–1950* (New York, 1960), pp. xiv–xvii.

[2] See David Gross, "Jacob Burckhardt and the Critique of Mass Society," *European Studies Review* 8 (1978): 393–410.

it seemed that culture was being inundated by pecuniary values and was, therefore, becoming reducible to mere monetary terms. Likewise, culture appeared to both sets of observers to be disintegrating into something flat and standardized as it got more and more caught up in the processes of capitalist mass production. And again, to both reactionary and progressive camps, it seemed that culture was becoming inherently meaningless and despiritualized and consequently was losing touch with people's inner lives or, as was said, with their "souls." Hence, both sides agreed that though material culture was growing extensively under industrial conditions, it was also declining intensively, losing its intrinsic quality, and turning into mass culture or what was often referred to as "cultural barbarism" (*Bildungsbarbarei*).

In the following pages, it is important to focus on several responses to modern culture, or what might be termed the "culture of everyday life," in just one country: Germany. The period dealt with here is the crucial one between the 1880s and the early 1920s when cultural criticism as a mode of analysis became a central and important undertaking. In the comments which follow, the main concern is not so much with the content of German cultural criticism as it is with both the *forms* this criticism took and the *methodologies* which were developed to analyze particular cultural phenomena. While the content of cultural criticism was often remarkably similar on the Right and the Left (that is to say, the same cultural facts or processes were singled out for criticism), the forms and methods of approach diverged radically because of fundamentally different sociopolitical assumptions which preceded (and underlay) the cultural attitudes of different commentators. These assumptions defined not only what the critic said about culture but how he said it. Even when the same cultural objects or values were analyzed, they yielded different symbolic meanings, depending on the perspective and presuppositions held by the individual critic.

The intention here is, then, to explain how a number of German critics in the late nineteenth and early twentieth centuries attempted to conceptualize the problem of culture in various ways and how each arrived at a different method for understanding what was wrong with modern culture and what needed to be done to remedy the situation. More specifically, what needs to be shown is the following: first, how a definitive methodology for cultural criticism slowly developed out of these early efforts at cultural analysis, a methodology which was at first crude but which in time grew more elaborate and sophisticated; second, how the critique of culture gradually moved from an abstract-philosophical starting point in the 1880s to a concretely social approach in the 1920s; and, lastly, how in the process of this transition the most rigorous German cultural criticism turned increasingly toward the Left until it finally became comfortably absorbed within a Marxist framework. This did not happen decisively until the advent of the Frankfurt School of Critical Theory in the 1920s and 1930s. Still, it is important to note that the groundwork for some of the major accomplishments of the Frankfurt School in the area of cultural criticism was laid long before, in the methodological breakthroughs achieved by some of the School's major intellectual predecessors.

II

The first totalistic critiques of culture in Germany appeared in the early years of the Second Reich, and they generally originated not, as one might expect, from the far Left but from the far Right (where they served as a rear-guard action against the "cultural rot" [*Kulturfäulnis*] of an emerging industrial civilization).[3] To be more precise, most cultural criticism before the late 1890s, with the exception of the brilliant insights and *aperçus* of a maverick like Nietzsche, came from not one but two main sources: the nationalist Right and the academic intelligentsia.

The cultural critique emanating from the nationalist Right was perhaps best exemplified by works such as Paul de Lagarde's *Deutsche Schriften* (*German Writings,* 1878) or Julius Langbehn's *Rembrandt als Erzieher* (*Rembrandt as Educator,* 1890), though both of these widely read authors were followed by a host of imitators.[4] This rightist

---

[3]The Marxist Left in Germany before the First World War was, by contrast, noticeably slow to initiate an adequate critique of culture because of its overly simplistic views about culture's being merely "superstructural." Though German Marxists naturally opposed bourgeois culture, they usually assumed that a change in economic relations would automatically bring about a change in cultural relations. Hence, the thrust of early left-wing criticism was directed toward economic, not cultural, issues.

[4]The most useful general discussion of these early critics can be found in the following works: Fritz Stern, *The Politics of Cultural Despair: A Study of the Rise of Germanic Ideology* (Berkeley, 1961); George L. Mosse, *The Crisis of German Ideology: Intellectual Origins of the Third Reich* (New York, 1964); and Hermann Glaser, *Spießer-*

critique was as sweeping as it was pessimistic. Virtually everything about modernity was viewed as degenerate, disintegrative, or spiritually vacuous. Whereas, so the argument went, Germany had once, in some unspecified preindustrial age, possessed true *Kultur*—which was described as soulful, creative, organic, and *Volk*-based—it had now, by the end of the nineteenth century, dissipated into a mere *Zivilisation*—that is, something vapid, materialistic, rationalistic, superficial, and rootless.[5] What had once been genuine culture had been transformed into its opposite because modern life was bereft of spirituality and depth, owing, as some said, to the loss of "German national feelings" or "German self-consciousness."

Since most of the critics of the far Right stood outside the academy (they saw the universities and the German school system as part of the problem), they flatly rejected the methods of cultural analysis which were associated with academic learning. This meant that, in their observations on contemporary culture, they shunned any approach that hinted at positivism or "soulless empiricism," both of which were equated with the mindless collection of facts. Consequently, as far as the methodology of their criticism is concerned, they turned away from a detailed analysis of culture and opted instead for metaphysical speculation *about* culture. Almost all their work stayed fixed at the level of generalities; very rarely were comments made about the specific, concrete phenomena of everyday life. In this respect, the opening lines of Langbehn's Rembrandt book are typical of this whole vague and abstract genre of cultural criticism. "The contemporary spiritual life of the German people," Langbehn wrote, "is in a state of gradual, and some say rapid, decay. . . . Science has degenerated into specialization. . . . Epoch-making individuals are no longer in evidence. . . . The visual arts lack monumentality. . . . [and our] whole present-day culture is regressive."[6]

Whenever the rightist critics became focused enough to conceptualize the main problems of modern culture—and this they did only occasionally—they usually conceptualized them by means of artistic categories, since most viewed themselves as artists in deadly opposi-

Ideologie: Von der Zerstörung des deutschen Geistes im 19. und 20. Jahrhundert (Freiburg, 1964).

[5] See Richard Hamann and Jost Hermand, *Stilkunst um 1900* (Berlin, 1959), pp. 102 ff.

[6] Julius Langbehn, *Rembrandt als Erzieher* (Leipzig, 1890), p. 1.

tion to a coarse, unharmonious, and "ugly" age. Hence, nearly all their judgments were grounded primarily in aesthetic considerations, and this severely limited the kind of in-depth, systematic analysis of culture they were able to achieve in their work. To make matters worse, most of them (in line with their artistic orientations) wrote in a highly impressionistic if not mystical-lyrical literary style, and this further hindered the amount of concreteness or specificity they could attain in their cultural criticism.

On the whole, the nationalist critics felt great animosity toward modern culture, but they did not have the intellectual tools for understanding exactly what was wrong with it or why. This was particularly true with regard to the "materialistic" culture of the urban masses, which most of the critics would not condescend to analyze or evaluate in detail because it seemed so debased and unworthy of comment.

The net result was a considerable lack of penetration, since even the best of their work was subjective and "aesthetic" rather than factual or precise. A similar limitation was the fact that the nationalist critics were closely wedded to a number of romantic concepts and modes of analysis which had outlived their usefulness by the end of the nineteenth century. One example was the rather overworked *Kultur-Zivilisation* dichotomy mentioned earlier. Nearly all the right-wing critics used this as the major scaffolding on which to hang their negative comments about the age in which they lived. Though it is true that this old-fashioned distinction afforded certain limited insights, it also hindered many others which were far more important and which could be arrived at only by abandoning such constrictive tools of analysis. Indeed, it seems fair to say that a careful, empirically grounded "critique of everyday life" could not emerge until the antiquated concepts on which the rightist critique depended were decisively overcome.

The second major source of cultural criticism in the 1880s and 1890s was the German academic community. Most of the academics who turned their attention to the broader cultural issues of imperial Germany—among them people like Friedrich Theodor Vischer (1807–87), Theodor Lipps (1851–1914), and Eduard von Hartmann (1842–1906)—felt that existing popular culture was "fallen," vulgar, and shallow.[7] They attributed this condition to the absence of genuine

---

[7] Friedrich Theodor Vischer, *Altes und Neues*, 3 vols. (Stuttgart, 1881–82); Theodor Lipps, *Grundtatsachen des Seelenlebens* (Bonn, 1883); Eduard von Hartmann, *Philosophie des Schönen* (Leipzig, 1887) and *Tagesfragen* (Leipzig, 1896).

Geist (by which they did not necessarily mean *deutscher Geist*, as the nationalist Right would have put it).[8] "Spirit," these academic intellectuals felt, had gone out of everday experiences, leaving only a culture full of dead objects without inherent meaning or value. Their response to this was, for the most part, not to try to change the world but to withdraw into a sphere of elite "high culture," to defend their own conception of the "spiritual personality" in a mass age, and to argue that the good life would have to be pursued outside the realm of ordinary culture, a realm they believed was being corroded by an insidious process of "Americanization." To many academics, the crisis of culture, narrowly conceived, was primarily a crisis of *Bildung*, or personal cultivation; and this crisis could be solved only by returning to a more "idealistic" form of education, which they hoped would spiritualize the German masses and restore quality to popular culture.

To the best and most perceptive German academics, however, there was the sense that the problem lay much deeper, in the very nature of modern industrial society itself. But, even with the majority of these individuals, there was still a hesitancy to immerse themselves in the empirical details of everyday life. The category of "the everyday" (*Alltäglichkeit*) continued to be looked upon as the commonplace realm of "petty practicality" and, therefore, almost beneath the dignity of serious analysis. In spite of this, a few notable critics, especially sociologists such as Ferdinand Tönnies (1855–1936), Max Weber (1864–1920), and Werner Sombart (1863–1941), at least went so far as to document, with scholarly thoroughness, the disenchantment and trivialization in modern cultural life.[9] This the Right never attempted to do, since it was most often content with simply criticizing and condemning, not describing and analyzing. Here, then, in the work of a few academic intellectuals, an important step was taken toward the concrete investigation of ordinary "lived reality," and hence toward the rudiments of a cultural critique of everyday life.

[8]There were numerous right-wing or *völkisch* educators—among them people like Moritz von Egidy, Ludwig Gurlitt, and Hermann Lietz—who need to be distinguished from those mentioned above. See Mosse, *Crisis*, pp. 46–50, 157–67.

[9]See, for example, Ferdinand Tönnies, *Gemeinschaft und Gesellschaft* (Leipzig, 1887); or Werner Sombart, "Technik und Kultur," *Archiv für Sozialwissenschaft und Sozialpolitik* 33 (1911): 305–47. There is an excellent discussion of this group of academic critics in Fritz K. Ringer, *The Decline of the German Mandarins: The German Academic Community, 1890–1933* (Cambridge, Mass., 1969); and Arthur Mitzman, *Sociology and Estrangement: Three Sociologists of Imperial Germany* (New York, 1973).

The reason that a minority of academics could move in this direction—and by and large they tended to be the more liberal thinkers within the universities—was that they, unlike the rightists, generally accepted modernity. Since they believed that the basic configurations of an industrial-technological society were here to stay, it seemed imperative to comprehend rather than resist them. (The nationalist Right, by contrast, spent much of its time searching for "solutions" to modernity. These they usually found in some type of revived "spiritual-religious *Volk* community," which they hoped would eliminate the traces of civilization and replace them with true German culture).[10] This greater sense of realism on the part of some German academics was an important factor in turning at least a few toward a closer look at actual cultural facts and processes. The best product of this social scientific tendency within the academy was the emergence of the field of cultural sociology (*Kultursoziologie*). But even this never became an area of hard-core empirical research which investigated the particularities of everyday cultural experiences. Instead, in the hands of Alfred Weber (1868–1958) and others, it became something more like a large-scale study of the social and historical *meaning* of culture in a theoretical sense.

III

In the 1890s and early 1900s some important advances toward a more adequate critique of everyday life were made by the sociologist and cultural philosopher Georg Simmel (1858–1918). Simmel was, for much of his life, a *Privatdozent* (instructor) and then, at the late age of forty-two, an *außerordentlicher Professor* (associate professor) at the University of Berlin. Hence, he was inside the academy, but personally and professionally he was not accepted as a bona fide member of the university community. Partly this was because of his Jewishness,[11] but it was also due to the fact that, especially in his later years, he did not write much specialized academic work, choosing instead to publish articles on broad cultural topics in the more popular journals. Simmel's conception of himself was that he was a "stranger" in the academy, but

---

[10] Hamann and Hermand, *Stilkunst*, pp. 36–47.

[11] See the revealing comments by Dietrich Schäfer in *Buch des Dankes an Georg Simmel*, ed. Kurt Gassen and Michael Landmann (Berlin, 1958), pp. 26–27.

precisely this marginality gave him the needed room to think more imaginatively and creatively about the problem of culture. It was out of this freedom and this liberating sense of "estrangement" that he arrived at some of his most interesting and original insights concerning the nature of everyday culture and the methods by which to analyze it.[12]

In contrast to the two modes of cultural criticism mentioned so far, Simmel developed an approach to culture which began with the concrete facts of everyday experiences—with what was immediate and given, not already prejudged and found wanting (as was the case especially with the rightist critics). This method of going back "to the things themselves," free from the biases of ideology, allowed him to see more clearly what other critics had missed, namely the singularity and specificity of the cultural objects or attitudes he wanted to write about. Most of Simmel's predecessors saw the world and everything in it from a tendentious point of view which they never questioned or transcended; consequently, they never really confronted the facticity of contemporary life but responded only to the interpretations and evaluations which they placed *over* the facts. Simmel, on the other hand, always tried to grasp things for what they actually were in themselves, not merely for what they reflected, in a mediated way, about a "bad reality." Also unlike the others, Simmel had a sharp eye for detail. He knew how to separate out what appeared to be minute and insignificant aspects of things and then to use them as starting points for his observations about everyday culture. Hence, one can find in his work numerous essays which focus on and elaborately discuss the simplest objects of ordinary experience: handles, meals, pitchers, fashions, coins, ruins, and the like. This alone—to go no further for the moment—was highly innovative, since earlier critics had never gotten to such a specific level of cultural analysis. Simmel was therefore perhaps the first in Germany to experiment in even a tentative way with what would later be called "the phenomenology of everyday life."

Simmel did not pursue this approach as far as he might have, however, for he used the empirical, presuppositionless method *only as a starting point*. Instead of following through with these promising be-

---

[12] For more on this aspect of Simmel, see Lewis A. Coser, "The Stranger in the Academy," in *Georg Simmel*, ed. Lewis A. Coser (Englewood Cliffs, N.J., 1965), pp. 29–39; and Margarete Susman, *Die geistige Gestalt Georg Simmels* (Tübingen, 1959).

ginnings (with what he called the "microscopic-molecular" approach),[13] Simmel chose to move rapidly from the isolated cultural fact to his own brand of abstractness, which was nevertheless different from the abstractness of his predecessors. What ultimately interested Simmel about cultural objects was not their substance or specificity but rather (1) what happens to them when they are used by human beings or placed in interaction with other cultural objects and (2) what *forms* these everyday things assume, as distinct from what contents they possess.

With regard to the first point, Simmel turned very quickly from a concern with concrete description to a concern with the social constitution of objects—that is, with the meanings they assume in the minds of those who interact with, exchange, use, or consume them. Hence, in the end, Simmel's attention went more toward understanding how things tend to be perceived by individuals—and what collective value and significance cultural phenomena are given by social actors—than toward a detailed exploration of the things themselves. As Simmel himself put it, it was not, for example, the actuality of a particular letter which one person writes to another which interested him, nor was it the *fact* of a dinner party, or the arrangement of city streets, or the details of a fashionable suit of clothes. Instead, he wanted to analyze something quite different, namely the fact that people "exchange letters and have dinner parties; . . . that one asks another to point out a particular street; that people dress and adorn themselves for each other"; and that these social experiences continually tie human beings together in reciprocity.[14]

What comes to the forefront of Simmel's cultural studies, then, are the numerous intangible relations between people and the (humanly constituted) objects or artifacts of everyday life. The social connection uniting both is, in fact, the main subject of his analysis, not the substance of cultural phenomena as such. But just to this extent the specific objects of culture slide out of focus or are dissolved in the social interactions which link together things and people. In the last analysis, it is not the concrete facts of cultural life (meals, pitchers, clothes, ruins) in and of themselves with which Simmel deals, though this is

[13] Simmel cited in Donald N. Levine, "Introduction," in Simmel, *Individuality and Social Forms*, ed. Donald N. Levine (Chicago, 1971), p. xxv.
[14] Simmel quoted ibid., pp. xxv–xxvi.

where he begins. Rather, his focus is on the connecting tissue of meanings and values attributed to these facts by the individuals who create, interpret, and make use of them in their daily lives.

The second thing Simmel did which drew him away from an empirical investigation of quotidian culture was to argue that the best way to comprehend the phenomena of everyday life was not through a careful study of the heterogeneous cultural contents which everyone is exposed to but through a study of the "forms" which shape and organize these cultural contents.

According to Simmel, every object of culture has two aspects: the first is its raw physical immediacy and particularity; the second is its form—that is, the hidden patterns and uniformities, as well as general social meanings and significations, which it contains as part of what it is. A clock, for instance, is, on a merely factual level, simply that: a clock and no more. A suit of clothes is simply a suit of clothes. But by their very presence in a culture both *produce* other relationships which seemed more important to Simmel—in these two cases, the clock engenders punctuality as a way of life and clothes create a consciousness of fashion (and along with it the whole fashion world). Only this second, social aspect of an object was centrally important to Simmel, because, in his opinion, this aspect alone contained a "form," and it was solely in the realm of forms that things could be meaningfully compared and contrasted. Hence, by discerning the forms inherent within specific objects, Simmel felt that more useful knowledge could be gathered about a particular culture than by analyzing a plenitude of chaotic or extraneous details. If it happened that certain kinds of forms were consistently and simultaneously found in divergent objets d'art within a culture—for example, a stress on symmetry and proportion in pottery or poetic expression—one would then expect to find identical forms in other parts of the same culture (for example, an emphasis on city planning). Similarly, if certain forms of modern urban life happened to create a need for "distance" in people, this same need would also show up in the kinds of art which metropolitan cultures supported—for instance, in symbolism, which, according to Simmel, was built upon a comparable desire for distance.[15]

[15] Ibid., p. xxix. See also Georg Simmel, "Sociological Aesthetics," in *The Conflict of Modern Culture and Other Essays*, trans. and ed. K. Peter Etzkorn (New York, 1968), pp. 68–80; and Simmel, *Philosophie des Geldes* (Leipzig, 1900).

Simmel's point was, then, that the forms reveal important structural truths about things in their social contexts which cannot be discovered by investigating only the specific contents of things. "The essence of a [cultural object]," went Simmel's argument, "is often more clearly revealed in its form than in its content. . . . [By] ignoring the content of social interaction as much as possible, one may achieve a liberation from coincidental, temporary, unnecessary elements. . . . The essence of culture is not revealed by searching for it in too much concreteness. . . ."[16] Appearances to the contrary, Simmel, too, when all was said and done, turned away from a detailed, empirical approach to cultural criticism.

To summarize: Simmel's cultural analysis unfolded in the following way. First, he began with some concrete phenomenon of cultural life, which he then isolated from the flux of familiar experience. Second, he examined this phenomenon very closely from all sides, as analytically and dispassionately as possible, looking for the multiplicity of elements which constituted it. Third, he tried to understand what social meaning the thing had by grasping its form. Once its essential form was discovered, the object could be compared with similar forms in the present (cross-culturally) or in the past (historically). But precisely here lay one of the major shortcomings of Simmel's method. By dealing with the form rather than with the content of things, he gained a certain conceptual transcendence over a plethora of detail, but at the same time he lost the specificity and concreteness which are essential for incisive cultural criticism. Fourth and finally, by giving so much attention to the lasting forms of cultural phenomena, Simmel fell into the trap of ahistoricity. He became accomplished at detecting the similarities and correspondences of forms throughout the ages, from ancient Greece to imperial Germany, but could not account very well for the different meanings and values people attributed to *even the same forms* at different moments in history. Simmel rightly pointed out that the cultural significance of things was socially constituted, but he failed to grasp how, over time, social relations change radically, and consequently how the cultural meanings or interpretations conferred upon objects and forms also change radically. One could not learn this simply

---

[16] This quotation, an excellent summary of Simmel's method, is taken from his student Leopold von Wiese. See von Wiese, "Simmel's Formal Method," in Coser, *Georg Simmel*, p. 55.

by comparing forms—unless one were also to compare the various historical (and class) interpretations the forms receive and to come to terms with just how much the contents *actually help shape and determine* the forms, rather than the other way around.

There is a final concept which was integral to Simmel's methodology, and that is his notion of the "tragedy of culture." A few words need to be said about this before turning to Simmel's successors.

Like many commentators during the 1890s and after, Simmel took note of the sheer number of cultural objects and artifacts available to people in the modern age. Thanks to the technology of mass production, the quantity of goods turned out had become practically limitless. The area of material and spiritual culture especially was being flooded with a surplus of assorted objects which were wholly unknown or even unimagined a few decades earlier. This realm of apparently boundless cultural products, this stark "magnitude of things," Simmel called *objective culture*.

Objective culture exists, however, for only one purpose: to be reintegrated by human subjects, who utilize it for their own personal growth and enrichment. Becoming cultivated simply meant, for Simmel, to experience and absorb the world of cultural objects subjectively, to internalize their qualities, and to incorporate their values into the living core of the personality. A cultivated person, as Simmel pointed out, is not one who simply knows a great deal, but one who incorporates objective cultural significations into "the vitality of his subjective development and existence."[17] This personal interiorization of objective culture Simmel called *subjective culture*.

With reference to the integral relation, or lack of it, between objective and subjective culture, Simmel perceived the following problem, which he termed "the tragedy of culture." Whereas the number of often useless cultural products had grown toward infinity, the capacity of individuals to experience or internalize even a small portion of them had greatly diminished. The reason had to do not simply with the quantities of things confronting people but with the fact that, by the beginning of the twentieth century, cultural objects had taken on an

---

[17] Rudolph Weingartner, *Experience and Culture: The Philosophy of Georg Simmel* (Middletown, Conn., 1962), p. 78. For Simmel, "cultivation" was impossible solely from within, through pure reflection; it always implied the evaluation and internalization of outside cultural objects.

independent, alien existence apart from both those who originally created them *and* those experiencing human subjects for whom they were
originally intended. Consequently, people had come to feel estranged
and helpless in their everyday life experiences because both the bulk
and the foreignness of things intimidated them. To be sure, "cultivation" still depended upon incorporating these seemingly alien objects
into the self; but since the intrinsic value and meaning of these objects
either had become lost altogether or were simply no longer readily
grasped by the majority of individuals in mass society, they were approached more as commodities to be devoured, accumulated, or displayed than as things whose qualities could be integrated into the soul.
The net result of this, according to Simmel, was that genuine culture
had atrophied to the same extent that the world of objects had expanded. Inevitably, people were becoming more and more inwardly
impoverished because the conditions of their existence were preventing them from assimilating all that would have to be internalized in order for an individual to be whole and complete.

This rupture between the two cultural realms was, in Simmel's
view, unavoidable and irreversible, since it was inherent in the very
nature of all mature civilizations. Consequently, Simmel ended on a
pessimistic note (which characterized so much of his theory of culture)
by calling the situation "tragic" because no solution could be found for
resolving this cultural dualism. Above all he made it clear, no doubt in
order to separate himself from the nationalist Right, that no activist
"cultural politics" could effectively overcome the "tragic discrepancy"
which lay at the heart of modern culture.[18] This split between subjective impoverishment and objective superfluity—something Simmel la-
beled a "logical development" of culture and part of a "general human-
spiritual fate"—was simply a fact of life that had to be accepted.[19]

Despite certain limitations, Simmel's method for analyzing popular
culture represented a significant breakthrough. For one thing, he dis-
pensed with the obsolete *Kultur-Zivilisation* distinction which had
dominated most earlier critiques. For another, he substituted a form-
content approach which helped shape a good part of German cultural

[18] Georg Simmel, "Die Zukunft unserer Kultur," in *Brücke und Tür*, ed. Michael
Landmann (Stuttgart, 1957), p. 97.

[19] See Georg Simmel, "On the Concept and Tragedy of Culture," in Etzkorn, *The
Conflict of Modern Culture*, pp. 41–46.

criticism well into the 1920s. For still another, he introduced into the field of cultural criticism some of Marx's most important conceptual tools (such as "reification" and the "fetishism of commodities"), but he did so within a watered-down, nonradical framework. Nevertheless, these concepts would prove to be extremely important to the younger critics who succeeded Simmel, many of whom discovered for the first time in his work the value of Marx for cultural analysis. Lastly, Simmel moved cultural criticism at least a small step closer to concrete, sociological analysis and hence away from the more impressionistic approaches of many previous critics. All of this made him a crucial link between the rightist critics who preceded him and the younger, more leftist-oriented critics who were to follow. Simmel was therefore the "stream of fire" through which cultural criticism had to pass in order to arrive at a greater sophistication of method.

IV

In the first and second decades of this century, a new generation came to the fore which advanced the methods of cultural criticism still further. This younger generation of critics was unified by a number of common characteristics. Most, for example, were born between the mid-1880s and early 1890s into middle- or upper-middle-class, often Jewish, homes. They received excellent university educations, usually at Berlin or Heidelberg, and were at first drawn to the dominant currents of thought at the time (neo-Kantianism, *Lebensphilosophie*); but they were also open enough to be attracted to Hegel and, more indirectly, to Marx, both of whom had a great methodological influence on them. Like the nationalist Right to some extent, most understood themselves to be "outsiders"; they felt profoundly alienated from their culture and the drift of events, and all experienced the ruptures of their age passionately, not merely intellectually as Simmel seemed to do. This led all of them toward a "romantic anticapitalism," but one with leftist rather than rightist overtones. Nevertheless, theirs was at first only a "metaphysical leftism" completely detached from socialist parties and organizations. Only later (after World War I) did many of them openly embrace Marxism and support the politics of the Soviet Union and the European Communist parties.

This younger generation began its speculations about culture heavily indebted to Georg Simmel, whose work decisively influenced their early formulations. Later, but while still in their twenties, they broke with some of Simmel's methods and presuppositions and moved off in directions of their own. In doing so, they placed cultural criticism in a new context, which gave it a different and more radical character.

Without discussing all their innovations in detail, it would be useful to mention briefly at least a few of them here before turning to some of the leading figures of the post-Simmel generation.

First, while accepting the form-content framework of analysis, the younger critics stood it on its head. For them forms were only appearances and therefore merely derivative of a deeper, more important content. Consequently, the primary focus of investigation needed to be on the living human reality behind or underneath the forms—which is to say, on the social and historical *praxis* that created the forms in the first place. The main goal, then, for Simmel's followers was not to accept and analyze the forms but to break through them, to reexperience the forgotten humanity within cultural objects and thereby to liberate the residues of *Geist* ensconced inside ossified cultural forms.[20]

Second, where Simmel tried to be purely analytical and avoid value judgments about culture, the younger generation did not hesitate to judge and condemn what it saw in the strongest possible terms. While Simmel cautiously talked about "the infinite ambiguity of the world" and tried to keep facts and values separate, his successors felt no qualms about making absolutistic statements about modern life. One, for instance, called the present "an age of utter sinfulness" (Georg Lukács), and another termed it a period wholly "abandoned by God" (Ernst Bloch). Both comments reflect an attitude and an intensity of language completely foreign to Simmel.

Third, the younger critics agreed that everyday culture was alienated, but they refused to believe that this was an inevitable part of the human condition. In their opinion, culture *became* alienated for historical reasons (mainly having to do with capitalism), and what was historically caused, they felt, could also be historically changed by going to the root of the problem: the existing social and economic conditions.

[20] The later Simmel, under the influence of Bergson and *Lebensphilosophie*, moved toward a similar position during the few years before he died in 1918. He offered no method for accomplishing this, however, only the hope that it could be done.

Put differently, capitalism—not a "general human-spiritual fate," as Simmel put it—was the source of cultural estrangement, and capitalism was viewed as something transitory, not an eternal economic arrangement that simply had to be put up with. There was, then, no inherent "tragedy of culture." The central problems of modern culture were seen as bound up with bourgeois society, but they could also be dispelled by eliminating the conditions that produced bourgeois society.

Fourth and last, the new generation argued that despite the bleakness of the cultural situation under capitalism there was reason to hope that things could be made better in the future. In contrast to the pessimism of Simmel and many other *fin-de-siècle* thinkers, the majority of younger critics were filled with almost utopian visions of a new kind of culture—one that would draw people together rather than separate them and would spiritualize everyday life rather than accentuate its worst aspects. Hence, most of the younger generation tended to be forward looking, even eschatological, in their thinking, since it seemed that transcendental values might soon enter into and utterly transform a decadent present, thereby ushering in an entirely new and purified cultural reality.[21]

There are several people who could be mentioned in this context, all of whom started with Simmel (many of them as his students) and then moved beyond to new modes of cultural criticism.

Karl Mannheim (1893–1947), for example, came from Budapest to Berlin to study with Simmel between 1912 and 1914; his earliest work—most of it focused on issues of cultural degradation and the need for cultural rejuvenation—reflected nearly all the above-mentioned attitudes and concerns of his generation. In fact, his interesting essay entitled "The Soul and Culture" (1917), written under Simmel's influence, encapsulates perhaps better than anything else the spirit of the younger generation of critics (though, unlike most of the others, Mannheim did not turn to Marxism to solve the problems of culture).[22]

Another Hungarian, Béla Balázs (1884–1949), also studied cultural sociology with Simmel and dedicated his first book, on "death aesthet-

---

[21] See Marianne Weber, *Max Weber: A Portrait*, trans. Harry Zohn (New York, 1975), p. 466.

[22] Karl Mannheim, "Seele und Kultur," in *Wissenssoziologie*, ed. Kurt Wolff (Berlin, 1964), pp. 66–84.

ics," to him. Later Balázs became a Marxist and turned his attention to the critical analysis of certain aspects of popular culture. His book on the "culture of the film," *Der sichtbare Mensch, oder die Kultur des Films* (*The Visible Man, or the Culture of the Film*, 1924), was an early classic in the field.

Similarly, the young Siegfried Kracauer (1889–1966) was greatly influenced by Simmel's approach to culture, though he, like the others, eventually moved well beyond it. Much of his best work centered on what he called "the analysis of the simple surface manifestations" of the age (dances, ornaments, films, and the like), which he thought provided the hieroglyphics through which the "underlying meaning of an epoch" could be deciphered.[23]

Still another prominent figure of this generation of cultural critics was Ernst Bloch (1885–1977). As a member of Simmel's private seminar before World War I, Bloch picked up from his teacher several core ideas which remained with him all his life. For example, he borrowed from Simmel certain key terms (such as the concept of the "horizon" or the "Not-Yet"), which he then made an integral part of his "philosophy of hope."[24] As a radical thinker with utopian and apocalyptical leanings, however, he could not help transforming Simmel's method in the process of appropriating it.[25] His approach narrowed in more on the "subjective spiritual factors" within the dead matter of everyday life. What especially interested Bloch was not mere facticity but the future possibilities locked within the decaying forms of bourgeois culture.[26] The task of criticism, then, was to emancipate these half-hidden potentialities by developing and expanding their "traces" in the present: that is, by releasing, as Jürgen Habermas summarized it, "the objective possibilities within the established reality."[27]

[23] Siegfried Kracauer, *Das Ornament der Masse* (Frankfurt-am-Main, 1965); see also Kracauer, "The Mass Ornament," *New German Critique* 5 (1975): 67–76.

[24] For a brief discussion of these terms, see my "Ernst Bloch: The Dialectics of Hope," in *The Unknown Dimension: European Marxism since Lenin*, ed. Dick Howard and Karl Klare (New York, 1972), pp. 107–30.

[25] Bloch's reflections on the limitations of Simmel's method can be found in his *Durch die Wüste* (Frankfurt-am-Main, 1964), pp. 91–92.

[26] Ernst Bloch, *Tendenz-Latenz-Utopie* (Frankfurt-am-Main, 1978). See especially chapter II (pp. 53–107), which contains Bloch's earliest work, dating from the years 1902–14.

[27] Ernst Bloch, *Spuren* (1930; reprint ed., Frankfurt-am-Main, 1969); Jürgen Habermas, *Theory and Praxis*, trans. John Viertel (Boston, 1973), p. 240.

Besides these, there are two other members of the post-Simmel generation who need to be singled out for further comment: Georg Lukács (1885–1971) and Walter Benjamin (1892–1940). Their contributions to a methodology of cultural criticism are especially important, and their influence on recent German (particularly Marxist) cultural analysis cannot be underestimated.

V

Georg Lukács was perhaps the most brilliant member of the younger generation. Though Hungarian by birth, his early upbringing and intellectual orientation were decidedly German. In 1906–1907, when he went to Berlin, Lukács fell under Simmel's influence; a short time later he became, with Bloch, a member of what Simmel called his "privatissimo" seminar. Consequently, many of Simmel's central concerns about the fate of cultural life and the alienation of cultural production can be found in Lukács's work dating from this period.

As time went on, however, Lukács undertook a "transformative criticism" of Simmel's cultural methodology, thereby imploding it from within. The result was that old concepts were charged with new meanings and pushed in directions quite different from what Simmel had in mind. During the succeeding years, up through and beyond his conversion to Marxism in 1918, Lukács opened up new avenues in cultural analysis which profoundly altered and radicalized Simmel's methods. For one thing, he attempted to understand the phenomena of culture not through timeless "forms" but through the actuality of socioeconomic conditions.[28] For another, he historicized his discussion of cultural reality by talking about it as a *process* rather than as a fixed object for metaphysical speculation. This allowed him to shoot beyond Simmel's more reflective, philosophical approach, which, because of its tendency to be ahistorical, notably limited the number of insights into modern cultural life he could achieve. Likewise, Lukács rejected the concept of a "tragedy of culture" and argued instead that an entirely new culture—a "new world-epoch," as he called it—was possible, though he often described this coming age in vague, eschatological

---

[28]This was true only after 1911–12. His earlier book, *Die Seele und die Formen* (written 1910, published 1911), still worked within a Simmelian (and Kantian) framework.

terms (as, for instance, an approaching "breakthrough of soul to soul" or a future "reconciliation of subject and object").

Also unlike Simmel, he expressed a passionate, though mostly poetic, anticapitalism in his early work. To Lukács, capitalism was the crux of the problem, the *cause* of a bad cultural life, because it represented the "rule of the economy" over culture.[29] Implicit (but not yet explicit until after 1918) in this position was the assumption that a healthy cultural life would emerge only when capitalism was overthrown and replaced by something radically different. But who would accomplish this? Until he became a communist, Lukács had no "agent" he could rely on to bring about such revolutionary changes. Consequently, he frequently fell back upon little more than utopian longings and expectations—on what his friend, the Hungarian poet Endre Ady, called "desire, hope, and dream."

By the time he had reached his late twenties or early thirties, Lukács felt he had "transcended" Simmel. He now saw him as only a "transitional phenomenon" (*Übergangserscheinung*), whose insights had to be taken further and completed by a "younger generation of thinkers."[30] Methodologically, Lukács complained in 1918 (in a note on the occasion of his mentor's death) that Simmel's work was too unsystematic and fragmentary. Though it was true that a viable "sociology of culture" could be erected only on the groundwork laid down by Simmel, this could not happen until he had been thought through and superseded. As Lukács put it, perhaps with himself in mind, Simmel was merely a Monet who needed to be completed by a Cézanne.[31]

In some respects, Lukács was that Cézanne who advanced beyond Simmel, but in other respects he was not. Though he expanded and refashioned many of Simmel's methods, he also, paradoxically, became "sociologically less concrete," and this, it would seem, was a step back-

---

[29] This was most clearly formulated in his 1920 essay "The Old and the New Culture" (translated and reprinted in *Telos* 5 [1970]: 21–30). Simmel was less specific than this, since his critique was directed less against capitalism than against a money economy as such. To Simmel, it was the presence of money in *any* society which caused quantification, a "numbers mentality," and an interest in the measurement and calculation of values.

[30] Georg Lukács, "Georg Simmel," in Gassen and Landmann, *Buch des Dankes*, p. 171.

[31] Ibid., p. 173. Later, in his *Zerstörung der Vernunft* (Berlin, 1954), Lukács was much more critical of his former teacher.

ward.[32] Simmel, as has been said, was right to start with "the most minute and inconsequential facts of everyday life," but wrong to make timeless observations about them, seeing them only as the embodiments of eternal forms. Lukács avoided this problem, but in an unsatisfactory way, by practically shunning empirical reality altogether. He felt, at a deep personal level, a great disgust for the degraded actuality of everyday culture, and hence all his early work was pervaded by an attitude of renunciation toward immediate experience (something he treated as spiritually exhausted, "a charnel-house of long dead inwardness").[33] Culture needed to be rescued, but not by immersing oneself in the chaos of ordinary life. The "merely existent," in its alienated and reified form, could be redeemed only by the "soul," which transforms and respiritualizes it inwardly. There is no other way for what is meaningless to be given meaning except by leaping beyond the quotidian and utilizing it as a "springboard to the ultimate."[34] In and of itself empirical life was treated as something worthless, which is why Lukács wanted "uncultural" reality done away with and replaced by something entirely different.[35]

In this regard, Lukács introduced a new concept which was diametrically opposed to what he called "the vulgar level of given facts": namely, the concept of "totality." Since ordinary cultural facts, taken by themselves, were seen as monadic, opaque, and impenetrable, they could be understood not in isolation but only "in relation" to other cultural facts—that is, through the connections and relationships which "dwell within" things "in their simple and sober everydayness."[36] For Lukács, then, in order really to grasp the meaning of a cultural object, one had to comprehend the *sum of relations* the object entered into— which is to say, one had to understand the whole or the totality of which it was a part. Cultural "things" were viewed as only concretizations of relationships. For example, Lukács believed that under capitalism every object had to be seen as a commodity and approached

---

[32] Andrew Arato, "Lukács' Path to Marxism," *Telos* 7 (1971): 130.

[33] Georg Lukács, cited in György Markus, "The Soul and Life: The Young Lukács and the Problem of Culture," *Telos* 32 (1977): 100.

[34] Georg Lukács, *Soul and Form*, trans. Anna Bostock (Cambridge, Mass., 1974), p. 15.

[35] Markus, "The Soul and Life," pp. 95–115.

[36] Georg Lukács, cited in István Mészáros, *Lukács' Concept of Dialectic* (London, 1972), p. 65.

mainly with regard to its function within the totality of capitalism; its true social meaning could be uncovered in no other way. Furthermore, according to Lukács, one must realize not only that every object is part of the whole but that it implicitly contains the whole in microcosm. The social and cultural totality therefore pervades all aspects of life and culture, even in their tiniest details, and if the whole is degraded, so too are all the aspects. This is why Lukács believed that any sound critique could be a critique only of the whole—not merely of the part or the fragment, as he thought was the case with Simmel's critique. If the compromised totality were not itself criticized and transformed, it would simply be repeated and no "new world-epoch" would emerge in the near future.

On a theoretical level, this may have been a correct interpretation. Still, Lukács seems to have had too much impatience with the vulgar, empirical character of everyday life, and consequently he was too eager to move as rapidly as possible from the part to the social and cultural totality, which he felt more comfortable dealing with on an abstract level. Even when Lukács thought he was looking at something concrete or specific, he was actually looking at, and was more interested in, the totality which manifested itself in and through the detail. All too often Lukács treated the details of everyday life not lovingly, as Simmel often did, but almost incidentally; to him they appeared to be a part of "soulless immediacy," which had to be transcended as quickly as one could.

The net result of Lukács's approach was that his early work was not as empirically based as even Simmel's was. The concept of totality, though extremely important and on the whole a positive contribution, tended to become counterproductive when it overwhelmed and virtually occluded the culturally specific and concrete aspects of everyday life. To be sure, this did not greatly bother the young Lukács, since at the time he was more interested in elaborating a "theory of culture" (which he *did* develop) than in analyzing closely the heterogeneous details of popular culture. But later, in the 1920s and after, Lukács gradually moved toward a closer fusion of the particular and the general in a way which tried to preserve both. He achieved this to some extent in *Geschichte und Klassenbewußtsein* (*History and Class Consciousness*, 1923), especially with his notion of "concrete totality," though he still showed hostility toward an excessive concern with empirical detail, a concern which seemed to him a typically "bourgeois" propensity.[37] Perhaps his most satisfying brief formulation of the proper approach to cultural criticism did not come until 1966. In a recorded conversation during that year, Lukács rejected the overly abstract method of analysis in which he had once excelled and argued instead for a methodology grounded in the concrete. One must "always start out from problems of everyday life," he asserted. "Developed science [wrongly] has a tendency to comprehend every form of life, every living phenomenon, in the highest forms in which it is found, and believes that this is the way to obtain the best analysis. . . . I believe that it is impossible to derive the lower form from the higher form. . . . [For instance], if I start from the categorical imperative, I will not be able to understand the simple practical behavior of everyday life. . . . In other words, we must attempt to investigate conditions *in their original forms of appearance*, and to see under what conditions these forms of appearance become ever more complicated, ever more mediated."[38] This statement was made five years before Lukács died at age eighty-six—too late for him to carry out in practice what he had succinctly, but only theoretically, articulated in this passage.

VI

Perhaps there was only one figure from the younger generation who combined an unusual sensitivity for the details of everyday life with a larger concern for totality and dialectics, and that was Walter Benjamin. Except for Kracauer, and then only occasionally, Benjamin was the only one who devised a method of analysis which stayed *within* the realm of the empirical (without feeling the need to rush beyond it to the "forms," the "totality," the "Not-Yet," or some other abstraction) and yet was able to explore fully the social ramification of cultural details. Benjamin learned this method not from Simmel as much as from two other sources: the Jewish mystical tradition, which taught him to see matter as epiphanic, alive with messages and revelations, and the

[37] Georg Lukács, *History and Class Consciousness*, trans. Rodney Livingstone (Cambridge, Mass., 1971), pp. 153–56.

[38] Hans Heinz Holz, Leo Kofler, and Wolfgang Abenroth, *Conversations with Lukács*, ed. Theo Pinkus (Cambridge, Mass., 1974), pp. 13, 15 (italics mine). This work was first published in Germany in 1967.

careful, idiographic approach to *objets d'art* suggested by the Austrian art historian Alois Riegl (1858–1905), who taught him how to re-create a world of meaning out of the "seemingly insignificant, atypical, or extreme." From the first source, Benjamin picked up not only an extraordinary close-sightedness but also a visionary, and at times almost mystical, mode of writing. From the second, the artistic-critical method of Riegl, Benjamin acquired an ability to re-create the whole of an epoch through its minutest details. In his work entitled *Spätrömische Kunstindustrie* (*Late Roman Art Industry*, 1901), Riegl turned his attention to ordinary objects of Roman life such as buckles, spoons, and earrings, but through them he was able to capture certain general qualities of the age which would otherwise not have been noticed. Benjamin was fascinated by this rare iconographic sense and tried to perfect it in a manner all his own. When later he spoke of "the gift of interpolating into the infinitely small, of inventing, for every intensity, an extensiveness to contain its new, compressed fullness," he was really speaking of the method of cultural analysis he had improvised for himself.[39]

This method came to have a significant impact on Theodor W. Adorno and, through him, on much of the Frankfurt School's later theory and practice of cultural criticism. More recently Benjamin's influence has appeared in the field of semiotics, especially in the emerging cultural criticism based upon the careful use of semiological analysis (developed most thoroughly by Roland Barthes and Umberto Eco). To a greater degree than perhaps any other German critic of this century, it seems to be Benjamin who has the most to offer methodologically for new directions in the analysis of everyday life.

Aside from chronology, it is hard to locate Benjamin in the history of German cultural criticism because he appears to defy all categories. In method he was in many ways closer to Simmel than other members of his generation, even though he did not study with him. Like Simmel, Benjamin took a microscopic approach to cultural analysis. His focus was on what he called the "concrete particular"—that is, the fragment or the apparently irrelevant detail which nevertheless contained important messages. Again like Simmel, Benjamin had a knack for isolating cultural facts and forcing the reader to view them in new

[39] Walter Benjamin, *Reflections: Essays, Aphorisms, Autobiographical Writings*, trans. Edmund Jephcott, ed. Peter Demetz (New York, 1978), p. 83.

and unfamiliar ways (for Benjamin part of the process of "deconstruct-ing" false consciousness). Nonetheless, he also differed from Simmel in significant ways—for instance, in his strong sense of the historicity of things and in his greater interest in the *objective content* of cultural objects, which he believed revealed much more than the structural forms.

In several other respects, Benjamin was not only unlike Simmel but also unlike other members of his own generation in his approach to culture. Where Lukács, for example, was concerned primarily with synthesis, holism, and integration, Benjamin was much more drawn to what was dissonant, contradictory, or ephemeral in modern cultural life. Likewise, while it could be said that both Lukács and Benjamin engaged in "redeeming criticism" (*rettende Kritik*),[40] which had as its goal the transformation of the world, each nevertheless understood the task of redemption in a different way. Lukács, in his early writings, was more apocalyptic: bourgeois culture had to be abolished in its entirety and replaced by something more intense and spiritual. Benjamin, by contrast, was interested mainly in liberating the truth *within* a banal reality, not in doing away with it altogether. The first step was to take an "inventory of the ruins" of contemporary culture, and then try to see how new beginnings could be effected through a rearrangement of the ruins.[41]

In many respects, Benjamin's approach to culture could be viewed as a creative synthesis of the best qualities of Simmel and Lukács. His starting point generally involved a close scrutiny of the part or the frag-ment, but always in a social context, where its social-cultural meaning was illuminated through its connectedness with other things. Ben-jamin, unlike most others, continually showed a willingness to im-merse himself in the particularities of mass culture in order to reveal and release the positive "subjective experiences congealed within them." For this reason, he was more favorably disposed than many of his contemporaries toward certain developments within mass culture (film, the telephone, urban architecture, photography), and he tried to give an *immanent* critique of each of these developments rather than

---

[40]The term is Habermas's. See Jürgen Habermas, *Kultur und Kritik: verstreute Auf-sätze* (Frankfurt-am-Main, 1973), p. 312.

[41]Benjamin, *Reflections*, p. 69.

simply to criticize them in an elitist way from without. In doing this, Benjamin had the ability to make general observations without noticeably leaving the realm of immediacy. Whether he was dealing with a smokestack, a banknote, an article of clothing, or a crooked street, he was always able to open it up to the reader, expose its multitudinous cultural significations, and elucidate its sociohistorical "aura." As Adorno put it, Benjamin's talent was "to allow the meanings [of cultural phenomena] to emerge solely through the shock-like montage of the material."[42] Though the cultural object had priority in this approach, the result was not a simple duplication or mirroring of reality but a surpassing of the given through an "active arrangement of [the] elements [and] the verbal articulation of their inner logic."[43]

Susan Buck-Morss has given one of the best descriptions of Benjamin's method of analyzing everyday life by comparing it to Simmel's. In his essay "The Sociology of Mealtime" (1910), Simmel studied the unnoticed interactions and rituals which occur at the dinner table, but he felt compelled to universalize his conclusions by uncovering the meal's timeless philosophical meaning. His chief interest, therefore, was in the meal's "regularity of time and place, the use of utensils and identical dishes, aesthetics and table manners," and the like.[44] Benjamin, on the other hand, looked for something different in the meal; his gaze was trained upon what was unique and singular and temporally determined about it, since this was likely to contain the most historically specific and culturally valuable information. For Benjamin, then, a meal was not simply an event characterized by a normative set of exchanges and gestures. To treat it so routinely would be to miss what was most important about it, for what takes place at mealtime is decisively shaped by the particular social, material, and cultural relations and expectations of those who participate in it. (Here Benjamin may have taken a cue from Marx, who once made a similar point by arguing that there was no such thing as hunger in the abstract, but only what he called ancient hunger, medieval hunger, and modern hunger. The reason for breaking hunger down in this way was that, for Marx,

---

[42] Theodor W. Adorno, cited in Susan Buck-Morss, *The Origin of Negative Dialectics* (New York, 1977), p. 134.

[43] Ibid., p. 90.

[44] Ibid., p. 75; Georg Simmel, "Soziologie der Mahlzeit," in Landmann, *Brücke und Tür*, pp. 243–50.

"being hungry" was always a social experience for human beings, since it implied some sort of relationship with a socially produced or processed object that was consumed; hunger was therefore inseparably bound up with the kinds of foods which were historically available to feel a hunger for, and these in turn were bound up with the whole history of production and the relations of production.)

"The way a dinner party has gone," Benjamin wrote in *Einbahnstraße* (*One-Way Street*, 1928), "can be told at a glance by whoever stays behind to view the placement of dishes and cups, of wine glasses and food."[45] Here Benjamin conveyed not only the notion that one must start with the minutest details of culture and move toward the whole contained within them but also the idea that something is best glimpsed when it is over or in decline, not when it is at the peak of its expressiveness. This explains, in part, his interest in ruins or in the remains left on an uncleared dinner table. If an object is studied in the full flush of its powers, when it is functioning properly within the system, then it signals only the "official" truths it is supposed to have. But if it is studied as it is waning, or when it has lost its status within the cultural whole, then the object reveals the darker underside of an age, which is precisely what Benjamin wanted to get at. This latter kind of signaling he called "unintentional truth," and his explorations of it were extraordinarily original. Benjamin was convinced that if the fractured and discredited things of everyday life were read in the right way, they would open up a world of meaning which no one else suspected was there.[46] The task of the cultural critic, then, was to decode or decipher quotidian objects no matter how insignificant they might seem, since it was by penetrating the apparently ephemeral minutiae of ordinary existence that the unspoken truth of the whole could be found.

VII

The distance between the cultural criticism of the 1880s (which barely condescended to look at the phenomenon of mass culture) and the cultural criticism of Benjamin in the 1920s (which gave ontological pri-

---

[45] Benjamin cited in Buck-Morss, *Origin*, p. 75.
[46] Ibid., pp. 77–81.

macy to the most banal objects of everyday experience) is almost immeasurable. With the nationalist Right, meaning was imputed to ordinary objects from an Olympian perspective, so much so that it was unnecessary actually to investigate the details of cultural life, only to make pronouncements about them. With Benjamin, by contrast, meaning was educed and extracted *from* things, which is exactly the opposite approach. Benjamin's tactile and sensuous (but nonetheless critical) method laid the foundation for the most promising beginnings of a thoroughgoing critique of mass culture in the twentieth century.

Today a rigorous *Kulturkritik* is virtually unthinkable without a methodological grounding in the entire German tradition from Simmel's work in the 1890s to the work of the leftist critics of the succeeding generation, especially Lukács, Bloch, and Benjamin. Most of these younger left-wing critics had formulated their basic approaches to the analysis of culture by the mid-1920s, and all had embraced, in varying degrees, a Marxist intellectual framework. But it remained for yet another group, coming half a generation or more later, to continue the project of cultural criticism into the 1930s and after. Some of the best of these cultural critics—among them T. W. Adorno (1903–68), Herbert Marcuse (1898–1979), and Leo Lowenthal (1900–)—became associated with the Frankfurt School and wrote their most interesting work under the influence of Critical Theory.[47] Collectively they, along with their predecessors, have succeeded in making an important point, which seems to have been hinted at at least as far back as Simmel: namely, that it is on the level of culture, perhaps more than politics or even economics, that modern life is most firmly secured and integrated. If this is so, then the first task on the way to changing the world would be to analyze closely, with the intention of making transparent, both the cultural forms and the cultural contents of ordinary experiences and values. This is what all the individuals mentioned above, be-

[47]Theodor W. Adorno, *Minima Moralia*, trans. E. F. N. Jephcott (London, 1974); T. W. Adorno and Max Horkheimer, "The Culture Industry," in *Dialectics of Enlightenment*, trans. John Cummings (New York, 1972); Herbert Marcuse, *One-Dimensional Man* (Boston, 1964); and Leo Lowenthal, *Literature, Popular Culture, and Society* (Palo Alto, 1961). For a general account of the Frankfurt School, see Martin Jay, *The Dialectical Imagination: A History of the Frankfurt School and the Institute of Social Research 1923–1950* (Boston, 1973).

ginning especially with Lukács and Bloch, tried to do, each in his own way. It is a project which continues still, since the "critique of everyday life" has turned out to be one of the richest and most fruitful approaches to an in-depth understanding of our "lived world" in all of its ramifications.

GORDON A. CRAIG

Irony and Rage in the German Social Novel: Theodor Fontane and Heinrich Mann

I

IT has often been noted that, in contrast to the situation in Britain and France, the national literature of Germany was not, in the nineteenth century, rich in works of social realism or authors who combined high aesthetic standards with gifts of political and social analysis. There were no Thackerays and Stendhals, or Flauberts and Dickenses, among the prose writers in the decades before unification, and indeed, the German writers who made any pretense of dealing with contemporary and social subjects before 1870—Jean Paul, E. T. A. Hoffmann, Karl Immermann, Gustav Freytag—rarely ventured beyond the realm of the idyllic or the fantastic or the parochial. Their works seldom awaken any shock of recognition among non-German readers and in general have an antiquarian flavor that may be charming but is usually remote from the realities of the modern world.

The explanation often given for this is that Germany was, in two senses, a retarded nation. Long after the Western countries had become powerful nation-states, Germany had continued to be fragmented into dozens of separate political entities, and the resultant lack of a cultural capital like London or Paris, where artists might gather and exchange ideas, had led necessarily to a narrowness of focus, a provincial perspective, and a lack of that urbanity which characterized the literature of the West.[1] Moreover, the effects of political disunity upon economic development, the relative slowness of industrial growth and of the rise of a strong middle class, and the late arrival of such concomitant fea-

---

[1] See Goethe's comments on this in *Goethes sämtliche Werke: Jubiläumsausgabe in 40 Bänden*, ed. Eduard von der Hellen, 40 vols. (Stuttgart and Berlin, 1902–1907), XXXVI, 139, which are balanced by his insistence that, by promoting cultural rivalry among German rulers, disunity had its positive side (*Conversations with Eckermann*, October 23, 1828).

tures of industrial society as urbanization, the proletarianization of the lower classes, and the disintegration of inherited social categories and values deprived German writers of the kinds of themes that challenged their colleagues in countries that were more advanced economically.

There is much to be said for this explanation, but it is not entirely satisfactory, else how would we account for the fact that, even after 1871, when the formation of the empire put an end to Germany's political divisions and the country experienced a surge of economic development that transformed it within a generation into one of Europe's leading industrial producers, German writers still, on the whole, avoided social and political themes? It was not until the 1880s, with the coming of the naturalist movement, that writers and dramatists showed any appreciable interest in such subjects as social justice, sexual discrimination, and the plight of the poor; and, even when they did so, their attention lacked persistence and was often disingenuous, for they tended to concentrate on prostitution, the more lurid aspects of urban crime, and other subjects that were calculated to titillate the palate of the middle-class reading public.[2] In the underlying values of society, the naturalists had little interest, and in its politics none; and by the end of the 1890s, when the vogue of naturalism was past, Germany's writers were little more concerned with serious problems of contemporary life than in the period before 1871. There was a good deal of talk in artistic circles in the 1880s about the need for German writers to emulate the work of Emile Zola and to write sociological novels—this was the stock-in-trade of Michael Georg Conrad and the group in Munich that founded the journal *Die Gesellschaft* in 1885[3]—but, in fact, few German imitators appeared.

The causes of this lack of social engagement must be sought, therefore, not in the slowness of the country's political and economic development but in German views of the proper function of literature. It had long been a strongly rooted prejudice that writers worthy of respect, true *Dichter,* should concern themselves with transcendental themes and spiritual values, that the problems and politics of contemporary society were no business of theirs, and that anyone who persisted in dealing with such questions was automatically deprived of his

[2] See R. Hamann and Jost Hermand, *Naturalismus,* 2d ed. (Berlin, 1968), p. 284.
[3] Ibid., pp. 278–82.

artistic status and relegated to the company of mere scribblers or *Literaten*.[4]

Erich Auerbach has suggested that this odd differentiation owes much to the towering figure of Goethe, whose interest in the actualities of social development was minimal, who found such things as the growth of industry and the increasing evidence of social mobility distasteful, and whose own novels were set in static social contexts, the actual conditions of life serving merely as immobile backgrounds against which the drama of Goethe's own ideological growth unfolded. To the emerging modern structure of life Goethe paid little attention, and such was his authority, Auerbach suggests, that his exclusive concentration on individuality and ideas came to be regarded as the criterion of art as opposed to mere literature.[5] Whether or not Goethe is really responsible for this is less important than the fact that the double standard prevailed. It is notable that Heinrich Heine, a writer of whom one would think any nation in the world would be proud, has never received his due recognition in the land of his birth, in part because political and social criticism was never far below the surface of anything he wrote. This confirmed bias against present-mindedness has doubtless served as a warning to countless writers with aspirations to lasting fame. In our own century, Thomas Mann, who proved that he was capable of writing superb social novels, seemed uncomfortable in this genre and once confessed, "Social problems are my weak point [although] this puts me to some extent at odds with my art form itself, the novel, which is propitious to the examination of social problems. But the lure of . . . individuality and metaphysics simply happens to be ever so much stronger in me. . . . I am German. . . . The Zola-esque streak in me is feeble."[6]

The inhibition imposed by literary tradition was reinforced by a concern for what the reading public would tolerate. Authors like to be read; and German authors after 1871 could not but be aware that a reading public that had made Heinrich von Treitschke's *German His-*

[4] On this, see especially Robert Minder, "Deutsche und französische Literatur—inneres Reich und Einbrüderung des Dichters," in *Kultur und Literatur in Deutschland und Frankreich* (Frankfurt, 1962), pp. 5–43.

[5] Erich Auerbach, *Mimesis: The Representation of Reality in Literature* (Princeton, 1953), pp. 452ff.

[6] Nigel Hamilton, *The Brothers Mann: The Lives of Heinrich and Thomas Mann 1871–1950 and 1875–1955* (New Haven, 1979), p. 213.

tory (Deutsche Geschichte im XIX. Jahrhundert, 1879–94) a bestseller
was hardly likely to welcome books that criticized the social foundations or political practice of the new Reich of which they were so
proud. The educated middle class of the Bismarckian and Wilhelmine
period was excessively preoccupied with its own social status and prestige, which were its substitutes for the political power that it did not
possess; its jealous regard for its position, which it felt was threatened
by the rising class of technicians and functionaries, made it vulnerable
to a process of ideological feudalization and robbed it of its intellectual independence.[7] Increasingly more conservative as the period advanced, this *Bildungsbürgertum* expected from the authors of its
books entertainment or moral elevation. It did not want to be told by
them that there were things in its world that ought to be put right and
that it was responsible to correct them; and it had the power to make
its disapproval felt. It took a determined writer to disregard this.

There were, nevertheless, writers who did disregard it. Some of
them were undistinguished artists and have been forgotten. Who today reads the novels of Friedrich Spielhagen (1829–1911) and Max
Kretzer (1854–1941) and Paul Lindau (1839–1919)? But two, at least,
were writers of distinction whose works are still extant in standard edi-
tions, in paperback and in cinematographic form. Theodor Fontane
and Heinrich Mann were both writers who had less respect for the literary conventions of their own country than for models they found
abroad; for Fontane, a descendant of French Huguenots on both sides
of his family, was an admirer of Sir Walter Scott and an imitator of
Thackeray, while Heinrich Mann, the son of Lübeck patricians, found
Voltaire a more congenial spirit than Goethe and was a follower of Balzac and Flaubert.[8] Both shared a scorn for self-proclaimed *Dichter* who
struck priestly attitudes and discoursed of ideas without social content,
and both strove, in imitation of their Western models, to write—in the
spirit of Trollope's title—about "the way we live now." Both were fascinated by the way in which the circumstances of the founding of the
new Reich and its tumultuous development affected the values of German society and the attitudes of the different classes, and both were
concerned with society's growing indifference to social injustice. Fi-

[7] See Klaus Vondung, ed., *Das wilhelminische Bildungsbürgertum: Zur Sozialgeschichte seiner Ideen* (Göttingen, 1976), pp. 30–33.
[8] See Heinrich Mann, *Essays* (Hamburg, 1960), pp. 15ff., 39ff., 82ff.

nally, both strove, although in different ways, to warn their fellow citizens of the dangers to which their country was prone; and, if their admonitions fell on deaf ears, this was doubtless due partly to the methods they employed, but even more to the persistence of the evils they detected and to their society's self-satisfaction and imperviousness to criticism.

II

Theodor Fontane (1819–98) did not begin to write novels until after the founding of the German Empire. His first experiment in that form, the historical novel *Before the Storm* (*Vor dem Sturm*), appeared in 1878, a few months before the publication of the first volume of Treitschke's *German History*, a work that was intended to create a historical tradition for the new nation by identifying Germany with Prussia. There were doubtless many readers who thought that Fontane's book was guided by the same purpose, for he was already known as the author of highly popular ballads, many of which glorified the Prussian past, as well as of a series of historically colored travel sketches called *Wanderings through Mark Brandenburg* (*Wanderungen durch die Mark Brandenburg*, 1862–82) and stirring accounts of the three wars of unification, and his new book also had a Prussian theme. In fact, the two books were significantly different. Treitschke began the first volume of his *German History* by advancing the thesis that Prussia (and hence Germany) was the creation of its rulers and by writing a eulogy of the Hohenzollerns from the Great Elector to Frederick the Great. Fontane's novel was not about the court but about society; it was the author's first attempt to emulate Thackeray by writing a panoramic account of typical people in typical circumstances at a particular moment in history. The moment chosen was 1813, the year of the Prussian rising against Napoleon, an event that Fontane believed—and had the protagonist of his last novel say—was infinitely more to be praised than the achievements that Treitschke admired, because "everything that happened had less of a command character and had more freedom and self-determination."[9]

---

[9]Theodor Fontane, *Sämtliche Werke*, ed. Edgar Gross, 24 vols. (Munich, 1959–1975), VIII, 283 (*Der Stechlin*).

In his very first novel, the fifty-nine-year-old writer therefore gave some indication of the direction in which his future work would lead him. He was interested in the familiar rather than the heroic aspects of life (to use a phrase of Thackeray's),[10] in the thoughts and activities of ordinary people; he was concerned about the degree of freedom and voluntarism that existed in a society; and he had a differentiated view of Prussia's past and its contribution to contemporary German society.

The last point is worth dwelling upon. Until the end of his life, Fontane considered himself to be a "dyed-in-the-wool Prussian"[11] and continued to admire the qualities of duty and dedication that had enabled his country to survive the great crises of the seventeenth and eighteenth centuries. But as early as 1848, as correspondent for a Dresden newspaper, he had written that "Prussia is a lie" and had criticized it as a police state in terms as uncompromising as those that Heine had used in his polemical poem "Germany, a Winter's Tale";[12] and, although this radicalism had faded in the years that followed, he remained uncomfortably aware that the Prussian legacy to a united Germany would always be ambiguous. In the very year of unification, in a curiously veiled passage in one of his war books, he spoke of the spirit of Potsdam as consisting of "an unholy amalgamation. . . of absolutism, militarism, and philistinism" and said that "a breath of unfreedom, of artificiality, of the contrived . . . blows through it all and oppresses any soul that has a greater need to breathe freely than to get in line."[13] And in the same work, speaking of the young Prussian lieutenants and assessors who were moving into occupied Alsace after the victory over France (and perhaps reflecting that Germany had been conquered by Prussia just as France had), he spoke of the dubious blessing of being ruled by "careerists, adventurers, the restless, and the ambitious."[14]

In the twenty years that followed the publication of *Before the Storm*, Fontane published fourteen novels. Through them runs a steady stream of careerists and adventurers and restless and ambitious men, beginning with Rittmeister von Schach in Fontane's second and last

---

[10] Cited in Walter Müller-Seidel, *Theodor Fontane: Soziale Romankunst in Deutschland* (Stuttgart, 1975), p. 100.

[11] Hans-Heinrich Reuter, *Fontane*, 2 vols. (Munich, 1968), I, 192.

[12] Ibid., pp. 190, 215ff., 221, 229.

[13] Fontane, *Sämtliche Werke*, XVI, 496 (*Aus den Tagen der Okkupation*).

[14] Ibid., pp. 485ff.

historical novel, *Schach von Wuthenow* (1883), including Landrat von Instetten and Major von Crampas in what is perhaps Fontane's greatest novel of society, *Effi Briest* (1895), and ending with Ministerialassessor von Rex and the mill owner von Gundermann in his last novel, *Der Stechlin* (1899). Hans-Heinrich Reuter has pointed out that there are other Prussians in these novels of admirable character and attractive temperament—the general in *Die Poggenpuhls* (1896), Effi's father in *Effi Briest*, Dubslav in *Der Stechlin*—but these are, with one conspicuous exception to be mentioned in a moment, men of advanced years who represent a dying generation.[15] It is the others, who in Fontane's stories are as ruthless in their dealings with their fellows as the young officials whom Fontane saw moving into Alsace, who represent the new Prussia that he detested and feared.

He feared it most of all, perhaps, because in the new Reich Prussianism had acquired an ideological weight that led many people to regard it as a superior form of culture.[16] Fontane always took an ironical view of this idea, for it was his conviction that the values that had sustained Prussia and had made it, for a time, a progressive element in German history were now in the process of atrophying and were, in their genuine form, hardly recognized any longer by those people who boasted most loudly of being Prussian. Nothing illustrates the soundness of his suspicion better than the reception accorded his novel *Trials and Tribulations* (*Irrungen, Wirrungen*) when it began to appear in the *Vossische Zeitung* in 1887. This is the story of a happy love affair between a young nobleman and a daughter of the people; both know that, because of the norms of society, it cannot last, and they are reconciled to this. The heroine of the novel, Lene Nimptsch, is one of Fontane's most fully realized creations, and she is also perhaps the most positively Prussian, as her lover recognizes when he says that her character is one of "simplicity, truthfulness, and naturalness" and that "she has her heart in the right place and a strong feeling for duty, right, and order."[17] Nevertheless, during the serial publication of the book, the *Vossische Zeitung* was bombarded with letters from members of the

[15] Reuter, *Fontane*, I, 483.
[16] Fontane, *Sämliche Werke*, VIII, 251 (*Der Stechlin*).
[17] Ibid., III, 170, 205 (*Irrungen, Wirrungen*).

Prussian aristocracy demanding to know when "this dreadful whore's story" was going to be terminated.[18]

The disintegration of values took several forms. It was, for one thing, clear to Fontane that the military virtues that had characterized the Prussian upper classes were in the process of degenerating into a blend of arrogance and braggadocio that, communicated to the general public, assumed the form of a dangerous kind of militarism. When he published his first novel, Fontane wrote to his publisher that "it struck a blow for religion, morality, and the fatherland, but was full of hatred against the 'blue cornflower' [the Prussian national flower] and against 'With God for King and Fatherland'—that is, against the windy spouting and caricature of that trinity."[19] On another occasion he noted that, if people insisted on decorating their lapels on every military anniversary, they ought to find something better than the "stupid" cornflower, something "with red trouser stripes" (the sartorial distinction of the General Staff).[20] In his novels, references to the pervasive militarism of society are numerous. In *Frau Jenny Treibel* (1892), Fontane caricatures the kind of person, all too numerous in Bismarckian and Wilhelmine Germany, who believed that the attainment of an officer's commission in the army reserve made him a superior being, whose opinions had more weight than those of mere civilians;[21] and, in *The Adulteress* (*L'Adultera*, 1882), Melanie van Straaten, reading the visiting card of a caller, says, "Lieutenant in the Reserve of the Fifth Dragoon Regiment. . . . Abhorrent, these everlasting lieutenants! There are no human beings any more!"[22]

One of the worst aspects of this progressive militarization of society was that it tended, in Fontane's view, to spread formalistic and artificial ethical concepts and taboos that had deleterious social effects. Thus, the old military concept of honor had, in civilian life, been translated into a cruel and unnatural code of etiquette that imprisoned the upper classes in a moral straitjacket. As early as 1883, Fontane hit out at this in his novel *Schach von Wuthenow*, which tells the story of a young

[18] Reuter, *Fontane*, II, 669.
[19] Ibid., p. 595.
[20] Kenneth Attwood, *Fontane und das Preußentum* (Berlin, 1970), p. 276.
[21] Fontane, *Sämtliche Werke*, VII, 25ff. (*Frau Jenny Treibel*).
[22] Ibid., IV, 41 (*L'Adultera*).

officer who kills himself because he is forced by considerations of military honor to take a course of action that he fears will lead to a degree of social ridicule that he will not be able to tolerate. After the young man's death, Fontane's spokesman in the novel, a staff captain named von Bülow, says:

> I have belonged to this army long enough to know that "honor" is its every third word. A dancer is charming "on my honor"; yes, I have even had money-lenders recommended and introduced to me as superb "on my honor." And this constant talking about honor, about a false honor, has confused the concept and made real honor dead. . . . To this cult of false honor, which is nothing but vanity and perverseness, Schach has succumbed, and better men than he will do the same. Remember what I say. . . . When the Ming dynasty was coming to its end, and the victorious Manchu armies had already penetrated into the palace gardens of Peking, messengers and envoys continually appeared to announce victory after victory to the Emperor because it was contrary to "the tone" of good society and the court to speak of defeats. Oh, this good tone! An hour later an empire was in fragments and a throne overturned! And why? Because all affectation leads to lies, and lies to death.[23]

Fontane's most extended treatment of the tyranny of honor comes in *Effi Briest*, after Effi's husband, the Prussian bureaucrat von Instetten, discovers that, six and a half years earlier, his wife had an affair with a Major von Crampas. Although he knows that she has had no relations with Crampas since that time and although he dearly loves her, Instetten challenges the major to a duel and kills him, then drives Effi from his home and takes her child away from her. As an intelligent man, he is well aware that his conduct is not rational, but, in order to render his doubts ineffectual, he tells a close friend, Baron von Wüllersdorf, of the affair, thus making it, as he sees it, impossible for him not to go forward with his drastic course of action. In what has been called "the greatest conversation scene in the German novel,"[24] Instetten says:

> We're not isolated individuals, we belong to society, and we must continually take society into account; we are dependent upon it. If one could live in isolation, I could let this go; I would then be bearing a burden that I had agreed to accept. . . . But with people living all together, something has evolved that exists here and now, and we've become accustomed to

---

[23] Ibid., II, 383, 384 (*Schach von Wuthenow*).
[24] K. Wandrey, *Theodor Fontane* (Munich, 1914), p. 285.

judging everything in accordance with its rules, other people and ourselves as well. And to violate that doesn't work. Society would scorn us
and, in the end, we would scorn ourselves and not be able to stand it, and
would shoot a bullet through our heads.

In any case, he adds, there's no keeping the secret now. He has to go
ahead. If he does not, then some day, when someone has suffered an
affront, and he suggests that allowances should be made because no
real harm has been done, he will see a smile pass, or start to pass, over
Wüllersdorf's face and will imagine him thinking, "Good old Instetten!
He's never been able to discover anything that smells too strong for
him!" Wüllersdorf, who has been trying to dissuade him, now strikes
his guns. "I think it's dreadful that you're right," he says, "but you *are*
right. . . . The world is how it is, and things go, not the way we want
them to, but the way others want them to. All that high-flown stuff
about a judgment of God is, of course, rubbish, and we don't want any
of it. On the other hand, our cult of honor is a form of idolatry, and yet
we must submit to it, as long as the idol is allowed to stand."[25]

Fontane's view that the Prussian aristocracy had submitted to a
kind of totemism convinced him that it was fast losing its originality,
spontaneity, and moral energy and was ceasing to be a vital force in
German life, a conviction that he expressed in the novel *Die Poggenpuhls*. But it had meanwhile corrupted other sections of society, the
educational establishment and the clergy, which repeated and sancti-
fied its prejudices, and the once self-reliant middle class. In the days
when, as he said, to be a *Bürger* meant to possess three qualities,
"property, respect for the law, and the feeling of freedom that flows
from the first two," Fontane had high hopes for the middle class and, in
1865, could say that its dominance of German life would be benefi-
cial.[26] But that was before its political energy had been sapped by its
final defeat in the constitutional struggle in Prussia and its moral instincts eroded by the easy affluence of the first years of unification. The
portraits of the *Besitzbürgertum* (propertied middle class) that Fontane gives us in his novels are increasingly unflattering and show that
he reprobated their materialism less than their attempts, at any cost,
to effect a symbiotic relationship with the aristocracy.

[25] Fontane, *Sämtliche Werke*, VII, 373–75 (*Effi Briest*).
[26] Reuter, *Fontane*, I, 92, 416ff.

In *The Adulteress* the parvenuism of the new bourgeoisie is symbolized in the acquisitive instinct of van Straaten, a typical entrepre-
neur of the *Gründerjahre* ("founding years" of the Reich) with preten-
sions to culture that he satisfies by buying copies of great paintings. In
Frau Jenny Treibel, Counselor of Commerce Treibel prefers to copy
the politics of the aristocratic classes and becomes a candidate for a
conservative seat in a rural district, while cultivating decayed gentle-
women to help his cause. One of them is bewildered by his ambitions
and lectures him on the politics of social stratification. "Aristocratic estate owners are agrarian conservatives," she tells him. "Professors belong to the National Liberal party; and industrialists are Progressives.
Become a Progressive! What do you want with a royal order? If I were
in your place I would go in for municipal politics and seek bourgeois
distinction!"[27] This is not the kind of advice Treibel wants, or his wife
Jenny, as ruthless a social climber as Proust's Madame Verdurin. As a
friend says, Jenny "really imagines that she has a sensitive heart and a
feeling for higher things, but she has a heart only for the ponderable,
for everything that can be weighed and that pays interest."[28] Finally, in
Der Stechlin, Fontane shows us, in the figure of the mill owner von
Gundermann, the kind of person who has squandered so much of himself to acquire an aristocratic title that he has forfeited all respect and is
generally regarded as a mean-spirited intriguer and sycophant. "Gundermann is a bourgeois and a parvenu," someone says, "therefore just
about the worst thing that anyone can be."[29]

It was the effect of all this on social relations that most concerned
Fontane. As early as January, 1878, in a letter to Mathilde von Rohr, he
wrote: "When I look around me in society, I encounter in the upper
strata of our people, among the aristocracy, the officials, the digni-
taries, the artists, and the scholars, a merely moderate decency. They
are narrow, covetous, dogmatic, without a sense of form and propriety;
they want to take and not to give; they respect the appearance of honor
rather than honor itself; and, to an unbelievable extent, they lack nobility of mind, generosity, and the gift of forgiveness and sacrifice.
They are self-seeking, hard, and unloving."[30] A society whose upper

---

[27] Fontane, *Sämtliche Werke*, VII, 28 (*Frau Jenny Treibel*).
[28] Ibid., p. 71.
[29] Ibid., VIII, 162 (*Der Stechlin*).
[30] *Fontanes Briefe*, ed. Gotthard Erler, 2 vols. (Berlin, 1968), I, 445.

classes were like this was unlikely to have much understanding of, or sympathy for, its most vulnerable members.

It has often been pointed out that Fontane's range of social vision was limited and that he did not write, for example, about the problems of the poor. This is true enough, but he did pay more attention than most of his contemporaries to another and larger group of victims of society—namely, women, who are the main characters of all but the first and last of his novels.[31] This was not because he held theoretical or doctrinaire views on the subject of women's rights, although he knew, of course, that this was becoming the subject of lively debate, and he was acquainted with August Bebel's widely read *Woman and Socialism* (*Die Frau und der Sozialismus*), which was published in 1883. Rather, his observations of German life convinced him that the current condition of women was a distressing commentary on the moral state of the country.

Fontane's reaction to the protests against the serialization of *Trials and Tribulations* illustrates his approach to the problem. He wrote to his son: "We are up to our ears in all sorts of conventional lies and should be ashamed of the hypocrisy we practice and the rigged game we are playing. Are there, apart from a few afternoon preachers into whose souls I should not like to peer, any educated and decent people who are *really* morally outraged over a seamstress who is having an unsanctioned love affair? I don't know any. . . . The attitude of a few papers, whose yield of illegitimate children well exceeds a dozen (the chief editor having the lion's share) and which are now pleased to teach me morality, is revolting!"[32] It was these hypocrisies that he sought to attack in his novels, exposing that double standard of morality which tolerated infidelity and sexual license on the part of males (in *Stine* [1890], for example) but outlawed women who acted similarly (in *The Adulteress*, for example, and *Effi Briest*). In two of his most interesting but least read stories, *Quitt* (1891) and *Cécile* (1887), and also in *Effi Briest*, he dealt with the tendency in upper-class society to educate women only in such things as would make them attractive to men and secure them good marriages, a practice he found shameful and degrading, since it deprived women of the opportunity for full development

---

[31] Reuter, *Fontane*, II, 643.
[32] *Fontanes Briefe*, II, 172.

of their talents and depersonalized or reified them by turning them into commodities in the male market or, as in the case of *Cécile*, into odalisques.

Finally, in his books about women, Fontane challenged the basic assumptions of a society that was male dominated and could read with complacency the views of people like Arthur Schopenhauer, Friedrich Hebbel, and Richard Wagner, who regarded women as an inferior species. In the relationship between Melanie and Rubehn in *The Adulteress*, Stine and Waldemar in *Stine*, Lene and Botho in *Trials and Tribulations*, and Mathilde and Hugo in *Mathilde Möhring* (1891), it is the woman who is the stronger partner, the more resilient under the pressures of society, and in every sense the educator of the man. It has been said of Mathilde Möhring that none of Fontane's other women possesses as many qualities, positive and ambiguous, that point to the future—that Mathilde, indeed, seems to the modern reader more a twentieth-century than a nineteenth-century woman.[33] If that is true, it is also true that she reflects the basic predicament of women in Wilhelmine society, for she is allowed to profit from the fruits of intellectual energy and social and political skills only as long as her husband is present to take credit for them. After his death, she is forced to return to the position out of which she lifted him. Nevertheless, she remains undefeated.

Having said all this about Fontane as a critic of his society, one must admit that the cultural and educational establishment of Fontane's own time was almost completely impervious to his strictures, apparently finding it impossible to regard the man who had written *Wanderings through Mark Brandenburg* as anything but a loyal subject, true to king, nobility, and the existing social order. It was only after the publication of his correspondence that it was realized that this was far from being the case, and this caused a small revolution in German studies.[34] That this is so, and that the reading public of Fontane's time read his stories with no deeper discomfort than an occasional twinge of moral outrage over his frankness in dealing with the relations between the sexes, gives some substance to the charges of critics like Georg Lukács who have written that, with all his social sensitivity, Fontane never

---

[33] Reuter, *Fontane*, II, 700.
[34] Robert Minder, *Dichter in der Gesellschaft: Erfahrungen mit deutscher und französischer Literatur* (Frankfurt, 1966), p. 151.

sought to explain the basic causes of the ills he revealed or to suggest any solutions for them. In novels like *Effi Briest*, Lukács has written, Fontane was really predicting that the Bismarckian Prussia-Germany was headed for another Jena. But "it was really a passive, a skeptical-pessimistic prophecy. The forces of German renewal lay outside his literary horizon."[35]

This last sentence is perhaps not wholly fair. Fontane's weakness, if that is what it was, was not so much a matter of lack of analytical depth as it was of choice. He believed that it was the function of the novelist not to tell his readers what to do but, rather, to explain to them the way things are. "The task of the modern novel," he once said, "seems to me to be that of portraying a life, a society, a circle of people who are an undistorted reflection of the life we lead."[36] If one can do that, with the intensity, clarity, perspicuity, comprehension, and feeling that are demanded of the artist, then readers should be able to understand their society and their lives better. Whether they will want to change them is really up to them.

Fontane's critical mode was one of detachment, ambiguity, and irony. It is no accident that there is more conversation than action in his books, for conversation is the ideal medium for expressing the differences of view and of perception of reality that we find in real life. As a private individual, Fontane might feel, as he said in a letter in 1898, that "everything that is interesting is to be found in the fourth estate. The bourgeoisie is frightful, and the aristocracy and clerics are old-fashioned. . . . The new, the better world begins with the fourth estate. . . . The workers have attacked everything in a new way; they have not only new goals but new methods of attaining them."[37] But he did not say this unambiguously in his novels. In *Der Stechlin*, the pastor Lorenzen says: "A new world is coming. I believe a better and happier one. Or, if not happier, at least a time with more oxygen in the air, a time when we can breathe more freely." But he gives no reasons for this optimism. A little later in the book, old Stechlin says, "Our whole social system, which prejudice rates so high, is more or less barbarism," but he does not reveal any prescription for changing this.[38] There

---

[35] Georg Lukács, *Deutsche Realisten des 19. Jahrhunderts* (Berlin, 1959), p. 306.
[36] Reuter, *Fontane*, II, 628.
[37] *Fontanes Briefe*, II, 395ff.
[38] Fontane, *Sämtliche Werke*, VIII, 154, 168 (*Der Stechlin*).

is hardly a major political issue that was canvassed during the Bismarckian and Wilhelmine years that does not surface in a conversation in one or another of Fontane's novels, but it is never discussed at length and is often dismissed with that ironical humor that is the hallmark of *Frau Jenny Treibel* and *Der Stechlin* without having afforded any clear indication of what the author thinks.

Robert Minder has lamented this failure to speak out and has written that, if only Fontane had been as forthright in his novels as he was, for example, in his letter to his friend Friedländer on April 5, 1897, when he shrewdly criticized the character and policies of William II and declared that the East Elbian aristocracy was Germany's misfortune,[39] the empire would have had, "along with Nietzsche and Wagner, an epic-writer of world rank."[40] This may be true. But it seems likely that Fontane chose his ironic and detached method with an eye to his audience, knowing its self-satisfaction and unresponsiveness to criticism and hoping that, if he helped it to understand what was happening to German society, he might at least trouble its complacency and stimulate doubt.

III

If Fontane was a gentle critic, as one American historian has called him,[41] Heinrich Mann (1871–1950) was just the opposite. Born in Lübeck in the year of unification, the eldest son of a merchant in grain who became a senator of the Hanseatic town in 1877, he showed his preference for the arts rather than for commerce at an early age and was making his first experiments in verse and prose before he was fifteen. His first literary hero was Heinrich Heine, and he may have derived some of his gift of satire and his rage over the crimes committed in the name of authority from that great enemy of social injustice. From Heine, too, it was an easy step to French culture, to Stendhal and Balzac and, from them, to Flaubert and Zola, who taught him, as he later wrote, that "the novel should not only portray; it should make things better."[42]

---

[39] *Fontanes Briefe*, II, 417–20.

[40] Minder, *Dichter in der Gesellschaft*, p. 152.

[41] See Joachim Remak, *The Gentle Critic: Theodor Fontane and German Politics, 1848–1898* (Syracuse, 1964).

[42] Mann, *Essays*, p. 158.

Fontane he also read at an early age and with mounting admiration, describing him in 1890 as "my favorite among the moderns . . . a brilliant critic without prejudices and . . . a novelist of pace and skill," although at that time his great predecessor's poetry, particularly the ballads, seems to have appealed to him more than the stories.[43] It may very well have been Fontane's influence, combined with that of Stendhal, that led Mann at the age of twenty-five to decide that he wanted to write novels about contemporary life in Germany, because, as he remembered later, he felt that German society no longer knew itself and was dissolving into fragments. He later wrote: "Do you think that democracy can grow [in Germany] without the portrayal of society? In terms of the future, it is the only thing that has any significance or meaning—not 'timelessness,' which is today still the highest aim [of literature]." Stendhal's novels, he added, were not "timeless" in the German sense of the word; "they portrayed their time with absolute critical sensitivity."[44] When Mann wrote his first novel in 1900, a story of Berlin life called *In the Land of Cockaigne* (*Im Schlaraffenland*), the influence of Stendhal's *Lucien Leuwen* was apparent, as was that of de Maupassant's *Bel Ami*; and to an even greater extent this first experiment could be described as a direct descendant of Fontane's *Frau Jenny Treibel*.

Indeed, Fontane's study of bourgeois life and social parvenuism influenced both Heinrich Mann's first work and the novel *Buddenbrooks*, written by his younger brother Thomas a year later.[45] *Buddenbrooks*, Thomas Mann's only real novel of society, tells of the rise and decline of a bourgeois family in a middle-sized city, whose fortune was founded, as was that of Fontane's Treibels, in the *Gründerjahre* immediately after the consummation of German unification. *The Land of Cockaigne* describes a new generation of parvenus that has consolidated its social position in the first years of the reign of William II and shows every sign of continuing to flourish. If its tone was sharper and its attacks upon the tuft-hunting proclivities of the bourgeoisie more savage than that of Fontane's novel, where the author regarded the social machinations of his protagonist with a degree of ironic affection, this was because Heinrich Mann recognized in the kind of people rep-

[43] Hamilton, *The Brothers Mann*, p. 32.

[44] Ibid., p. 212.

[45] Müller-Seidel, *Theodor Fontane*, p. 316; Ulrich Weisstein, *Heinrich Mann* (Tübingen, 1962), pp. 22ff.

resented in his novel by the Türkheimer family a new and dangerous force. These parvenus were not like those who, a generation earlier, had sought status by means of social and cultural collaboration with the aristocratic classes and who had generally been fobbed off with meaningless trifles. They resembled neither the effete bourgeois intellectuals who were to become the subject of Mann's novel of Munich life, *The Hunt for Love* (*Die Jagd nach Liebe,* 1904), nor the Austrian liberal bourgeoisie whose frustrations are described in Carl F. Schorske's book about *fin-de-siècle* Vienna.[46] The Türkheimers represented the new power of finance capital, which threatened to be the solvent of all forms of status and all the values that held society together.

The Land of Cockaigne, in other words, was really about power, and it marked the beginnings of Heinrich Mann's fascination with the dimensions assumed by this problem in Wilhelmine society, with the growing obsession with power, and with the infinite ability of power to corrupt. In contrast to Fontane, who was inclined to believe that the working classes might be immune to the ills that he saw afflicting the aristocracy and the working classes, Mann made no such distinction. In each of his three great social novels, representatives of all classes are shown as equally vulnerable to the seductions of power and equally unrepentant when their ambitions are defeated. *The Land of Cockaigne* is a kind of distorted *Bildungsroman* about an ambitious young man from the country named Andreas Zumsee. He is advised by a journalist of his acquaintance that, if he wants to make his way to fortune and fame, he must attach himself to the Türkheimers and become part of their system. This adviser says:

> Türkheimer is, in fact, a reasonably enlightened man. He even recognizes that the communism that is so popular today represents a contemporary need. Provided, of course, it is a sound communism that stays within appropriate bounds. . . . But the family has many branches and extends, on the one side, even to princely personages who are accustomed to plant trees here and there in the Türkheimer garden. . . . And, at the other end, it reaches to people like us, who, if we show skill and agility, can pick this or that fifty-mark note out of the air.[47]

Zumsee is easy to persuade. He becomes an attendant lord at the court of these flashy but powerful parvenus, has a giddy series of pre-

[46] Carl F. Schorske, *Fin-de-Siècle Vienna: Politics and Culture* (New York, 1980).
[47] Heinrich Mann, *Zwei Romane* (Berlin, 1966), p. 183 (*Im Schlaraffenland*).

ferments, and then makes a mistake and is cast aside. He has by then, however, been so completely corrupted by the system that he is incapable of resentment against his former patrons. At the end of the book, as he watches them driving down the Leipziger Straße, swollen with new commercial successes in eastern Europe, "stupid, profligate, and happy," and learns that Türkheimer has just received a decoration from the Crown, Andreas feels only anger at the inadequacy of his own social adroitness; he has, he says, "cravings that cannot be stilled and an endless regret."[48]

Heinrich Mann's second important novel is better known to Western audiences than any of his other works because, in 1931, it was made into a popular motion picture called *The Blue Angel*, starring Marlene Dietrich and Emil Jannings and directed by Joseph von Sternberg. A powerful study of sadism, the film tells the story of a martinet schoolmaster who is destroyed by an infatuation for a cabaret performer, to whom he sacrifices his career and his social position.[49] But the film has little of the analytical incisiveness and bite of the novel, *Professor Unrat*, which was published in 1905 and was less a story about sexual attraction than it was about power and its affinity with anarchy.

In *Professor Unrat*, and, indeed, in his later trilogy about the Wilhelmine Reich, Mann was in a sense writing a commentary on Nietzsche's statement in *The Twilight of the Idols* that obsession with power deprives a society of the vital energies that it needs to sustain civilization.[50] The schoolmaster Rath (or, as he is called by his students, Unrat, or garbage) has no interest in his calling as a teacher or in the world of scholarship. He is wholly possessed with the idea of the power that his position gives him over his charges and, by extension, over society in general. He hates everyone with whom he comes into contact because he senses that he is not respected:

> He went among these people unesteemed and even ridiculed, but in his own consciousness he belonged to those who ruled. No banker and no monarch had a greater share in power or was more interested in maintaining the existing order than Unrat. He was zealous in behalf of all authorities and raged in the secrecy of his study against the workers, who,

[48] Ibid., pp. 368ff.

[49] See Siegfried Kracauer, *From Caligari to Hitler: A Psychological History of the German Film* (Princeton, 1947), pp. 215–18.

[50] Friedrich Nietzsche, *Götzendämmerung* (Stuttgart, 1964), p. 125.

had they attained their goals, would probably have seen to it that Unrat too was better paid. He warned young teachers . . . against the baleful disease of the modern spirit that was shaking the pillars of order. He wanted those foundations to be strong: an influential church, a reliable army, strict obedience and sound morals. . . . As a tyrant, he knew how one controlled slaves: how the mob, the enemy, the fifty thousand refractory students who afflicted him were to be tamed.[51]

When this monster of rectitude and adulator of authority fell in love with the singer Rosa Gründlich and was dismissed from his post and accused of spreading a pestilence among right-thinking people by his example, the notion of his being able to do such a thing, the prospect of revenging himself by poisoning society, had an exciting effect upon him;[52] he proceeded, with the assistance of his paramour's attractions, to debauch the town by running a combination of gambling hell and bordello for the very people who condemned him. "In the midst of those who rushed, by way of the tables, towards bankruptcy, disgrace, and the gallows," Mann writes, "Unrat, with his knock-knees and impassive mien, was like an old schoolmaster whose class had fallen into a dissolute frenzy and who, from behind his eyeglasses, was taking note of the ringleaders so as to be able later to ruin their character references. They had dared to set themselves up against the power of the ruler; very well, he would loose them from restraint so that they could beat each others' ribs in and break each others' necks. Out of the tyrant, the anarchist had finally emerged."[53]

Moreover, as an anarchist, gloating over his success in disclosing what lay beneath the respectability of the town's leading citizens, Unrat made an important discovery—namely, that what is ordinarily called morality is merely a form of stupidity or philistinism, used by the powerful and cynical to maintain their control over those who think that they cannot do without it. It has no real depth or strength and can be stripped away by the clever practitioner of power, who knows how to arouse and mobilize the baser impulses for his own purposes.[54] We are reminded of Fontane's definition of the spirit of Potsdam as "an unholy amalgamation . . . of absolutism, militarism, and philistinism";

---

[51] Mann, *Zwei Romane*, pp. 403ff. (*Professor Unrat*).
[52] Ibid., p. 513.
[53] Ibid., pp. 546ff.
[54] Ibid., pp. 518.

but Mann's insight had a disturbing forward thrust and was a chilling premonition of things to come in Germany.

So, finally, was the so-called Empire (*Kaiserreich*) trilogy, which Mann intended to be the crowning achievement of his preoccupation with the social novel. Theodor Fontane had never tried to deal directly in his novels with the real stuff of politics, with the struggles of the parties, the political influence of agriculture, industry, and high finance, the relationship between interest groups and foreign policy, and the whole complicated web of relationships between the activities of government and the life of ordinary people. Heinrich Mann conceived the daring notion of dealing with all of this in three novels, whose action was set in the years from 1890 to 1914. It seems clear that he was inspired by the example of Zola's novels about the end of the Second French Empire; and, like Zola, he sought to add verisimilitude to his account by having his characters move against the background of real events, like the workers' riots in Berlin in 1892, the debate on the military law in 1893 and the dissolution of the Reichstag, the court scandals of the late 1890s, the beginning of the naval agitation, the *Daily Telegraph* affair of 1908, and the gathering tension before 1914. This did not always work well.

The first and most successful of the three novels was *The Man of Straw* (*Der Untertan*), finished in 1914 but not published until four years later. In the broadest sense, this is the story of the defeat in a small town of what is left of the liberal tradition of 1848 by special interests and political jobbery in the form of an alliance between a new "Kaiser's party" and an unprincipled local Social Democratic organization. Within this framework Mann has set the young careerist Diederich Hessling, who, by modeling himself in speech and manner, and as far as possible in appearance, upon the young emperor, by making undeviating loyalty to him a personal attribute and a weapon against his rivals and enemies, and by disregarding considerations of professional integrity and human decency, tramples his way to eminence in his community. The second novel, *The Poor* (*Die Armen*), written during the war and published contemporaneously with *The Man of Straw*, continues Hessling's career, focusing now upon his direction of a gigantic industrial complex and upon the unscrupulous methods that he uses to keep his workers at minimal wages, to exploit them by making them live in company quarters and eat company food, to use strikebreakers and spies to defeat their attempts to organize, and to discredit their leaders and describing how, when the workers are finally goaded into rising against him, vigorous government intervention frustrates them and leaves him with undiminished power. The conclusion of the trilogy, *The Head* (*Der Kopf*), published in 1925, is a *roman à clef* in which the protagonist, a humanist with the improbable name of Claudius Terra, seeks to defeat the dangerous policies of figures who resemble Bülow, Tirpitz, and Bethmann Hollweg in the decade before the war.

Only the first of these novels can be considered a successful work of art, and even it seems hardly to merit the praise lavished on it by Kurt Tucholsky and other left-wing intellectuals during the Weimar period.[55] Even so, it is a powerful indictment of a society that seemed increasingly to be composed of the tyrannical and the servile, a system that rested upon brutality and Byzantinism and seemed to be inspired by a secret death wish, which is hinted at in the paean to power that comes to Diederich's mind as he sees the emperor riding through the Brandenburger Gate: "The Power that rides over us and whose hooves we kiss. . . . Against which we are powerless, because we all love It. Which we have in our blood, because we have submission in our blood. . . . Living in It, sharing in It, showing no mercy toward those who are further from It, and triumphing even as It smashes us; for thus does It vindicate our love for It!"[56]

Despite Mann's relentless insistence upon the moral obliquity of nearly every character whom he presents to our gaze, the socialist leader being shown to be as self-seeking as the protagonist, the book has undeniable satirical power. The burlesque association of Diederich's oratorical style with that of his royal master is well sustained, and the passages dealing with Diederich's university career, his membership in the New Teuton fraternity, and his interruption of his honeymoon to follow the emperor to Rome are rich in comic invention.

In the novels that follow, these qualities are sadly diminished. If *The Poor* was intended to be another *Germinal*, it fell far short of the

---

[55] See the interesting analyses of the trilogy in Weisstein, *Heinrich Mann*, pp. 111–41; and R. Travis Hardaway, "Heinrich Mann's *Kaiserreich* Trilogy and the Democratic Spirit," *Journal of English and German Philology* 53 (1954): 319–33.

[56] Heinrich Mann, *Der Untertan: Roman* (Munich, 1969), p. 47.

mark, for Mann's workers lack the elemental savagery of Zola's, and their leaders hover between tortured indecisiveness and Germanic sentimentality. Mann's hatred of the system that he was portraying was beginning to make him forget the requirements of his craft, and sometimes the motivation of his characters—Diederich's decision, for example, that to expose his son to the risk of murder was an acceptable price to pay for eliminating the chief labor agitator—was contrived and improbable.

Yet Mann's powers of social analysis remained as acute as ever. His treatment of the activities of the Pan-German League in *The Head* has the realistic sharpness of his earlier treatment of the theme of money and power in *The Land of Cockaigne* and was perhaps a sign of concern that this danger had not been eliminated with the fall of the empire, a feeling also expressed in his powerful novella *Kobes*, which appeared in the same year as *The Head* and was inspired by the role of the magnate Hugo Stinnes in Weimar politics. But his method of presentation was now departing from the realism that Theodor Fontane had insisted should be the novelist's principal concern. Perhaps because he wanted his books to change things rather than merely describe them, Mann was resorting increasingly to exaggeration, and his language was beginning to resemble that of the expressionists in its passion and intensity. After reading *The Poor*, his admirer Arthur Schnitzler wrote to him: "The realities that you present in all their shattering power strike me at times as being distorted into caricature and often as being elevated into symbols, without it generally being clear to me what principle determines these distortions and enhancements. . . . Certain oversimplifications, which I think I find not so much in the action as in the willful, precipitate stylistic execution that you have chosen this time, have distressed me—perhaps because it's almost as if I were watching you distrust your own genius."[57]

This was shrewd enough, although, if Mann was beginning to have doubts, they were less about his own gifts than about the importance and usefulness of what he was doing. The reading audience that had tolerated Fontane's irony had no similar patience with Mann's rage.

[57] Klaus Schröter, *Heinrich Mann in Selbstzeugnissen und Bilddokumenten* (Hamburg, 1967), p. 90.

The social novels after *The Man of Straw* were not successful; indeed, Mann never again had a significant success until he wrote his great historical novels about Henry IV of France, and that happened when he was in exile from his own country. Years later he reflected upon the reasons for the failure of his earlier books and wrote to a friend, "What I had to suffer for was my feeling for public life. It alienated people in Germany at the time I began writing, despite Fontane, who was there." Later on, he added, he was rejected for his foresight. "I wrote in advance of what would actually become of Germany. People blamed me for it, as if I had been the one who caused it."[58]

IV

In 1955 Gottfried Benn addressed himself in a public lecture to the question, Should writers improve life? and concluded that they couldn't and shouldn't try to do so.[59] This was not surprising, coming from a writer whose lack of political responsibility was such that he had actually accepted the presidency of the Literature Section of the Prussian Academy of Arts in 1933, after Heinrich Mann had been forced from that post by Nazi pressure and had left the Academy, along with his brother, Käthe Kollwitz, Ricarda Huch, and other distinguished artists.[60] Benn's view was a restatement of the traditional German attitude that *Dichtung* was a sphere unto itself, elevated above the crass realities of ordinary existence.

Both Fontane and Heinrich Mann rejected that view of literature, Fontane with jocularities, Mann with bitter reflection on *la trahison des clercs*.[61] Both tried to change their worlds by using art to illumine the problems of their time, and both failed, for reasons that we have noted. But their failure was at least an honorable one, and it was by no means complete. By rejecting the inherited convention of the novel, they showed German writers the way to break out of the provincialism that had for long years denied them a hearing outside their own coun-

---

[58] Heinrich Mann, *Briefe an Karl Lemke und Klaus Pinkus* (Hamburg, 1964) (to Lemke, December 10, 1948).

[59] Gottfried Benn, *Essays, Reden, Vorträge*, 2d ed. (Wiesbaden, 1962), pp. 583ff.

[60] See Hildegard Brenner, *Ende einer bürgerlichen Kunst-Institution: Die politische Formierung der Preußischen Akademie der Künste ab 1933* (Stuttgart, 1972).

[61] Mann, *Essays*, p. 13 ("Geist und Tat," 1910).

try; and, by demonstrating that it was possible to combine great art with social engagement, they set a standard for the writers of contemporary Germany to follow, one that is being followed to an extent that would have been inconceivable before 1945. This was no mean achievement, and it is certainly no accident that their memories are green and their readers numerous in both parts of Germany today and that there are constant reruns, not only of *The Blue Angel* but also of Wolfgang Staudte's film of *The Man of Straw,* made in the German Democratic Republic in 1951, and of Rainer Werner Fassbinder's much-admired recent production of *Effi Briest*.

GARY D. STARK

Cinema, Society, and the State:
Policing the Film Industry in Imperial Germany

I

ON November 1, 1895, the audience at the Wintergarten, one of imperial Berlin's most popular vaudeville theaters, sat impatiently through the regular program of singers, dancers, magicians, and comedy skits. Most of the patrons were waiting for the last act of the evening, an attraction billed as the "Bioscope," which was to make its debut that night. At last, two brothers rolled out and switched on their new invention; as the audience watched in amazement, Max and Emil Skladanowsky's Bioscope projected moving pictures onto the wall. Thus the world's first performance of a film to a paying audience took place that chilly autumn night, and a new entertainment medium was born.[1] Before long, the commercial cinema would captivate millions of viewers throughout Germany and the world. By the outbreak of the First World War in 1914, some sixty thousand cinema theaters had sprung up across the globe, and next to sex and drink the cinema had become *the* entertainment medium of the masses.

It was, curiously enough, not in the large cities but in the countryside that the German cinema attracted its first audiences. During the first decade of its existence (1895 to 1905), the German film industry centered around roving tent shows (*Wanderkinos*). Like the traveling sword-swallowers, fire-eaters, and penny arcade operators, cinema shows wandered between the numerous local carnivals, fairs, and

---

[1] Oskar Kalbus, *Vom Werden deutscher Filmkunst*, 2 vols. (Altona, 1935), I, 11; Friedrich Zglinicki, *Der Weg des Films* (Frankfurt, 1956), pp. 232ff.; Peter Dittmar, "Berlin und die deutsche Filmindustrie," in *Berlin und die Provinz Brandenburg im 19. und 20. Jahrhundert*, ed. Hans Herzfeld (Berlin, 1968), pp. 845–48; and Horst Knietzsch, *Film, gestern und heute: Gedanken und Daten zu sieben Jahrzehnten Geschichte der Filmkunst*, 3rd ed. (Leipzig, 1972), pp. 15ff. August and Louis Lumières are often credited with holding the first public film showing in Paris, but their performance occurred almost two months after the Skladanowsky brothers', on December 28, 1895.

shooting festivals that were held regularly in Germany's small towns and rural villages. Using tents or hastily constructed portable booths, a crude projector, and a few short strips of film, cinema operators charged awestruck peasants and townsmen a pfennig or two to watch moving pictures of speeding locomotives, everyday street scenes, or other commonplace events. Occasionally, a primitive short story or crude comedy sketch might also be included.[2]

Economic considerations were primarily responsible for the itinerant nature of the early commercial cinema. For the cinema operators had to purchase all the films they wished to show, and few could afford to acquire new films very often. Showing the same shorts over and over, however, rapidly exhausted the local market. So, rather than attempting to maintain audience interest by frequently changing the films he showed, the early cinema owner found it more profitable to keep the same set of films and to change his audience instead—that is, to move on to a new location every few weeks. Only about 1904–1905, when the first film rental and exchange companies were established, did it become possible for German cinema operators to acquire new films on a regular basis at reasonable cost.[3] Now that they were able to offer an audience a different program every few weeks, cinema operators began abandoning their itinerant existence and settling in one location.

Huge profits could be had, and had quickly, by opening a cinema in a fixed location. After purchasing a projector and renting a vacant shop, an empty hall, or the back room of a local pub, the aspiring cinemateur could rent a complete thirty- to forty-five-minute program (consisting of six or seven short films) for one or two hundred marks. By running this program continuously from morning to night, it was not uncommon for a cinema proprietor to take in as much as five hundred to six hundred marks a day.[4] Because it held out the alluring prospect of quick and easy gains with a minimum of capital outlay, the early cinema industry attracted hordes of ambitious men, each hoping to attain

---

[2] Max Kullmann, *Die Entwicklung des deutschen Lichtspieltheaters* (inaugural diss., Hindenburg-Hochschule; Kallmünz, 1935), pp. 33ff.; Kalbus, *Filmkunst*, I, 11 ff.; Knietzsch, *Film gestern und heute*, pp. 15ff.; Roger Manvell and Heinrich Fraenkel, *The German Cinema* (New York, 1971), p. 2.

[3] Zglinicki, *Weg des Films*, pp. 320–27.

[4] Ibid., pp. 298ff.; Kullmann, *Entwicklung des Lichtspieltheaters*, pp. 33ff.; Emilie Altenloh, *Zur Soziologie des Kinos* (Jena, 1914), p. 18.

instant wealth by exploiting the public's seemingly insatiable appetite for this new form of entertainment. In the period between 1905 and the First World War, cinemas sprang up in German cities and towns at a staggering rate. While there had been no more than a handful of permanent cinema theaters in Germany before 1905, by 1910 there were over five hundred. After 1910, the spread of the cinema reached truly epidemic proportions, with over five hundred new movie houses being founded each year. By the outbreak of war in 1914, there were between twenty-five hundred and three thousand cinemas scattered throughout Germany.[5]

Unlike the roving tent shows, these permanent cinemas were most heavily concentrated in the larger cities, and it was there that the most hectic proliferation took place. Berlin, for example, which enjoyed some 20 cinema houses already in 1905, had about 200 by 1912; if some estimates are to be believed, by the time the war broke out in 1914 the number of Berlin cinemas had risen to nearly 350 and had a total seating capacity of 120,000.[6] While no other German city could rival the capital in this regard, other urban centers such as Hamburg could boast of over 40 cinemas by 1914, while Munich, Leipzig, Breslau, Hannover, and Frankfurt each had over 30. Even small provincial towns like Mannheim, Elberfeld, Dortmund, or Jena housed about ten cinemas each.[7] These film theaters varied greatly in size, from the

[5] Estimates on the number of cinemas in prewar Germany vary widely. Figures for 1910 range from 456 to 1000, but there is general agreement that by 1912 Germany had 1500 cinemas and that by 1913 there were 2370. Estimates for 1914, however, range from 2446 to 3000. See Kullmann, *Entwicklung des Lichtspieltheaters*, pp. 33ff.; Zglinicki, *Weg des Films*, pp. 298, 320, 328; Curt Moreck, *Sittengeschichte des Kinos* (Dresden, 1926), p. 22; Jerzy Toeplitz, *Geschichte des Films*, vol. 1, *1895–1928* (Munich, 1975), p. 105; and Karl Brunner, *Der Kinematograph von heute—eine Volksgefahr*, Flugschriften des Vaterländischen Schriften-Verbandes, Nr. 24, (Berlin, 1913), pp. 8–9.

[6] Berlin police report of October 7, 1912, Zentrales Staatsarchiv (hereafter cited as ZStA) Merseburg, Rep. 77, Tit. 1000, Nr. 20, Bd. 1; Arthur Wolff, *Denkschrift betreffend die Kinematographentheater, die durch ihr Überhandnehmen geschaffenen Mißstände, und Vorschläge zu einheitlichen gesetzlichen Maßnahmen: Im Auftrage des Präsidiums des Deutschen Bühnenvereins* (Berlin, 1913), p. 7; Arthur Wolff, "Theaterrecht," in *Wörterbuch des Deutschen Staats- und Verwaltungsrechts*, ed. Max Fleischman, 2d ed. (Tübingen, 1914), III, 593–94; Brunner, *Kinematograph von heute*, pp. 8–9. Dittmar, however, maintains there were only 195 cinemas in Berlin in 1914 ("Berlin und die Filmindustrie," pp. 848–50).

[7] Hans Werth, *Öffentliches Kinematographenrecht* (Hannover, 1910), app.; Zglinicki, *Weg des Films*, p. 320; Wolff, *Denkschrift*, p. 7; Altenloh, *Soziologie des Kinos*, p. 52;

small neighborhood pub that doubled as a movie hall two or three times a week to the mammoth "cinema palaces" that could seat 900 or 1,000 patrons at a time. On the average, however, most prewar cinemas could accommodate 200 or 300 people.

As the number of cinemas skyrocketed, so did cinema attendance. A survey of moviegoers in one typical German city on the eve of the war revealed that about one-third visited the cinema at least once a week, and most went more often than that.[8] By 1914, an estimated ten thousand people were attending the cinema each day in medium-sized towns like Mannheim or Stuttgart, while for the nation as a whole daily film attendance was believed to be nearly one and one-half million. Some of the larger Berlin cinema palaces, such as the Union-Theater, could boast that their annual paid admissions surpassed the total population of the city.[9]

The customers who flocked to Germany's movie houses came primarily from the lower social strata, and from the burgeoning industrial working class in particular. As the length of the average workday steadily declined in Germany after 1900 and as real wages rose, workers were able to devote more of their leisure time and their disposable income to entertainment and popular amusements.[10] Increasingly, they spent their time and their money at the cinemas. As one noted film historian observed,

> The cinema developed into the true entertainment of the masses, of the common people. The proletariat, which was more or less shut out of the respectable theaters and concert halls, and which was hardly capable of reading or appreciating worthwhile literature, sought an alternative to these in the cinema. At the annual fairs and religious festivals, peasants gawked at filmstrips in booths and tents; in the darkened rooms of the city

---

and Hessisches Hauptstaatsarchiv (hereafter cited as HHStA) Wiesbaden, Abt. 407, Nr. 418, 420.

[8]Altenloh, *Soziologie des Kinos*, p. 55. The city was Mannheim.

[9]Ibid., p. 52; *Deutsche Reichspost*, December 14, 1912; Brunner, *Kinematograph von heute*, pp. 8–9; Toeplitz, *Geschichte des Films*, I, 106; Moreck, *Sittengeschichte des Kinos*, p. 33. One authority (Wolff, *Denkschrift*, p. 9) cites the following annual cinema attendance in the town of Elberfield (population 180,000): 1906—126,000; 1907—259,000; 1908—332,000; 1909—449,000; 1910—555,000; 1911—880,650.

[10]Between 1900 and 1913, real wages in Germany rose 13 percent; by the war, the average worker was able to spend 4 percent of his annual income on "geistige und gesellige Bedürfnisse." Jürgen Kocka, *Klassengesellschaft im Krieg: Deutsche Sozialgeschichte 1914–1918* (Göttingen, 1973), p. 152, n. 6.

bioscopes, the factory worker and artisan found satisfaction for his inner needs. Like the pulp penny novels that could be purchased cheaply, like the circus, the traveling musicians, and the touring vaudeville companies, the early cinema served as an art substitute for the proletarian public.[11]

Indeed, Germany's semiliterate masses found the new cinematic medium perfectly suited to their situation and their needs. For the cinema was, above all, cheap entertainment: the least expensive seats or standing places in the theater could be had for only a few pfennigs, and even the best seats at the most luxurious houses seldom cost more than a mark.[12] The cinema was also an undemanding, totally passive medium, one that barely required concentration, much less sophisticated interpretation; thus it taxed neither the modest educational levels nor the limited attention spans of its mass viewers. Finally, the cinema had grown directly out of popular forums that had long been preserves of the lower classes. For nearly a decade, before they finally settled in permanent movie theaters, cinema shows had been held in physical settings that the common man found familiar and comfortable: the vaudeville or music hall, the circus or itinerant carnival tent, the neighborhood pub. Even after fancy cinema theaters were constructed in an attempt to appeal more to the tastes and habits of the respectable middle classes, the character and ambience of these movie houses continued to resemble more closely the casual, raw settings of the beer hall or vaudeville stage rather than the formal, proper milieu of the genteel private theaters or concert halls. Unlike the legitimate theater, for example, one did not need to dress up to attend the cinema or feel that one had to be on one's best behavior. Rather, moviegoers frequently ate, drank, smoked, necked, and petted in the darkened rooms during the film.[13] The police chief of Bremerhaven noted in 1912, for instance, that "although today the largest and most popular cinema theaters are generally well lit and the audience no longer finds much opportunity for immoral behavior, it is still apparent that cinemas are often sought out by lovers in the expectation that during the darkness they will have the chance to engage in actions that normally shun the

[11] Toeplitz, *Geschichte des Films*, I, 14.

[12] Staatsarchiv (hereafter cited as StA) Bremen, 3-F.1.b.1.—Nr. 203; Zglinicki, *Weg des Films*, pp. 298, 328; Frankfurt police report of November 5, 1909, HHStA Wiesbaden, Abt. 407, Nr. 420.

[13] I. C. Jarvie, *Towards a Sociology of the Cinema* (London, 1970), p. 216.

light of day."[14] Indeed, since the noisy commotion and restless comings and goings of the audience did not really interfere with one's enjoyment of the silent film on the screen, prewar cinema theaters were usually raucous, uninhibited places where juveniles, salesgirls, the unemployed, and others of ill repute often hung out. It was not uncommon, for example, for signs to be posted in cinemas warning the unruly patrons that "the demolition of the seats and benches is strictly forbidden."[15]

For all these reasons, the cinema appealed strongly to the lower social classes, and the largest portion of moviegoers came from the lower social strata, especially the urban working class. Industrial or port cities such as Hamburg, Essen, or Elberfeld or densely populated working-class districts like those in north or east Berlin usually had a higher-than-average concentration of cinema theaters and a higher rate of cinema attendance. A survey of devoted moviegoers in Mannheim on the eve of the war revealed that the majority of patrons were workers and artisans.[16] In short, the commercial cinema in imperial Germany was an entertainment medium of the masses; as one scholar has observed, "It spoke not to hundreds, or to thousands, but to millions of viewers. They were spellbound by the pictures of daily life and of the wider world that passed before them on the screen. Since the age of the Elizabethan theater, there had never been a form of entertainment in European civilization that was so rooted in popular [volkstümlich] culture, and yet was so universal in its appeal."[17]

II

As cinema theaters sprang up across Germany in the decade before the First World War and as millions sat each week before the silver screen, a growing array of police officials, religious leaders, educators, and

---

[14]Bremerhaven police report, September, 1912, StA Bremen, 4,20—Nr. 352.

[15]Altenloh, *Soziologie des Kinos*, p. 52; Siegfried Kracauer, *From Caligari to Hitler: A Psychological History of the German Film* (Princeton, 1947), p. 16.

[16]Altenloh, *Soziologie des Kinos*, pp. 55, 64. See also Dittmar, "Berlin und die Filmindustrie," p. 848; Zglinicki, *Weg des Films*, p. 319; and Albert Hellwig, "Die maßgebenden Grundsätze für Verbote von Schundfilme nach geltendem und künftigem Rechte," *Verwaltungsarchiv: Zeitschrift für Verwaltungsrecht und Verwaltungsgerichtsbarkeit* 21 (1913): 447, 453.

[17]Toeplitz, *Geschichte des Films*, p. 14.

other assorted cultural crusaders became deeply concerned over the appeal and the effects of this new entertainment medium. They warned in particular of the dangerous psychological and moral impact that popular films were having upon their mass audience. To some, the evils of the cinema were direct. Uneasy over their vaudeville origins and alarmed over the social composition and undisciplined nature of their audiences, observers such as the police chief of Bremerhaven or the Interior Minister of Hesse warned that movie theaters were in themselves centers of immorality, for the darkened cinemas attracted all types of disreputable characters and provided an irresistible opportunity for immoral hanky-panky between the sexes.[18] Such critics were fond of citing a recent American case where a Chicago man had been sentenced to nine and one-half years in prison for seducing an underage girl by taking her to the movies regularly. According to the judge in this case, the films had made the girl more pliable and less willing to resist the man's advances—all of which proved, to the judge's satisfaction at least, that "there is no greater danger to the integrity and honor of our girls than the cinema."[19]

Other concerned Germans saw the insidious effects of the new cinematic medium as more oblique. They argued, for example, that a film, regardless of its plot or its technique, was inherently sensationalistic and exercised a potentially dangerous suggestive influence over its audience. For silent films, by necessity, had to appeal directly to the viewers' visual sense, and any medium that was so totally dependent on visual images was compelled, by its very nature, to concentrate on what was sensational and lurid. Thus the cinema expert attached to the Berlin police force argued that, because it had to rely on exaggerated pantomime rather than on dialogue to portray events and human emotions, the cinema was incapable of depicting subtlety and finer nuances. All films, consequently, had to focus "on the strongest and most dramatic emotional states possible, and thus on the most vivid, agitating, and provocative types of scenes."[20] Moreover, since actions carried a greater dramatic impact than mere words and exaggerated, sensationalistic actions more so than subdued ones, the influence of the cinema

[18] Memorandum of Bremerhaven police chief, September, 1912, StA Bremen, 4,20—Nr. 353; memorandum of Hessian Interior Minister, January 18, 1909, StA Darmstadt, G15 Friedberg, XX. Abt., Konv. VI.

[19] Cited in Wolff, *Denkschrift*, p. 12.

[20] Brunner, *Kinematograph von heute*, p. 27.

over its audience was considered to be far stronger than with other forms of entertainment such as the traditional theater.[21] Worse still, it was feared that the cinema's direct, profound impact upon its viewers would ultimately undermine their sense of reality. For in the legitimate theater or even in a vaudeville show, the audience always felt a certain criticial distance from what it saw portrayed before it on the stage; however realistic or convincing the performance, the formal theatrical setting, the artificial stage scenery and props, and numerous other factors always reminded theater patrons that what they were viewing was not reality but, rather, something fictional and staged. By contrast, some critics of the cinema argued, the photographic realism of films, the outdoor locations where films were frequently shot, and the sheer immediacy of the cinema's visual images were so powerful that even the most sophisticated moviegoer could temporarily be deceived into thinking he was watching reality itself rather than a mere film. If this were so, then the immature adolescents and ill-educated lower-class patrons who made up the bulk of cinema audiences and who sat for hours each week in the movie houses might completely lose their ability to distinguish between reality and the illusions and fantasies they saw portrayed before them on the screen.[22] In short, many critical observers considered it an indisputable fact that, "compared to the traditional theater, the cinema exerts an infinitely more sustained impact upon the broad masses, that the cinema audiences are more susceptible to suggestive influences, that cinema shows have a more suggestive effect on their viewers, and that the type of entertainment shown [in the cinema] more often appeals to one's baser instincts."[23]

But if German authorities were apprehensive about the general nature of the cinematic experience, they were both apalled and alarmed over the types of films that were so popular with the masses of moviegoers. As they do today, the cinema patrons seeking diversion and entertainment at the turn of the century craved spine-tingling, hair-raising films that they knew would frighten, titillate, shock, horrify, or even nauseate them, and the more so the better. By far the most popular—and profitable—films in prewar Europe were harrowing, action-packed adventure stories teeming with bloodthirsty violence. These films, like the immensely popular ten-penny novels or

---

[21] Hellwig, "Die maßgebenden Grundsätze," p. 448.

[22] Ibid., pp. 447–48.

[23] Ibid., p. 453.

pulp fiction on which they were often based,[24] were invariably set in some exotic location, especially the underworld, and portrayed the heart-stopping exploits of criminals and detectives, slaves and masters, cowboys and Indians, soldiers and spies. They carried such provacative titles as *Hell of Death, Game of Death, Dead or Alive, The Man Without a Conscience,* or *Ghostly Nights.* They had flimsy plots with characters who were motivated primarily by greed, fear, hatred, revenge, jealousy, or lust, and they abounded with violent crimes, bloody gun battles and knife fights, grisly suicides, executions, horrible accidents, bloody medical operations, or other equally chilling and tasteless scenes. Besides acts of ghastly violence and savage brutality, audiences then—as now—also reveled in lurid, suggestive films about illicit love. Thus films such as *Sinful Love, White Slave Women, Slave of Love, Burning Love, Flaming Hatred, Death in the Nude, Burning Desires,* or *Queen of the Night* capitalized on the voyeurism of the mass audiences by depicting for them an endless cycle of lust, seduction, adultery, and prostitution. One tenacious pastor who investigated some 250 of these low-grade thrillers and trashy melodramas claimed he saw depicted a total of twenty-seven murders, fifty-one adulteries, nineteen seductions, twenty-two kidnappings, forty-five suicides, 176 thieves, twenty-five prostitutes, thirty-five drunks, and a veritable army of police, detectives, and executioners.[25] Such fare was daily viewing for millions of Germans; hundreds of these "junk films" (*Schundfilme*) were produced and distributed each year, and it was estimated that the more popular ones might reach audiences of perhaps thirteen million viewers each.[26]

[24]"Cinema [in those days] was in many ways simply a filming of those pulp fiction pamphlets, a pictorial recitation of their contents, but one that was far more effective because the actions and adventures were actually portrayed visually." Walter Panofsky, *Die Geburt des Films: Ein Stück Kulturgeschichte: Versuch einer zeitgeschichtlichen Darstellung des Lichtspieles in seinen Anfangsjahren* [1895–1913], 2d ed. (Würzburg, 1944), p. 22. On the popularity and content of pulp fiction in imperial Germany, see Rudolf Schenda, *Volk ohne Buch: Studien zur Sozialgeschichte des populären Lesestoffes 1770–1910* (Frankfurt, 1970); and Ronald A. Fullerton, "Toward a Commercial Popular Culture in Germany: The Development of Pamphlet Fiction, 1871–1914," *Journal of Social History* 12 (1979): 489–511.

[25]Pastor Conrad, quoted in Albert Hellwig, "Die Kinematographenzensur: Zugleich ein Beitrag zur Frage der Umgrenzung der Gewerbe-, Presse-, und Versammlungsfreiheit," *Annalen des Deutschen Reiches* 43 (1910): 909–10.

[26]Knietzsch, *Film gestern und heute,* pp. 15–27; Toeplitz, *Geschichte des Films,* I,

In the eyes of many of imperial Germany's leading officials, these low-grade popular films endangered both the body and the spirit of the viewer. Authorities in Prussia and Hesse, for example, were convinced that watching fast-paced, action-packed thrillers or vividly gruesome horror scenes ruined one's nerves and produced such ailments as bad dreams and hypertension.[27] Likewise, the Württemberg state government warned that "exciting, arousing scenes, such as those in criminal, detective, and horror films, where the viewers are kept in a state of constant suspense and tension over the fate of the hero—these can lead to severe mental agitation, high excitability, and even nervous disorders, especially in children or in persons with a minimum of nervous resistance."[28]

Even more distressing to observers was the presumed effect of these junk films upon the nation's moral spirit. It was not merely (as some charged) that suggestive or indecent films about illicit love aroused men's baser passions and incited lust.[29] Rather, many believed that all the grotesque, repulsive, or downright silly films being shown in German cinemas were slowly debasing the spiritual faculties of the

105; Brunner, *Kinematograph von heute*, pp. 6–9. On the outcry against prewar *Schundfilme*, see the following works by Albert Hellwig: *Schundfilme: Ihr Wesen, ihre Gefahren, und ihre Bekämpfung* (Halle, 1911); "Die Schundfilme," *Zentralblatt für Volksbildungswesen* 11 (1911): 129–36; "Schundfilme und Filmzensur," *Concordia: Zeitschrift der Zentralstelle für Arbeiterwohlfahrtseinrichtungen* 18 (1911): 187–91, 260–62; and "Die Beziehung zwischen Schundliteratur, Schundfilme, und Verbrechen: Das Ergebnis einer Umfrage," *Archiv für Kriminalanthropologie und Kriminalistik* 51 (1913): 1–32. For a representative list of *Schundfilm* titles, from which those cited above were drawn, see Wolff, *Denkschrift*, p. 6; memorandum of Baden Interior Minister, October 31, 1911, Generallandesarchiv (hereafter cited as GLA) Karlsruhe, Abt. 362 Mannheim, 1976/16, Nr. 202; report of Berlin-Charlottenburg police president, August 13, 1908, StA Potsdam, Rep. 30 Berlin C, Tit. 74, Th. 96; and Brunner, *Kinematograph von heute*, pp. 4–6.

[27] Memorandum of Prussian Culture Minister, March 8, 1912, StA Potsdam, Rep. 2, Abt. I, Nr. 3446; memorandum of Hessian Interior Ministry, January 18, 1909, StA Darmstadt, G15 Friedberg, XX. Abt., Konv. VI; decision of Prussian Kammergericht, June 1, 1911, as quoted in Brunner, *Kinematograph von heute*, p. 17; and Hellwig, "Schundfilme und Filmzensur," p. 189.

[28] "Entwurf eines Gesetzes betreffend öffentliche Lichtspielvorstellungen: Begründung," *Stenographischer Bericht der Württembergischen Ersten Kammer*, Beilage 4, of February 19, 1913 (also contained in Hauptstaatsarchiv [hereafter cited as HStA] Stuttgart, E 151c/II, Nr. 270c).

[29] Memorandum of Baden Interior Minister, March 19, 1908, HStA Stuttgart, E 151c/II, Nr. 270a; memorandum of Schwetzingen Bezirksamt, June 18, 1910, GLA Karlsruhe, Abt. 362, Nr. 174.

masses. For, by focusing on the seamy underside of life rather than on the noble and beautiful, it was feared that popular films corrupted the aesthetic sensibilities of the viewer. Because they familiarized people with and accustomed them to the baser aspects of human behavior, low-grade thrillers were also thought to brutalize the spirit. And, so the charges went, by overexciting the imaginative powers with make-believe fantasies, popular escapist films blunted one's sense of reality. Thus, in the words of the Prussian minister of culture, popular junk films were dangerous because they

> exercise a harmful effect on the ethical sensibilities in that they portray unsuitable and ghastly scenes that excite the senses and unfavorably stimulate the imagination. Viewing such material poisons the impressionable minds of the young just as much as reading trashy pulp fiction or looking at pornography does. Seeing such material on the screen is bound to corrupt one's sense of good and evil, of what is proper and what is low and vulgar. The unspoiled character of many a child can be pointed down the wrong path [by these junk films]; the aesthetic sensibilities of the young are also perverted, for the senses become more and more accustomed to what is strong and provocative, while the ability calmly to contemplate great works of art is steadily eroded.[30]

What the authorities of imperial Germany seemed to fear most, however, was that watching too many violent or sexually suggestive films might slowly wear down the viewers' inner inhibitions and moral standards and ultimately prompt them to imitate the kinds of actions they saw portrayed before them on the screen week after week.[31] The state government of Württemberg, for example, warned:

> When people constantly see scenes of criminality and suicides, acts of viciousness, gross sensuality, and the many other unethical things that recur with sickening regularity in our so-called "criminal and sexual films," then their sense of what is ethically reprehensible is gradually blunted. This danger exists especially for children and adolescents, whose ethical perceptions are still in the formative stage, and also for adults whose characters are insufficiently developed or whose mental faculties are weak. Eventually, when the temptation arises in their own lives to commit morally reprehensible acts, the moviegoers' consciences and the lessons of

---

[30] Memorandum of March 8, 1912, StA Potsdam, Rep. 2, Abt. I, Nr. 3446.

[31] Ibid.; "Entwurf eines Gesetzes," HStA Stuttgart, E 151c/II, Nr. 270c; Hellwig, "Schundfilme und Filmzensur," p. 189; letter of Leipzig police president, February 20, 1909, HStA Stuttgart, E 151c/II, Nr. 270a.

their ethical upbringing will be so undermined that they will no longer hold them back. One must also consider the powerful suggestive influence that movies can exert upon the young mind; the cinema can push a child into actually imitating the crimes and misdeeds that he sees portrayed.[32]

This danger seemed especially real given the social composition of most cinema audiences. For, as one leading jurist pointed out, the popular movie theaters were frequented mostly by members of the lower social classes, and it was generally believed that these kinds of people were more susceptible to evil suggestive influences than were the more educated classes, whose moral inhibitions were greater and who had less incentive to commit crimes than did the lower social strata.[33]

Official concern about the link between popular films and criminality must be seen against the background of imperial Germany's rising crime rate. Since about 1890, the total per capita crime rate had risen rapidly, and by the outbreak of the First World War it stood some 20 percent above what it had been in the 1880s. During this period, crimes against property and morality, the rate of criminal recidivism, and juvenile deliquency had increased much faster than the growth of the population.[34] In light of these disturbing trends, many religious, judicial, and political figures were quick to blame low-grade popular films as an indirect cause of rising criminality in general and as a direct cause of juvenile crime in particular. The police chief of Leipzig charged, for example, not only that the popular cinema glorified criminals but also that many films actually showed youngsters in detail how to pick a pocket, break into a store or house, or commit other criminal acts. He cited the fact that a number of hardened juvenile burglars had recently been apprehended in his city; when questioned as to how they had acquired their nefarious talents, many replied that they had "seen at the movies how one is supposed to do it."[35] Albert Hellwig, Germany's leading authority on cinema law, conducted an extensive survey of the

[32] "Entwurf eines Gesetzes," HStA Stuttgart, E 151c/II, Nr. 270c.

[33] Hellwig, "Die maßgebenden Grundsätze," p. 447.

[34] See Vincent McHale and Eric Johnson, "Urbanization, Industrialization, and Crime in Imperial Germany," *Social Science History* 1 (1976): 45–78 and 2 (1977): 210–47, especially pp. 212–15. See also my forthcoming article "Pornography, Society, and the Law in Imperial Germany," in *Central European History*.

[35] Letter of Leipzig police president, February 20, 1909, HStA Stuttgart, E 151c/II, Nr. 270a.

link between popular crime films and criminality; all the juvenile judges he talked to, he said, generally agreed that

> popular crime films have a decided effect on juvenile criminality. Although it is not possible to demonstrate this link with any certainty in even a single specific case, the correctness of this view can undoubtedly be deduced from general psychological principles. It is simply self-evident that crime films, as well as other brutalizing popular junk films, create a favorable disposition toward criminal acts. That popular crime films cloud one's sense of reality, that they strengthen antisocial passions and instincts, such as vulgarity and cruelty, that they glorify the criminal and thereby erase the distinction between justice and injustice, that they are inclined to weaken and ultimately to break down completely the inner inhibitions and mental barriers that might hold youngsters back from embarking on a life of crime, and that they destroy a person's ability to resist the temptations and seductions of life—all this has been demonstrated by criminal psychologists and confirmed time and again by judges, police officials, teachers, and other experts in these matters.[36]

The police chief of Bremerhaven concurred wholeheartedly that there was "no denying a certain causal connection between criminal acts and the influence of low-grade junk films and pulp fiction. . . . This connection has been observed repeatedly in criminal cases involving juveniles." As proof, he cited the example of a young domestic servant in his city who had attempted to poison her employer and his family shortly after she had seen a film about a similar crime.[37] Judges in Baden and Württemberg, although unable to cite such dramatic examples, pointed nonetheless to several local cases where boys had lied and cheated in order to get money to attend the cinema. This showed, the judges concluded, that the cinema was at the very least an indirect cause of juvenile delinquency.[38]

III

To combat the presumed physical, moral, and social dangers of the popular cinema, a number of teachers, clergymen, and representatives

[36] Albert Hellwig, "Der Kinematograph vom Standpunkt der Juristen," *Die Hochwart* 3 (1911): 19; Hellwig, "Schundfilme und Filmzensur," p. 189; and "Hellwig, "Beziehung zwischen Schundfilme und Verbrechen."

[37] Letter of Bremerhaven police chief, September, 1912, StA Bremen, 4,20–Nr. 352.

[38] Memorandum of Schwetzingen Berzirksamt, June 18, 1910, GLA Karlsruhe, Abt.

from various cultural organizations such as the Dürer League joined together around 1905 into a "cinema reform movement."[39] This movement, which eventually formed its own small political pressure group, the Cinematic Reform Party (Kinematographische Reformpartei), demanded that the programs of German cinema theaters be censored and that objectionable films be banned. Under the influence of these moralistic reformers, German officials began imposing controls over the types of films shown in the public cinemas.

Police in Germany's largest cities were generally the first to act: beginning around 1906, a score or more individual cities enacted various ordinances to censor or otherwise regulate local cinema theaters. A few years later, several of the larger states stepped in and began to standardize and centralize cinema censorship within their respective jurisdictions.

The first step toward film censorship in imperial Germany was taken in Berlin, where in May, 1906, the police imposed upon movie halls the same precensorship to which legitimate theaters in the city had long been subject. Henceforth, no film could be publicly shown in Berlin without first obtaining the express approval of the police; the operators of each cinema theater had to submit the films they wished to show at least three days in advance to the police, who could prohibit the showing of any film judged objectionable.[40] Berlin's action encouraged other large cities to take similar steps, although not all imposed the same strict controls over films as did the capital. Authorities in some cities, for example, believed the dangers posed by the cinema could best be met by merely restricting the exposure of children and adolescents to popular films. Thus Brunswick, Karlsruhe, Halle, Hamburg, Mülhausen, and Strassburg banned all school-age children (roughly ages six to sixteen) from the cinema unless they were accompanied by a parent or adult guardian. Elsewhere, such as in Leipzig, Chemnitz, Dresden, Oldenburg, and the Prussian province of Westfalen, chil-

362, Nr. 174; letter of Stuttgart judge to Württemberg Minister of Justice, April 21, 1910, HStA Stuttgart, E 151c/II, Nr. 270a.

[39] Dittmar, "Berlin und die Filmindustrie," p. 848; Heiner Schmitt, *Kirche und Film: Kirchliche Filmarbeit in Deutschland von ihren Anfängen bis 1945* (Boppard, 1979); Volker Schulze, "Frühe kommunale Kinos und die Kinoreformbewegung in Deutschland bis zum Ende des ersten Weltkrieges," *Publizistik* 22 (January–March, 1977): 6–71.

[40] Berlin police decree of May 5, 1906, StA Potsdam, Rep. 30 Berlin C, Tit. 74, Th. 123.

dren and adolescents were barred altogether from the regular cinema performances and could attend only special children's matinees. The films shown at these separate performances were closely supervised, for the cinema owner had to submit his proposed program to the police several days in advance and obtain their approval. Other cities, such as Stuttgart, Dresden, Düsseldorf, Oldenburg, Strassburg, Mülhausen, and Karlsruhe, followed Berlin's example and demanded that all films, whether intended for adults or for children, be subjected to prior police censorship.

Cinema theater operators, of course, vehemently protested these restrictions. Submitting their films to police censors days in advance, they complained, was both expensive and impractical. For theaters rented their film for only a few days, and they usually did not receive them from the distributor until immediately before the scheduled showing. Waiting a day or two for police approval cut into the rental period deeply and greatly limited the number of times a film could be shown. And should a film be banned by the police, cinema proprietors were seldom able to produce a replacement for it on such short notice and often had to cancel their planned performances altogether.[41] More importantly, spokesmen for the cinema industry protested that film censorship violated the German press law, which prohibited the censorship of "any printed material or pictorial representations that have been reproduced mechanically or chemically for the purpose of public distribution."[42] By splitting some very thin hairs over the issue, however, German courts concluded that motion pictures were not protected under the press law. For, it was argued, what one sees at a cinema performance is not the actual celluloid film itself but merely its incorporeal projected image, and the moving pictures one thinks one sees are in fact an optical illusion, a deception that is created by the rapid, successive projection of the many distinct individual frames on the film. Since, strictly speaking, no actual, tangible pictures were physically exhibited or distributed to the public at the cinema, the courts ruled that cinema performances were not protected by freedom of the press and could be censored.[43]

[41] See Otto Buss, *Eingabe betreffend polizeiliche Beschränkungen des Kinematographenwesens* (Berlin, 1911).

[42] Alexander Elster, "Kinozensur und Kinokonzession," *Recht und Wirtschaft* 2 (1913): 104.

[43] Prussian Oberverwaltungsgericht decision of May 1, 1908 and Prussian Kammer-

Once the legality of film censorship and other police restrictions on the cinema had been firmly established, the German state governments began standardizing the confusing patchwork of local regulations. Generally, the interior minister in each state would suggest that all communities in the state adopt the same cinema ordinances that were in force in the state capital. By 1914, cities and towns in virtually every German state had enacted the same general decrees, which banned young children under six from cinemas completely, allowed youths under fourteen or sixteen to attend only specially supervised children's matinees, and required that any film to be shown publicly be first submitted to the police for their approval.[44]

As long as film censorship was handled separately by each municipality, however, problems were bound to arise. The standards by which films were judged varied radically from locality to locality. For example, some films were banned completely in one town but could be shown even in the children's matinees in a neighboring community, or vice versa.[45] This situation created confusion and economic hardship for film distributors, who sought to market their films throughout the Reich, and for local cinema house operators, who could never be sure that the police in their town would allow them to show the films they had already rented and paid for. Examining scores of films each week also proved burdensome for many local police forces, especially in smaller communities that lacked the manpower and resources for such a task. The police chief in one Württemberg city, for example, complained that his constables were spending an inordinate amount of

gericht decision of June 21, 1909. See Albert Hellwig, "Öffentliches Kinematographenrecht," *Preußisches Verwaltungsblatt* 34 (December 21, 1912): 202–203; and Hellwig, "Die Kinematographenzensur," pp. 101–12.

[44] Württemberg memorandum of November 17, 1908, HStA Stuttgart, E 151c/II, Nr. 270a; Saxony memorandum of April 6, 1909, ibid.; Baden memorandum of June 13, 1910, GLA Karlsruhe, Abt. 362 Mannheim, 1976/16, Nr. 202; Prussian memorandum of December 16, 1910, StA Potsdam, Rep. 2, Abt. I, Nr. 3446; Bavarian memorandum of January 14, 1911, as quoted in Albert Hellwig, *Die Rechtsquellen des öffentlichen Kinematographenrechts: Systematische Zusammenstellung der wichtigsten deutschen und fremden Gesetze* (Mönchen-Gladbach, 1913), p. 87; and Hessian memorandum of July 19, 1912, StA Darmstadt, G15 Alsfeld, Abt. XIX.

[45] Memorandum of Regierungspräsident Frankfurt-Oder, July 3, 1912, StA Potsdam, Rep. 3B, Abt. I, Bd. 1431; report of February 29, 1912 by Landrat for Kreis Niederbarnim, StA Potsdam, Rep. 2, Abt. I, Nr. 3446; Breslau police president to Berlin police president, January 3, 1912, StA Potsdam, Rep. 30 Berlin C, Tit. 74, Th. 1252; and complaints by the Stuttgart police in HStA Stuttgart, E 151c/II, Nr. 270a, Büschel 13.

time each week sitting in movie theaters, running between theaters, and waiting for the projectionists to set up the films for the special police screenings. Moreover, these local cops were unqualified for the task of cinema censorship and were often being duped by clever cinema proprietors into approving films they should not. "If one of my constables raises an objection to this or that film," the chief moaned,

> he is told that it's Shakespeare, and that he would be a narrow-minded philistine to object to it. What is the poor policeman to do? If the cinema house owner tells him it is one of Shakespeare's works, then he no longer has the courage to ban it. Or it sometimes happens that in the middle of the private screening someone drops a bunch of keys and the policeman, wishing to be helpful, bends down to pick them up. Weeks later, it turns out that during this little diversion with the keys one of the most ghastly murder scenes ever put on film was taking place up there on the screen.[46]

Some film producers or distributors who knew their films were not likely to pass the diligent censors in the larger cities and state capitals often submitted them instead in other communities where the police censors were more liberal, gullible, or careless. Once a film was passed by one police office, it was more likely to be routinely accepted by others as well, especially as the censors became deluged with more and more films to screen. In this way, a film that would normally have been banned could gain a fairly wide circulation.[47]

To close the more egregious of these loopholes and establish more uniform standards for film censorship, in 1912 the major state governments began centralizing their censorship procedures by removing film censorship from the hands of local police and investing it instead in a central state office. In January, 1912, the Bavarian Interior Ministry designated the Munich police as Bavaria's central film censors (Landesstelle zur Prüfung von Bildern); they were now required to examine every film that was to be shown anywhere in Bavaria, and cinemas in the state would be permitted to show only those films that had been approved by the Munich censors.[48] Saxony followed suit in Feb-

[46] Stuttgart police chief Bittinger, as quoted in *Amts- und Anzeigeblatt der Stadt Stuttgart* (1912), p. 318.

[47] See memorandum of Prussian interior minister, April 30, 1911, January 27, 1912, and July 6, 1912, StA Potsdam, Rep. 2, Abt. I, Nr. 3446; Moreck, *Sittengeschichte des Kinos*, pp. 48–52; and Berlin police president to Minister of Trade and Commerce, March 6, 1918, ZStA Merseburg, Rep. 120 BB, IIb1, Nr. 37, Adh. 2, Bd. 1.

[48] Bavarian Interior Ministry decree of January 27, 1912, HStA Stuttgart, E 151c/II, Nr. 270b.

ruary, appointing the Leipzig police force as that state's central film censor. In July, the Prussian government centralized cinema censorship in Germany's largest, most populous state by dramatically expanding the powers of the Berlin police and curtailing the independence of local police in cinema matters. All film companies that wished to have their films shown in Prussia were now required to submit these to the Berlin police for censorship, and local authorities were obliged to accept Berlin's decisions in all but the most exceptional of circumstances.[49] Finally, in March, 1914, after receiving numerous petitions and pleadings from public-interest groups, the state of Württemberg, too, centralized its film censorship in the hands of the Stuttgart police.[50] By 1914, then, film censorship in each of the major states of Germany was being handled by a single, central state film censor's office, usually the police in the state's capital city.

Of the different censorship offices, Berlin was by far the most important. For, although technically not bound to do so, it soon became common practice for all film companies to submit their new films to the Berlin censors before releasing or distributing them anywhere else in the Reich.[51] Not only was the capital the most lucrative market for films, but once a film was passed by the Berlin censors it was unlikely to be banned by Bavaria, Baden, or the other states, as these generally deferred to Berlin's judgment.[52] Thus, just as Prussia led and domi-

---

[49] Memorandum of Prussian Interior Minister, July 6, 1912, StA Potsdam, Rep. 2, Abt. I, Nr. 3446; also Albert Hellwig, "Zentralisierung der Filmzensur in Preußen," *Preußisches-Kommunalarchiv* 4 (1912–13): 227–43.

[50] Württemberg Interior Ministry to Württemberg State Ministry, November 19, 1912, HStA Stuttgart, E 130a, Nr. 408; "Gesetz betreffend öffentliche Lichtspiele, vom 31. März 1914," *Regierungsblatt für das Königsreich Württemberg (1914)*, Nr. 9, pp. 87–92; "Verfügung des Ministeriums des Innern, betreffend die Vollziehung des Gesetzes über öffentliche Lichtspiele (31. März 1914), vom. 3. Juli 1914," in HStA Stuttgart, E 151c/II, Nr. 270b.

[51] Legally, it was the individual cinema theater proprietors who were required to submit the films they intended to show. When a film was banned by the police, it was the cinema proprietor who suffered, for he was usually unable to obtain another film on such short notice and had to cancel his performances altogether. After cinema operators complained of this to film production and distribution companies, these latter began voluntarily submitting all their films to the Berlin censor before releasing them to individual cinema theaters, thereby relieving the individual cinema propietors of any risk. Moreck, *Sittengeschichte des Kino* pp. 48–52.

[52] Memorandum of Baden Interior Minister, May 23, 1911, GLA Karlsruhe, Abt. 362, 1976/16, Nr. 202; memorandum of Bavarian Interior Minister, January 27, 1912, HStA Stuttgart, E 151c/II, Nr. 270b.

nated the rest of the German Reich, so too did the rulings of the Prussian film censors come to prevail over those of other states.

Initially, film censorship in Berlin had been handled by the same officials who censored theatrical productions. After Berlin was named the central film censor for all Prussia (and, in effect, for the entire Reich), this arrangement proved unworkable, and a special Film Censorship Office (Filmprüfungsamt) was created. Eventually, four Berlin police inspectors (*Polizeiräte*) were employed to screen the twenty to thirty films that were submitted for approval each day.[53] The office was placed under the supervision of Professor Karl Brunner, a forty-year-old former *Gymnasium* history teacher who had made a national name for himself earlier by crusading against pulp fiction and sensationalistic penny novels, which, he claimed, were corrupting the minds of the nation's youth. Brunner made no attempt to conceal the fact that he held the popular cinema in equal disdain. He once told reporters that the cinema had no artistic merit, indeed no social justification whatsoever, and that it represented a dire threat both to the nation's aesthetic standards and to its morality.[54]

The Berlin censors had the option of approving a film for all age groups, approving it for adults but banning it from children's matinees, ordering certain offensive scenes cut out, or banning the film completely. Decisions to ban a film could be appealed through the Prussian administrative courts, although it was extremely rare for a decision of the censors to be reversed. In reaching their decisions, the censors in Berlin considered only the probable effect a film might have upon its audience (*Wirkungszensur*); the motives or intentions of the film producer or distributor, however noble or innocuous, were irrelevant.[55]

---

[53] Albert Hellwig, "Die Filmzensur in Württemberg: Ihre Notwendigkeit, ihre rechtliche Grundlagen, und ihre zweckmäßigste Gestaltung," *Zeitschrift für die freiwillige Gerichtsbarkeit und die Gemeindeverwaltung in Württemberg* 55 (January, 1913): 27n; Hellwig, "Schundfilme und Filmzensur," p. 188; Altenloh, *Soziologie des Kinos*, p. 41; Wolff, *Denkschrift*, p. 14. Also Hellwig, "Zentralisierung der Filmzensur," p. 288.

[54] *Tägliche Rundschau*, May 30, 1912, as quoted in Panofsky, *Geburt des Films*, p. 69. On Brunner's background, see Berlin police to Prussian Interior Minister, April 25, 1912, StA Potsdam, Rep. 30 Berlin C, Tit. 74, Th. 125; Prussian Interior Minister to Prussian Finance Minister, July 24, 1913, ZStA Merseburg, Rep. 77, Tit. 380, Nr. 7, Bd. 10; and Baden Ambassador in Berlin to Baden State Ministry, March 28, 1914, GLA Karlsruhe, Abt. 233/12655.

[55] Hellwig, "Die maßgebenden Grundsätze," p. 436.

This approach, of course, allowed the censors the widest possible latitude. For, however educational or artistically praiseworthy a film's intent, if the public was likely to ignore its positive aspects, misinterpret its message, or in any way be shocked by it, then the film had to be banned. Moreover, it was not merely the film's direct effect upon the audience's behavior that was at issue; rather, censors were also to consider its possible indirect impact upon the internal values or general outlook of the viewers. This meant, in effect, that even if a film posed no clear and present danger to public order or to the public welfare it could nevertheless be banned if there were a chance it might arouse or reinforce attitudes that were judged contrary to morality or public order.[56]

As a rule, Brunner's censors banned any material that might endanger public order or the general welfare, that might corrupt or brutalize the public's moral values, or that, because of its excessively vivid or shocking nature, might be physically or psychologically harmful to young viewers. Five basic types of films met these broad criteria.

First, the censors banned many crime and detective films. They prohibited the portrayal of serious felonies (such as murder, arson, assassination, armed robbery, or counterfeiting) and were careful not to allow films that seemed in any way to glorify criminality or to sympathize with criminal heroes. Indeed, they refused to allow even minor crimes to be committed on the screen if the perpetrator went unpunished in the film. For the police feared that unless audiences explicitly saw that criminals were always apprehended and punished for their misdeeds, some viewers might be tempted to imitate the criminal behavior they saw portrayed before them.[57] The film *Tom Butler's Secret Adventures* was banned in 1912, for instance, because in the eyes of the authorities

> the entire film more or less glorifies Tom Butler's criminal inclinations, and never are his transgressions portrayed as being illegal or immoral. Up to his very last breath—where he must make the decision either to escape out the window or to be captured—Butler's actions are presented as the

[56] Ibid.; and Hellwig, "Filmzensur in Württemberg," p. 27.

[57] Berlin police president to Essen police president, September 24, 1909, memorandum of Berlin Polizeirat Glasenapp, July 22, 1910, and Berlin police president to Vienna police president, August 7, 1912, as quoted in Hellwig, "Die maßgebenden Grundsätze," p. 413.

triumphs of a renegade and as humiliations of the authorities, who are always shown in a bad light in this film. . . . When, at the end, Butler falls to
his death from the window, this is hardly presented as being a just retribution for his long string of successful crimes. . . . There is no question that
the repeated showing of [this film] to the broad public would lead to a dangerous deterioration of ethical values and that this would be most detrimental to the public welfare. Finally, it must be noted that it is not feasible
simply to cut out the offensive parts of the film, for the criminal thrust of
the entire film pervades every part of it.[58]

Police censors even refused to allow the 1913 comedy short *A Cheap
Meal*, in which a disgruntled diner, after being harassed by a surly
waiter, stomps out of restaurant without paying his bill. In the view of
the censors, such a film might encourage others, too, to skip before
paying their bills.[59]

Second, German film censors banned any immoral scenes that
were, as they put it, "likely to arouse base instincts in the viewer or
offend his sense of decency."[60] Scenes depicting prostitution, adultery,
seduction, abduction, and the like fell into this category. One amusing
example involved the 1912 burlesque comedy *A Servant Girl's Prank*,
in which both the father and the son in a household make advances on
their servant girl, Nini, who finally decides to teach both a lesson. She
tells each to come to her room one night at an appointed time. The
father arrives first, excitedly undresses, and slips under the covers of
her bed to await her. When the son arrives and sees a figure in the bed
that he assumes to be Nini, he too undresses in a fit of passion and
crawls in, only to discover his father. To the stern police censor,

the humorous aspects of this story are far overshadowed by the detrimental effect it will have on the moral sensibilities of the viewer. Father and
son each excitedly prepare themselves for a night of illicit love with their
servant girl, and this is portrayed in the film as vividly as possible. The fact
that they both fall victim to the girl's prank in no way negates the erotic,
and at the same time highly cynical, impression that this scene makes upon
the viewer. The fact that father and son, unintentionally, suddenly find
themselves together precisely at the moment that they are about to give

---

[58] Decision I A 151/1912 (December 6, 1912) of Berlin Bezirksausschuß, upholding
the police ban, as quoted in Hellwig, "Die maßgebenden Grundsätze," p. 426.

[59] This ban, however, was later repealed by the Prussian Oberverwaltungsgericht
(decision of III. Senat, April 24, 1913).

[60] Berlin police president to Vienna police president, August 7, 1912, quoted in Hellwig, "Die maßgebenden Grundsätze," p. 413.

themselves over to the pleasures of forbidden love is likely to have a most harmful impact upon young people and upon those whose moral values are not sufficiently developed. And even to those in the audience who do have strong moral characters, the crucial final scene in Nini's bedroom will be offensive and shocking.[61]

Third, any material considered politically, socially, or religiously inflammatory was prohibited by the film censors on the ground that it could lead to public disturbances that might endanger civic peace and order.[62] It was not merely a matter of banning blatantly subversive or blasphemous material, as when police prohibited a film about the Portuguese revolution of 1910 because they believed it glorified revolution.[63] Rather, the police sought to keep virtually all controversial political, social, or religious issues off the movie screen. They applied especially strict standards to any film that portrayed a member, living or dead, of the ruling Hohenzollern dynasty. In 1910, for example, the Berlin censors sought to ban an otherwise complimentary film about Frederick the Great because, as the police chief explained, certain incidents from Frederick's boyhood were depicted in a rather silly or unflattering way. Considering the fact that cinema audiences were composed primarily of lower-class individuals and adolescents, the chief argued that it was "important that precisely among these kinds of people no film be shown that might leave a false impression about the personalities or actions of any member of our ruling dynasty or that might undermine popular loyalty toward the royal family."[64] He asked the Prussian interior minister to issue a general decree that in the future

[61] Decision I A 162/1912 (December 20, 1912) of Berlin Bezirksausschuß, upholding the police ban, as quoted ibid., p. 427.

[62] Berlin police president to Vienna police president, August 7, 1912, quoted ibid., p. 413.

[63] Ibid., p. 428. When they could not keep politically subversive material off the screen, the authorities tried the next best thing: keeping audiences out of the theater. Thus in February, 1911, soldiers in Halle were ordered by their commander not to attend the cinema because newsreels featuring the funeral of socialist leader Paul Singer were being shown. See Alex Hall, *Scandal, Sensation, and Social Democracy: The SPD Press and Wilhelmine Germany 1890–1914* (Cambridge, 1977), p. 53.

[64] Berlin police president to Prusian Interior Minister, August 3, 1910, ZStA Merseburg, Rep. 77, Tit. 1000, Nr. 5, Bd. 4. Such an order was issued in 1844 regarding all theatrical pieces in which Hohenzollerns appeared either directly or indirectly. The Interior Minister, although in full sympathy with the police president, ruled that the 1844 decree could be applied only to the live theater and that for complex legal reasons it could not be extended to the cinema (Interior Minister's letter of August 7, 1910).

no film about any of the Hohenzollerns, however favorable the portrayal, be allowed without first obtaining the express approval of the kaiser himself. The Prussian film censors guarded with equal care the cinematic image of the ruling dynasties of other German states. On the eve of the war, for instance, the Berlin censors, acting at the behest of the Bavarian authorities, banned a film about the tragic life of the mentally disturbed King Ludwig II on the ground that it "might damage patriotism."[65]

If the censors were fearful of permitting the hereditary political sovereigns to be portrayed on film, they were adamantly opposed to any cinematic depiction of the founder of the Christian religious system. In 1913 the Prussian government issued a decree categorically banning any motion picture about the life of Christ, however religiously inspired or reverential the film might be:

> The story of the life and suffering of Christ forms the basis of the Christian faith and of all Christian-religious life within the Church and the home. Christ's life would be stripped of its holy, consecrated aura if it were to become part of a show in a commercial cinema. In our opinion, the public portrayal of the life and Passion of our Savior on film constitutes an offense to religious sensibilities and would likely cause disruptions of the public order. For this reason, any such film can be banned by the police.[66]

Fourth, the police censors proscribed any violent, gory, or bestial scenes that could brutalize the spirit of the viewer. This meant that "horrifying or repulsive medical conditions" such as surgical operations, accident victims, catalepsy, epileptic seizures, and suicides were banned from the screen, as were any wanton acts of cruelty or sheer barbarism.[67] Thus in 1910 a graphic film of a cockfight was prohibited on the ground that the film presented "an image of repulsion and bru-

[65] Berlin police letter of February 24, 1914, StA Bremen, 4,20–Nr. 353. Not only was this film banned in Prussia, but police throughout the Reich were also requested by their state governments to ban it, and it appears that they complied. StA Darmstadt, G15 Friedberg, XIX. Abt., III. Abschnitt, Bd. II.

[66] Memorandum of Prussian Interior Minister, May 27, 1913, StA Potsdam, Rep. 2, Abt. I, Nr. 3446. The local censors in Breslau also proclaimed that "portrayals from the Old and New Testament, namely of the life and passion of Jesus Christ, are absolutely not permitted." Breslau police president to Berlin police president, January 3, 1912, StA Potsdam, Rep. 30 Berlin C, Tit. 74, Th. 1252.

[67] Berlin police president to Essen police president, September 24, 1909, memorandum of Polizeirat Glasenapp, July 22, 1910, and Berlin police president to Vienna police president, August 7, 1912, quoted in Hellwig, "Die maßgebenden Grundsätze," p. 413.

tality that is certain to pervert and brutalize the ethical standards of anyone, including mature adults."[68] Likewise, a film of the famous Johnson-Jeffries prizefight was banned in 1911—not because police feared that the victory of the black Johnson over the white Jeffries would incite race riots, as in the United States, but because it was felt that, according to prevailing moral standards, the sight of two adult men pounding each other bloody for fifteen rounds was intolerably brutal.[69] Berlin censors even went so far as to ban the film *Dante's Divine Comedy* on the ground that its portrayal of the torments and agonies of souls in hell was too graphic and revolting. In this case, however, the ban was later lifted by the courts because "behind the horrible, shocking sufferings depicted in the film stands the great ethical principle of God's retribution in the hereafter, the concept of divine justice."[70]

Finally, each film was examined by the censors to see whether, from a psychological or pedagogical standpoint, it was appropriate viewing for children and adolescents. If it was thought a film might somehow detrimentally influence the psychic or intellectual development of tender minds, then it was passed for adult audiences but was banned from the children's matinees. One particularly interesting decision of this kind involved the 1910 futuristic science fiction film *A Look into the Future*. This motion picture contained a sequence about an imaginary war of the future, with scenes that the Berlin censors considered totally unsuitable for young viewers. "The absurd fantasies of this film," the police claimed,

> would have little effect if shown to adults with even minimal intelligence. But on children it could have a very detrimental impact. For children lack the factual knowledge and mature judgment that most adults have, and hence they are liable to believe even the most improbably absurd things. [This film shows] the horrors of an explosive torpedo being dropped from the sky by an airship and turning a city to ashes; it shows the airship in turn being pursued and shot at by an automobile, but the auto and its passengers are blown up by the airship in the nick of time; and finally the

[68] Decision A I 70/1910 of Berlin Bezirksausschuß, upholding the police ban, as quoted ibid., p. 424.

[69] Ibid., p. 420; and *Frankfurter Zeitung*, September 17, 1911 and September 24, 1911.

[70] Prussian Oberverwaltungsgericht decision of May 2, 1911, as quoted in Hellwig, "Die maßgebenden Grundsätze," p. 428.

airship is shown being hit by an air torpedo and crashing into the sea. Seeing such things is likely to cause extreme mental agitation and serious nervous disorders in children. It is also clear that showing such utterly fantastic and horrible war scenes of the future can cause serious moral harm to children by arousing in them a desire to imitate what they see and by evoking pleasure at the sight of cruelty and horror.[71]

It was ironic that within months these scenes of horrible mechanized warfare, which the censors had condemned as improbably absurd and inhumanly cruel, became stark reality as Europe sank into the First World War.

Although film producers and distributors naturally complained that the criteria applied to popular films were too strict, the work of the Prussian film censor's office seemed to enjoy relatively broad support, at least within the middle-class press. Brunner had helped see to that through some deft public relations work. In December, 1912, he invited members of the Association of Berlin Newspapers (Verein der Berliner Presse) to a special closed screening of several banned films in order to give the press a better understanding of the censor's work. As one Berlin daily later reported, the evening proved a magnificent success, and rallied most of the capital's press firmly behind the censorship office:

> The cinema censor, who has snatched so many sure hits from the film producers, has himself achieved a great hit with his special performance [of banned films]. Not one of the police decisions on these films was challenged or questioned by this select audience of critics. Not only did the actions of the film censor find unanimous support, but often the audience shouted their hearty approval that this or that particularly brutal or repulsive scene had been banned. Many skeptical critics who had previously condemned the Berlin censors are now singing a different tune after seeing the films for themselves. Press reports now unanimously approve of the basic principles of cinema censorship and of the way the authorities are carrying it out. Indeed it has been a long time since so many different newspapers, representing such a variety of different outlooks, have been so united in their unbounded approval of the government's actions. With one stroke, the cinema censor has won the eternal gratitude of the Berlin press.[72]

---

[71] Decision A I 66/1910 of Berlin Bezirksausschuß, upholding the police ban, as quoted ibid., p. 425.

[72] *Berliner Volkszeitung*, December 22, 1912, as quoted in Brunner, *Kinematograph von heute*, p. 25.

The central film censorship office for Bavaria, which began its work in April, 1912, followed the same general guidelines as the censors in Berlin, banning any film or scene that was "contrary to state institutions, public order, religion, morality, or decency." Two film reviewers and two assistants, all with at least a *Gymnasium* education, were employed in Munich to screen about fifteen films per day. Unlike their Berlin colleagues, however, the cinema censors in Munich were not allowed to distinguish between the films destined for adult audiences and those for children's shows; every film they passed had to be suitable not only for adults but for children as well. As a result, a larger percentage of films was banned by the Bavarian censors than by the Prussian, and many of the films that had been approved for adults in Berlin were prohibited altogether in Munich.[73]

Germany's other major film censorship office in Stuttgart had barely begun operation when its work was interrupted by the war. Although the framers of Württemberg's 1914 film law had intended that the state's censors be highly educated, the Stuttgart cinema censorship office was placed under the control of Lieutenant Wilbur Höfling, a reserve officer and former railway secretary with police experience in the areas of gypsies, chocolate smuggling, and identity papers. He also had acquired a passing familiarity with the Munich film censor's office, and for this reason he was hired (at eleven marks per day) to serve as Württemberg's film censor. The Stuttgart police also hoped he would be able to help out in the force's antiespionage and antismuggling divisions. Höfling was soon aided by another part-time censor, a thirty-two-year-old elementary school teacher. Between them, they screened about five films a day in the months before the war.[74] The Württemberg law stipulated that a film was to be banned from public showing if

[73] On the Munich film censors, see Bavarian Interior Ministry order of January 14, 1911, in Hellwig, *Rechtsquelle*, p. 86; and Munich police president to Bavarian Interior Minister, August 22, 1912, HStA Stuttgart, E 151c/II, Nr. 270b. Between April 1, 1912 and August 22, 1912, the censors examined a total of 2,330 films. Of these, 192 (8.2 percent) were banned completely and portions of 227 others (9.7 percent) had to be cut before the film could be passed. Corresponding data on the decisions of the Berlin censors exist only for the months of September and October, 1911. During that time, 986 films were submitted for censorship in Prussia; 29 of these (2.9 percent) were banned completely, while 119 (12 percent) were passed only for adult audiences but were declared unsuitable for children. Wolff, *Denkschrift*, p. 14.

[74] Stuttgart police president to Württemberg Interior Minister, May 8, 1914, June 22, 1914, June 23, 1914, and September 18, 1914, HStA Stuttgart, E 151c/II, Nr. 270b.

"its subject matter, or the way the material is presented, is likely to endanger the health or morality of the viewer, offend his religious feelings, brutalize his senses, deprave or overexcite his imagination, or blunt and disorient his sense of justice and public order."[75] As in Prussia, a film in Württemberg could be passed for adults but banned from children's matinees if it were deemed inappropriate for those under sixteen. In questionable cases, or whenever the censors' decisions were challenged, a panel of physicians, teachers, pastors, journalists, artists, youth workers, and other experts was to be consulted.

IV

As early as 1901, Charles Pathé, one of the early pioneers of the cinema industry, had predicted that "the cinema will be the theater, the newspaper, and the schoolroom of tomorrow."[76] By 1914, those who worried that the perceptions and behavior of the masses were indeed being shaped more by the popular cinema than by the press or the schools had succeeded in subjecting the German cinema to rigorous censorship. Yet for those who feared the cinema would, as Pathé predicted, also supplant older forms of entertainment such as the legitimate theater, mere censorship of film content offered no solace at all.

Without a doubt, the rapid proliferation of cinema halls and the general cinema craze that swept Germany and other nations after 1905 represented a serious threat to other traditional amusements. Owners of music halls, variety shows, circuses, and even pubs and beer halls found it increasingly difficult to compete with the attractions of the new cinematic medium. In 1911, for example, it was reported that two thousand small pubs in and around Berlin had closed down, presumably because their nightly male clientele had been lured into the movie theaters.[77] But the group that claimed to be hardest hit by the popularity of the cinema—and that was the most vocal about it—was the owners, actors, and employees of Germany's legitimate dramatic

---

[75]Article 2, "Gesetz betreffend öffentliche Lichtspiele, vom 31. März 1914," *Regierungsblatt für das Königsreich Württemberg (1914)*, Nr. 9, pp. 87–92.

[76]Quoted in Zglinicki, *Weg des Films*, p. 1.

[77]Panofsky, *Geburt des Films*, p. 71. Women, according to Panofsky, tended to visit the cinema in the afternoon, but men did so in the evening after work. Previously, men had spent most evenings drinking in pubs.

theaters. Small towns such as Hildesheim reported that theaters there were losing one-third to one-half of their audience to the cinemas, while in larger cities such as Stuttgart or Berlin cinemagoers soon outnumbered theater patrons by as much as seven to one. In 1912 alone, some twenty-two theaters were forced to close in Berlin, while twenty-nine Austrian theaters shut their doors for good, throwing sixteen hundred people out of work. According to those in the theater industry, these closings were in large part a result of the intense competition that theaters faced from the commercial cinema houses.[78]

To combat the dire economic menace posed by the motion-picture industry, those in the legitimate theater quickly banded together into lobbies or interest groups such as the Guild of German Stage Employees (Genossenschaft deutscher Bühnenangehöriger), the Association of Berlin Theater Directors (Verein Berliner Bühnendirigenten), the German Stage Association (Deutscher Bühnenverein), or the League of German Playwrights (Verband deutscher Bühnenschriftsteller). Some of these organizations forbade their members from directing, acting in, or writing for the commercial cinema; others merely issued a series of ringing anticinema proclamations, pamphlets, and public petitions designed to awaken the nation to the peril that faced the German theater.[79] One such manifesto, for example, declared:

> A few years ago an enemy of the German theater appeared. We must finally undertake an energetic struggle against this enemy, if it isn't already too late. The havens of dramatic art are in danger, threatened by an ingenious wonder of technical inventiveness—the cinema. . . . This is no struggle against some other art form. On the contrary, the cinemas are a dangerous, almost invincible force that is working against all artistic effort; cinemas push aside the mighty word and the actor's noble gesture, and offer only a pitiable [visual] substitute. Purely mechanical reproductions [such as films] necessarily exclude art as it has been traditionally understood; the cinema's mechanical performances are devoid of any higher artistic purpose. The cinema and the legitimate dramatic arts are born enemies.[80]

[78] Toeplitz, *Geschichte des Films*, I, 105; Knietzsch, *Film gestern und heute*, p. 27; Kracauer, *From Caligari to Hitler*, p. 16; *Deutsche Reichspost*, December 14, 1912; and Wolff, *Denkschrift*, p. 10.

[79] Dittmar, "Berlin und die Filmindustrie," pp. 848–50; Kracauer, *From Caligari to Hitler*, p. 17.

[80] Wolff, *Denkschrift*, pp. 3, 16.

Theater owners complained bitterly that cinema houses enjoyed an unfair competitive advantage because they were not subject to the same close state supervision as the theater industry was. For although theatrical performances in most German cities had to submit to prior police censorship just as cinemas did, private theaters were, in addition, tightly regulated by the German Commercial and Trades Code (*Gewerbeordnung*). This code required that every private theater be licensed by the local police; before any such license was granted, authorities investigated whether the community needed and could support another theater, and they probed deeply into the professional qualifications, financial assets, and even the moral character of the applicant. Once a theater license was granted, it was often limited to specific types of dramatic or operatic performances and could be revoked at any time. Furthermore, the commercial code laid down strict guidelines for the operation of a private theater: the number of performances per week was specified, as was the minimum interval between them; theaters were required to close on all major holidays; no beer or alcoholic beverages could be served in theaters; and the like. Since early court decisions had ruled that cinema performances could not, strictly speaking, be classified as "theatrical performances," cinemas were exempt from all these regulations.[81] Operators of private theaters, at once jealous and alarmed about the popularity of the cinemas, naturally blamed the economic plight of the theaters on the unfair competitive edge that cinemas enjoyed because of this exemption from the commercial code.

According to spokesmen for the theater industry, the lamentably low aesthetic and ethical standards of the popular cinema could also be traced to the fact that no licensing or controls of any kind were imposed on those who wished to open a new movie house. While the background of legitimate theater operators was carefully scrutinized before they were granted a theater license, any shady, irresponsible, or unscrupulous character with a little ready cash could open a cinema and exploit the film craze. Critics were fond of citing the case of one Aurel Zacharias. Zacharias had been convicted of arson, breaking and entering, two counts of willful destruction of property, and ten counts of

---

[81] Decision of Prussian Oberverwaltungsgericht, May 11, 1903, and of Prussian Kammergericht, June 10, 1907 and June 11, 1908.

armed robbery; he had, in addition, been declared mentally disturbed and a danger to society and was committed for several years to an insane asylum. Upon his release, however, he had opened a movie theater in Berlin and was soon enjoying a comfortable income.[82] More seriously, theater spokesmen charged that it was precisely the unchecked, almost frantic proliferation of cinemas that was inundating the nation with dangerous sensationalistic "junk" films. For as a community became saturated with more cinemas than it could possibly support, the cinema operators were forced to compete more fiercely and more unscrupulously with each other. To attract new customers, each cinema owner was inevitably tempted—indeed, forced—to outbid his competitors by offering the public increasingly more lurid, horrifying, or titillating films than they.

To ensure the survival of the legitimate theaters and to raise what they regarded as the deplorable moral level of the popular cinema, several theatrical lobbies mounted a concerted campaign around 1911 demanding that the spread of cinemas and their daily operations be more tightly regulated.[83] During the next two or three years, the imperial government was deluged with numerous petitions from theatrical groups, state parliaments, and even from the Reichstag requesting that the commercial code be expanded to cover cinemas and, in particular, that movie theaters be licensed like legitimate theaters and their reckless proliferation halted. One such petition stated:

> In the name of the many stage actors who are hard-pressed and often unemployed because of the rapidly growing excesses of the cinema, we hereby petition the Bundesrat to enact, as soon as possible, licensing for cinemas before the harm—which today is already bad enough—becomes even worse for our entire profession. . . . We request a speedy passage [of the proposed amendments to the commercial code] so that the cinema epidemic, with all its unhealthy consequences, may thus be finally stopped once and for all, before it is too late.[84]

As the cinema industry was faced with the threat of licensing and still tighter regulation, its members, too, organized into lobbies and

[82] Mayor of Berlin-Reinickendorf to Berlin Landrat, May 21, 1912, StA Potsdam, Rep. 2, Abt. I, Nr. 3448.

[83] Wenzel Goldbaum, *Denkschrift über die Kinematographentheater, im Auftrage des Verbandes Deutscher Bühnenschriftsteller* (no date, ca. 1912); and Wolff, *Denkschrift*, pp. 10–16.

[84] Petition dated April 10, 1913 to Deutscher Bundesrat, copy in GLA Karlsruhe,

pressure groups to protect their interests. During 1912 and 1913, organizations such as the Protective League of Cinema Associates (Schutzverband der Kinobranchen), the Protective League of German Film Theaters (Schutzverband der deutschen Lichtspieltheater), the Union of Cinema Owners (Verband der Kinobesitzer), and the Central League of German Film Distributors (Zentralverband der Filmverleiher Deutschlands) issued counter-manifestos and sent petitions of their own to the imperial government protesting the imposition of further controls on German cinemas. Any move to require the licensing of movie house owners, they argued, would violate constitutionally guaranteed freedoms of trade and occupation.[85]

Throughout 1913, as theater and cinema lobbies wrangled, and as the imperial government undertook a laborious study as to whether the provisions of the commercial code should be extended to movie theaters, several individual cities took ad hoc measures of their own to curb the growth of the commercial cinema and to halt the decline of their local private theaters. First Berlin, then other municipalities imposed special amusement taxes on their cinemas in the form of a 5 to 20 percent surcharge on every movie ticket sold. By raising the price of tickets, it was hoped the tax would discourage somewhat cinema attendance and cut into the industry's huge profits. In many cities, such as Berlin, the tax resulted in the closure of several cinemas.[86] Cinema taxes were also popular because of the revenue they provided; in Bremen, for example, the city fathers anticipated that such a tax could net the city 175,000 marks annually.[87] In some cases, as in Barmen, the

---

Abt. 234/5281. See also Baden Interior Minister to Baden Foreign Minister, December 6, 1911, and reply of Reich Interior Minister to Baden Foreign Minister, December 19, 1911, GLA Karlsruhe, Abt. 233/10972. The German Reichstag (which, according to the constitution, could merely approve laws but not initiate them) passed resolutions on April 14, 1912 and January 22, 1913 requesting the imperial government to draft a revision of the commercial code and submit it to the Reichstag for approval. *Stenographische Berichte über die Verhandlungen des Deutschen Reichstages*, XIII. Legislaturperiode, I. Session 1912/14, Drucksache 204.

[85] *Neuste Nachrichten*, January 3, 1913; and *Berliner Börsen-Courier*, January 12, 1913.

[86] Altenloh, *Soziologie des Kinos*, p. 42. The actual number of cinemas to close in Berlin in 1913 because of the *Lustbarkeitssteuer* is a matter of dispute. Zglinicki (*Weg des Films*, p. 327) claims 150 cinemas closed, while Dittmar ("Berlin und die Filmindustrie," pp. 848–50) maintains the number was closer to 65.

[87] StA Bremen, 3-F.1.b.1.—Nr. 203.

proceeds from the cinema tax were used to subsidize the city's legitimate theaters.[88] Although cinema owners and film industry lobbies protested these taxes bitterly, their protests were in vain.

Finally, in February, 1914, the imperial government submitted to the Reichstag the long-awaited draft bill that would revise those portions of the commercial code pertaining to popular amusements. Citing the dangers when children spend too much time and money in movie theaters and pointing to the way most cinemas exploit the baser instincts and sensationalistic cravings of the mass audience, the imperial government warned that the modern cinema preyed "on that segment of the population which lacks the education [*Bildung*] to resist the evil influences of popular films. . . . The attraction of the cinema for youth and for the undereducated classes—an attraction that is enhanced by the cheap admission prices and by the nature of the film advertisements—represents a moral threat to the nation that must absolutely be resisted."[89] Under the government's bill, not only would all new cinema houses in Germany have to be licensed, but in addition these licenses would be difficult to obtain, especially in the large cities. For a cinema license could be denied to an applicant on any of the following grounds: first, if there was evidence that the applicant was morally, professionally, financially, or otherwise unqualified to operate a movie house; second, if the premises of the cinema did not meet police safety specifications; third, if it appeared the applicant had insufficient capital (when authorities deemed it necessary, they could grant a permit on the condition that the applicant first put down a security deposit as a guarantee of any future claims against him). Lastly, and most importantly, cinema licenses could be denied when authorities decided that, in relation to the size of the population, the locality already had a sufficient number of cinemas. This last stipulation, of course, was a means of protecting private theaters in the area against excessive competition from the cinema and of protecting the public from the presumed evils of excessive competition between cinema owners.

The government's bill clearly represented a victory for the legitimate theater industry and another blow to the cinema. These new re-

[88] Altenloh, *Soziologie des Kinos*, p. 42.
[89] Draft law of February 25, 1914, *Stenographische Berichte des Reichstages*, XIII. Legislaturperiode, I. Session 1912/14, Drucksache 1431.

strictions were to be voted on in the summer of 1914, and they would almost certainly have passed, had not the bill been overshadowed and quickly forgotten in the rush of events when war erupted on August 1.

V

The gathering war clouds had cast their shadows over the German cinema already before August, 1914. In the tense months prior to the outbreak of war, film censors became increasingly sensitive to the international and military implications of certain popular films. The 1913 film *The Enemy Is Here*, for example, was banned in cities near the German-French border not only because it depicted a "hypothetical" German-French war but also because the authorities thought it cast the German army in a bad light.[90] Of even greater concern, however, were the spy films that were so popular with prewar German audiences. Films like *The Fortress Spy* frequently showed foreign agents bribing German civilians and military officers for defense secrets. In the summer of 1913 the War Ministry expressed concern about these popular spy films and in a secret memo declared: "In view of the brisk activities of foreign espionage agents in Germany, showing such films is extremely detrimental to our counterespionage efforts. For not only do these films stir up public interest in espionage, but they might be a factor in prompting irresponsible persons to commit espionage."[91] In the interest of national security, therefore, the War Ministry urged all state governments to ensure that all films treating the topics of espionage or treason were banned.

When the First World War broke out in August, 1914, a dramatic new phase in the government's policy toward the cinema began. Ever since the film industry had appeared in the late 1890s, many German authorities had viewed it with suspicion, if not outright hostility, and as this new mass entertainment medium grew, increasingly stringent regulations had been imposed upon it in hopes of limiting its mass impact. To those who most feared the power of the mass cinema, the war pre-

---

[90] *Frankfurter Warte*, October 11, 1913, reporting Essen's ban of the film.

[91] Secret memorandum of Hessian Interior Minister to Kreisämter, July 30, 1913, StA Darmstadt, G15 Friedberg, XIX. Abt., III. Abschnitt, Bd. II; and memorandum of Baden Interior Minister to Bezirksämter, August 6, 1913, GLA Karlsruhe, Abt. 234/5821.

sented a unique opportunity to restrict even further the offerings and operation of movie theaters. For, under the state of siege (*Belagerungszustand*) that went into effect during the war, district military commanders assumed control over much of Germany's civil administration. These military authorities, who exercised their powers independently of the civilian government or parliamentary bodies, proved highly receptive to demands for more constraints on the cinema. They eagerly used their temporary emergency powers to subject the popular cinema to far tighter controls than had been possible in peacetime. At the same time, however, the war convinced some imperial officials, especially the high military officers, that the popular cinema might not represent such a grave threat to the established order after all. Toward the latter years of the war, as the prospects of German victory dimmed and as popular support for the imperial order rapidly evaporated, the German high command came to appreciate the potential power of the cinema and to see it as a medium that, if properly used, might help shore up the sinking imperial state.

As soon as the war began, military authorities began intruding into cinema affairs. The German general staff, for example, took over the censorship of all films that in any way touched upon military affairs or war industries.[92] For their part, civilian film censors during the early days of the war simply urged cinema operators to show only films that corresponded to the patriotic mood of the nation; yet, at the same time, the censors sought to ensure that no films were shown that might arouse overzealous patriots to commit acts of violence against foreign nationals residing in Germany.[93] Although more patriotic documentaries and educational shorts were inserted into cinema programs, by and large Germany's cinemas continued during the early months of the war to offer the same popular escapist films as before. To the austere military authorities, such frivolous kinds of mass entertainment during a time of national crisis seemed almost sacrilegious. By late 1914, the Prussian war minister began complaining that, given the gravity of the times, far too many shallow, even downright silly foreign films were being shown and that these were "poisoning [the people's] healthy na-

[92] War Press Office to Württemberg War Minister, December 1, 1917, HStA Stuttgart, E 151c/II, Nr. 286.
[93] Berlin police memorandum, August 11, 1914, StA Potsdam, Rep. 30 Berlin C, Tit. 74, Th. 134.

tional sentiment." Rather than offering all that imported "trash," the minister suggested that the cinema houses show more serious films that would strengthen the nation's patriotic will and promote good morals.[94]

What disturbed many wartime observers, however, was not that popular films lacked serious content but that popular romances, melodramas, comedies, and adventure films threatened the established social order. After 1915, especially, as the Reich's initial wartime solidarity broke down and as bitter internal political and economic conflicts again surfaced, a number of local authorities warned that popular films exacerbated Germany's class tensions by portraying the upper classes in inaccurate, stereotyped ways and by generating envy and resentment among the lower classes. One Reichstag delegate, for instance, complained that in the movies barons and industrial magnates were always portrayed as being "filthy rich" and as leading

> a kind of life that simply does not exist in reality. [In the films] they always drive big automobiles, carry bulging pocketbooks but never pay for anything, are constantly drinking champagne, and generally lead a life of total pleasure and sensuality. . . . By portraying in such a matter-of-fact way things that, in real life, are rare individual cases, and by raising these almost to a norm, many popular films not only falsify and distort people's view of the world but also distort the social behavior of certain types of people.[95]

A Prussian school inspector charged that popular films invariably depicted the upper classes as an elite that never worked, lived in opulent luxury, led decadent lives, and tended either to scorn or to mistreat those lower down on the social ladder. "What false perceptions and distorted images are perpetuated in the minds of countless moviegoers concerning the lives of the better-situated social classes," he complained, "especially when most moviegoers come from the lower classes. Hardworking, honest industrialists who feel deeply responsible for the millions of marks and thousands of workers in their charge; the anxious, often frantic existence of our great merchants; the responsible work being done by our higher civil servants and officers; the unceas-

---

[94] Memorandum of Prussian War Minister, December 15, 1914, to all local military commanders, StA Potsdam, Rep. 2, Abt. I, Nr. 3446 and Rep. 30 Berlin C, Tit. 74, Th. 134.

[95] Quoted in Zglinicki, *Weg des Films*, p. 367.

ing exertions of the productive middle classes—of these, one never catches even a glimpse in the cinema. The masses, in short, are getting only a social caricature [of the upper classes]." Similar sentiments were expressed by a county director in Baden, who warned of the "false images and misperceptions" that the great box-office hits were creating about the values and life-styles of the propertied classes.[96]

Growing concern over cinema programs soon led to the imposition of new wartime controls on the film industry. In such areas as Baden, where legal restraints on police power had prevented the enactment of censorship before the war, military commanders now used their emergency powers to subject all films to prior censorship.[97] Next, the German government banned the importation of all new foreign films. For not only were most of the popular films that authorities found objectionable produced in France, England, and Italy, but it was also feared that films from these enemy nations, however innocent they might appear, could surreptitiously be spreading false, anti-German ideas among the nation's cinema audiences. Censors thus were instructed in 1915 not to pass any films that had been produced in foreign nations since the outbreak of the war, regardless of the actual content of the film.[98] Finally, in order to stamp out undignified, frivolous forms of entertainment for the duration of the war, local military commanders across Germany ordered that all low-grade adventure films, comedies, and other "junk" movies be completely banned from their districts on the ground that these films were, by their very nature, unsuitable to the "gravity of the present times."[99] Under these stricter wartime

[96] Guben county school inspector to Regierungspräsident Frankfurt/Oder, September 27, 1915, StA Potsdam, Rep. 3B, Abt. I, Bd. 1431; Bezirksamt Schwetzingen to Baden Interior Minister, May 2, 1917, GLA Karlsruhe, Abt. 362, Nr. 174. See also the comments by the Prussian War Minister about the film *Sword and Hearth* in his memorandum of April 19, 1917, HStA Stuttgart, E 151c.II, Nr. 287.

[97] Military decree of March 6, 1916 and directives of Baden Interior Minister, March 14, 1916 and April 7, 1916, GLA Karlsruhe, Abt. 233/10972 and Abt. 357/13077.

[98] Memorandum of Prussian Interior Minister, February 7, 1915, StA Potsdam, Rep. 2, Abt. I, Nr. 3446; order of Ninth Army Corps commander, October 23, 1915, StA Bremen, 4,20—Nr. 352; memorandum of Hessian Interior Minister, May 21, 1915, StA Darmstadt, G15 Friedberg, XIX. Abt., III. Abschnitt, Bd. II. See also Knietzsch, *Film gestern und heute*, p. 31; and Dittmar, "Berlin und die Filmindustrie," p. 850.

[99] *Merkblatt für Kinematographen-Theater*, January 13, 1915, in StA Potsdam, Rep. 30 Berlin C, Tit. 75, Th. 134. Also memorandum of Ninth Army Corps commander, December 22, 1914, StA Bremen, 4,20—Nr. 352; commander of Fourteenth Army Corps to

guidelines, films like *Detective Braun*, an action-packed police story that censors had earlier passed for adult audiences, were now banned from cinemas altogether.

Other facets of the cinema industry were also subjected to tighter state regulation during the war. Concerned that, as more fathers were called to the front and more mothers went to work, children would spend more of their time and money at the cinema, military commanders in 1916 raised the minimum age for cinema admission. German authorities moved also to restrict the use of the garish posters that were often used to advertise new films. For as the number of the cinemas continued to rise, even during the war,[100] and as tighter censorship prevented cinema owners from showing the most profitable thrillers and potboilers, movie houses had to compete more and more fiercely with one another for patrons. Cinema operators sought to lure audiences through attention-getting flyers, banners, posters, and placards, some of which might be several square meters large. Many conservative Germans found these cinema posters, with their vivid, often crass colors, their tantalizing and eye-arresting illustrations, and their screaming, suggestive slogans to be both highly offensive and completely contrary to the austere wartime mood. To some, these sensationalistic movie placards were even more vulgar than the low-quality films they advertised; indeed, the less interesting the film, the more provocative or suggestive its posters tended to be. After receiving complaints from local police, religious leaders, and others, in 1916 military commanders in Prussia, Baden, Bavaria, Hesse, and other states cracked down on the plague of crass cinema posters. The size of posters was strictly regulated; they could be displayed only in movie theaters and could not be visible from the street; they could announce only the titles of coming attractions, without any embellishment or commentary; and they could contain only printed words, no illustrations. In some localities, posters, like films, had to be approved by the police before they could be displayed.[101]

Baden Interior Minister, December 21, 1914, and memorandum of Baden Interior Minister to Baden Bezirksämter, January 6, 1915, GLA Karlsruhe, Abt. 357/13077.

[100] In 1914 there were 2,446 cinemas in Germany; by 1917 here were 3,130, an increase of 27 percent. Zglinicki, *Weg des Films*, p. 328; and Kullmann, *Entwicklung des Lichtspieltheaters*, p. 43.

[101] See, for example, the Baden decree of March 6, 1916 and memorandum of Baden

Many observers, however, maintained that all these new wartime measures attacked merely the symptoms, not the basic cause of the cinema industry's problems. All the excesses of the commercial cinema, they believed, could be traced back to the ruthless, unscrupulous competition between cinema owners, a competition that had been caused by the excessive proliferation of cinemas in recent years. Although prewar efforts to license cinema owners and to control the number of new movie houses had come to naught, the solemn new public mood after 1914 and the suspension of normal administrative procedures created a new opportunity for the state once again to attempt to curb the inordinate spread of cinemas. Thus in 1916 the military commander for Berlin-Brandenburg decreed that no new cinemas could be opened there for the duration of the war unless specifically approved by the local authorities. Inspired by this move, several prominent private individuals organized the German Committee for Cinema Reform (Deutscher Ausschuß für Lichtspielreform) a few months later. Supported by the Center, the Conservative, and the National Liberal parties, this committee began another campaign to impose licensing on the entire German cinema industry. In March, 1917, this movement succeeded in convincing the Reichstag to ask the imperial chancellor to resubmit that ill-fated bill of February, 1914, which sought to revise the commercial code and subject all cinema operators to licensing. The imperial cabinet, however, feared that reopening parliamentary debate on this issue would simply stir up a bitter controversy between pro- and anticinema interest groups and exacerbate the serious economic and political divisions that were beginning to surface in war-weary Germany.[102]

The following year the cabinet suddenly reversed its stand and drew up a new law on cinemas for the Reichstag to consider. Cinemas had become an important, accepted element of national life, the cabi-

Interior Minister, May 11, 1916, GLA Karlsruhe, Abt. 357/13077, Abt. 233/10972, and Abt. 357/1907/32, Nr. 13077; Bavarian decree of March 7, 1916, HStA Stuttgart M77/1, Bü. 60; Berlin decree of July 11, 1916, StA Potsdam, Rep. 30 Berlin C, Tit. 74, Th. 12; and Hessian decree of November 14, 1916, StA Darmstadt, G15 Friedberg, XIX. Abt., III. Abschnitt, Bd. II.

[102] Reichstag resolution of March 23, 1917, in Stenographische Berichte des Reichstages, XIII. Legislaturperiode, II. Session, 1914/18, p. 2625; March 9, 1918 draft of "Reich Lichtspielgesetz, Begründung" in ZStA Merseburg, Rep. 120 BB IIbl, Nr. 37, Adh. 2, Bd. 1, Bl. 279–83.

net explained as it submitted this bill, and the cinema industry would surely continue to expand after the end of the war. But the war had made apparent many serious abuses within the industry that had to be eliminated, and the future growth of cinemas had to be made more orderly. While the ad hoc actions of the military commanders since 1914 had successfully alleviated some of the problems with cinemas, the cabinet pointed out that these measures were merely temporary and would expire when the state of war ended. Therefore, to ensure that recent advances in cinema control would not be undone when the war ended and to control the development of the cinema industry in the future, the Reichstag was urged to pass this new bill that would impose licensing on all cinema operators and empower the authorities to close down extant cinemas if these were operated in ways contrary to the provisions of the commercial code.[103] Ironically, just as the outbreak of war in August, 1914, had prevented passage of the first proposed national cinema bill, the collapse of the imperial order in November, 1918, intervened before this new cinema law could be debated and voted upon.

While the war had confirmed the worst suspicions of many German authorities about the evils of the popular cinema and had provided them with a welcome excuse to subject the cinema industry to increasingly stringent state supervision, at the same time the exigencies of war and national mobilization caused other high imperial officials to appreciate, for the first time, the tremendous potential of the popular cinema as a state-supporting medium. Although district military commanders had initially condemned the cinema and its unwarlike frivolities, before long one war minister could be heard proclaiming that "movie theaters are an essential part of the war economy in that they offer diversion and amusement to wide sectors of the nation, and they can be effective tools of enlightenment and education."[104] Indeed, during the war the German high command even constructed special cinemas near the front lines to provide relaxation and needed distraction for the German troops. On the home front, too, government officials in some industrial areas ordered that local movie houses hold special per-

---

[103] Draft bill of March 9, 1918, in *Stenographische Berichte des Reichstages*, XIII. Legislaturperiode, II. Session 1914/18, Drucksache 1376.

[104] Hessian War Minister to Hessian Kreisämter, November 26, 1917, StA Darmstadt, G15 Friedberg, XIX. Abt., III. Abschnitt, Bd. II.

formances on holidays and weekends to serve those munitions workers who, because of their work schedules, were unable to attend the regular shows.[105]

In fact, during the war the imperial government itself—which previously had been apprehensive about if not outright hostile toward the film industry—began producing films for the German cinemas. Prompted by a concern over the low quality of most popular films and by the belief that the cinema could play an important role in arousing the nation's patriotic spirit and in maintaining wartime morale, in 1916 the War Ministry began commissioning a private firm, the German Bioscope Company (Deutsche Bioscop Gesellschaft), to produce some entertaining feature films that would subtly propagandize the German cause and cultivate anti-French sentiment. To ensure the widest possible circulation of these films, the War Ministry strongly urged all local film censors to pass them without question. Local authorities were told to keep the government's involvement with these films secret from the public. The military also used its considerable influence to have the film censors pass all the films of the German Cinematographic Company (Deutsche Lichtspielgesellschaft), another private firm, which, with government assistance, turned out propagandistic documentaries and feature films for domestic and overseas consumption.[106]

By 1917, the German high command declared that the cinema had become so important for the war effort that the production and distribution of patriotic films could no longer be left to private initiative. In a secret memorandum to the War Ministry in July, 1917, General Ludendorff pointed out that the longer the war dragged on, the more imperative it became to influence and direct mass opinion in a deliberate way; every possible medium had to be mobilized and systematically applied in this gigantic struggle for the minds of men. Until now, the general noted, the cinema had been used only sporadically and halfheartedly by Germany to influence public opinion. Yet, he continued,

[105] Kracauer, *From Caligari to Hitler*, p. 22; memorandum of Hessian Interior Minister, September 20, 1917, StA Darmstadt, G15 Friedberg, XIX. Abt., III. Abschnitt, Bd. II.

[106] Secret memorandum of Prussian War Minister to Württemberg War Minister, January 12, 1917, HStA Stuttgart, E 151c/II, Nr. 287; Kracauer, *From Caligari to Hilter*, p. 22; Manvell and Fraenkel, *German Cinema*, pp. 8–9. The Deutsche Lichtspielgesellschaft (Deulig) was financed by the right-wing press magnate Alfred Hugenberg and stood close to heavy industry, the Pan-German League, and the military.

this war has made clear the immense power of pictures and films as a means of enlightening and influencing the public. Our enemies, unfortunately, have so thoroughly exploited their advantages in this area that we have suffered great harm. Precisely because of the powerful political and military influence that films will continue to wield for the duration of the war, our victory absolutely depends on our using films to exert the greatest possible persuasion wherever people can still be won over to the German cause.[107]

In order to undertake a "vigorous indoctrination" of the broad masses by means of the cinema, the general advocated that the state unify the German film industry so as to simplify and coordinate the production and distribution of propaganda films. Key elements of the commercial cinema industry should be secretly acquired by the government for that purpose, Ludendorff recommended.

At Ludendorff's urging, the high command created a special Photographic and Film Office (Bild- und Filmamt [BUFA]) to coordinate the use of visual materials that were directly related to the war effort. This agency collected war photos, sent cameramen to the front to film battles, and produced short newsreels and documentaries about Germany's war effort. BUFA was also responsible for supplying programs for the soldiers' cinemas near the front; to hold the audience's attention and to guard against propaganda overkill, it concluded that these programs must be carefully balanced, with approximately one and one-half hours of harmless light entertainment and one-half hour of documentary or propaganda material. BUFA officials were so impressed with the success of these cinema programs that they also attempted to convince civilian cinema theaters back at the home front to run them. Great pains were taken, however, to keep the activities and the very existence of BUFA secret from the German public that viewed its films.[108]

A few months after the creation of BUFA, in November, 1917, the

---

[107] Ludendorff to Prussian War Minister, July 4, 1917, reprinted in *Innenansicht eines Krieges: Deutsche Dokumente, 1914–1918*, ed. Ernst Johann (Frankfurt, 1973), pp. 242–46.

[108] Memorandum of Hessian Interior Minister, September 20, 1917 and November 26, 1917, StA Darmstadt, G15 Friedberg, XIX. Abt., III. Abschnitt, Bd. II; memorandum of Baden Interior Minister, May 22, 1917, June 6, 1917, and November 2, 1917, GLA Karlsruhe, Abt. 357/13077; Kracauer, *From Caligari to Hitler*, p. 35; Paul Monaco, *Cinema and Society: France and Germany in the Twenties* (New York, 1976), p. 26; Zglinicki, *Weg des Films*, p. 363; Manvell and Fraenkel, *German Cinema*, p. 8.

German government secretly established the Universal Film Company (Universum Film A.G. [UFA]), which was to plan and supervise the production and distribution of patriotic feature films in the same way that BUFA oversaw war documentaries. Using some twenty-four million marks in state funds, front organizations quietly bought up private film companies like the Nordisk Company, which were then merged into the huge UFA enterprise. UFA's task was to produce pro-German entertainment films for showing in military cinemas and civilian theaters and, it was hoped, also in nations that Germany wished to woo. UFA had barely begun its work by the time the war ended and the German Empire collapsed.[109] (During the postwar years, however, UFA grew into a gigantic film enterprise that came to dominate the entire German cinema industry.)

VI

Imperial Germany's encounter with the popular cinema represents one of the first attempts by a society to come to grips with the modern mass media. By the end of the nineteenth century, urbanization and a mature industrial economy had produced in Germany, and in most other Western nations, a mass urban population that enjoyed an increasing amount of leisure time and disposable income. With more vacant time to fill, these masses sought amusement and diversion. Entire new industries arose, such as the popular press and the commercial cinema, to supply these mass consumers with the inexpensive entertainments and regalements they craved. The popular cinema was one of the first true mass entertainment media, and its appearance in the 1890s marked one of the earliest and most significant transitions from a traditional folk culture to a modern mass culture.[110]

In recent years, leftist critics such as Herbert Marcuse have maintained that the mass media are reactionary forces that help preserve

---

[109] Monaco, *Cinema and Society*, p. 26; Manvell and Fraenkel, *German Cinema*, pp. 8–9; Kracauer, *From Caligari to Hitler*, p. 35. For a detailed account of UFA, see Otto Kriegk, *Der deutsche Film im Spiegel der UFA* (Berlin, 1943); H. P. Manz, *UFA und der frühe deutsche Film* (Zurich, 1963); and Hans Taub, *Die UFA* (Berlin, 1943).

[110] Hannah Arendt, "Society and Culture," in *Culture for the Millions? Mass Media in Modern Society*, ed. Norman Jacobs (Boston, 1959), p. 47; Oscar Handlin, "Mass and Popular Culture," ibid., p. 66.

the power and privileges of traditional social elites. For the banality of mass culture, they argue, tranquilizes and stupefies the masses, diverting them from political activism and from pushing through social reforms. In this way, the mass media and the mass culture they disseminate are said to help thwart reform and to conserve the status quo.[111] Whether or not this is true today, the case of imperial Germany demonstrates that when the first mass media appeared at the end of the nineteenth century they were seen not as a prop for the established social and political order but rather as a dangerous threat to it. For the rise of a commercial mass culture challenged the traditional cultural dominance of the educated German elite. As a huge new market for the popular arts emerged in imperial Germany, and as the numbers, fortunes, and influence of cinemateurs and other cultural popularizers rose accordingly, the old cultural elite found its once secure monopoly under attack. Faced with the prospect, either real or imagined, of declining social influence and falling economic status, representatives of the educated elite often reacted by assailing the producers, purveyors, and consumers of mass culture, who, in their eyes, threatened the long-standing predominance of "high" culture.[112] Thus German state officials, clergymen, educators, theater people, and others denounced the commercial cinema as a direct threat to "high culture" and aesthetic principles in general and to the legitimate theater industry in particular. Like so many other social groups in imperial Germany, the university-educated, self-appointed "guardians" of high culture organized themselves into lobbies and pressure groups to protect their social position and economic interests from the competition of commercialized mass culture. And because the "culture-bearing" *Bildungsbürgertum* was able to utilize the power of the German state, they were able to impose a series of increasingly stringent legal restrictions upon the media of mass culture. Indeed, in the decade before the

---

[111] See Marcuse's "Repressive Tolerance," in R. P. Wolff, Barrington Moore, and H. Marcuse, *Critique of Pure Tolerance* (Boston, 1965), pp. 81–117, esp. pp. 94–99, 111; and Herbert Marcuse, *One-Dimensional Man* (Boston, 1964). Also Herbert J. Gans, *Popular Culture and High Culture* (New York, 1978), p. 48.

[112] Gans, *Popular Culture*, pp. 53–55. In this regard, see also Fritz K. Ringer, *The Decline of the German Mandarins: The German Academic Community, 1890–1933* (Cambridge, Mass., 1969); and Klaus Vondung, "Zur Lage der Gebildeten in der wilhelminischen Zeit," in *Das wilhelminische Bildungsbürgertum: Zur Sozialgeschichte seiner Ideen*, ed. Klaus Vondung (Göttingen, 1976), pp. 20–33.

First World War, the imperial government did not seek merely to censor and control the popular cinema but launched a general assault on other forms of popular culture, such as pulp fiction (*Schundliteratur*) and pornography, as well.[113]

This antipathy toward the emergence of a mass culture was part of a broader reaction by the German elite against the rising influence of the masses. As Herbert Gans has pointed out, the reaction against mass culture and mass media represents a reaction of the cultured against the uncultured, the educated against the uneducated, the affluent upper classes against the less affluent lower classes.[114] Anxiety over the cinema in imperial Germany was closely linked to class tensions, and the state's efforts to control the popular cinema clearly sprang from upper-class fears of the urban lower classes. For it was assumed by officials and other participants in high culture that the intensified consumption of popular films and other objects of mass culture by the lower classes would disorient and deprave those classes, undermine their attachment to traditionally sanctioned values, and lead to moral, perhaps even to social, anarchy.[115] Thus, in contrast to modern critics who believe the offerings of the mass media will narcotize and paralyze the masses, the cultured elite in imperial Germany feared just the opposite—namely, that media like the commercial cinema would activate the masses and impel them toward antisocial behavior that would endanger the established order.

But just as the First World War brought momentous changes in all areas of European civilization, so too did it bring a fundamental shift in official German policy toward the cinema. For the governing elite in imperial Germany, as elsewhere, soon realized after 1914 that victory in the war demanded not only that the military and the economy be mobilized but also that the collective energies of the masses be mobilized. To sustain civilian morale and public support of the regime's war effort, German leaders sought to organize, cultivate, and direct popular enthusiasm and nationalist passions;[116] to do this, they began to

[113] See Fullerton, "Toward a Commercial Popular Culture in Germany," and my "Pornography, Society, and the Law."

[114] Gans, *Popular Culture*, p. 3.

[115] Ibid., p. 4.

[116] Jack Roth, ed., *World War I: A Turning Point in Modern History* (New York, 1967), p. 109.

organize, cultivate, and direct mass media such as the commercial cinema. Through systematic manipulation of the cinema, Ludendorff and others in Germany's ruling elite hoped to manipulate mass opinion and thereby fortify the shaky imperial order.

While this newfound appreciation for mass media such as the cinema came too late to save the Second Reich, it foreshadowed the far more successful policy of the Third Reich. After the brief liberal interlude of the Weimar Republic, when the government remained officially indifferent toward the cinema and tried neither to suppress nor to manipulate it, the Nazis once again picked up where Ludendorff had left off. Goebbels and other Nazi propagandists, from the very outset, relied heavily on popular films, popular music, and other mass media to manipulate mass opinion systematically and to generate and sustain mass support for the Nazi order.[117] Where the elites of the authoritarian Second Reich had feared the urban masses and had sought to construct tight barriers around them and their media, the ruling elite of the Third Reich sought to harness and manipulate the power of the masses and of their cultural media. Herein lies the essential difference between nineteenth-century conservatism and twentieth-century fascism. And, as in so many other areas of modern history, it was the experience of the First World War that provided the bridge between the two.

[117] On the Nazis' use of the cinema, see Kracauer, *From Caligari to Hitler*, pp. 275–331; Joseph Wulf, *Theater und Film im Dritten Reich* (Gütersloh, 1964); David S. Hull, *Film in the Third Reich: Art and Propaganda in Nazi Germany* (Berkeley, 1969); Gerd Albrecht, *Nationalsozialistische Filmpolitik* (Stuttgart, 1969); Dorothea Hollstein, *Antisemitische Filmpropaganda: Die Darstellung des Juden im nationalsozialistischen Spielfilm* (Munich, 1971); François Courtade and Pierre Cadars, *Histoire du cinéma nazi* (Paris, 1972); Wolfgang Becker, *Film und Herrschaft: Organisationsprinzipien und Organisationsstrukturen der nationalsozialistischen Filmpropaganda* (Berlin, 1973); and Erwin Leiser, *Nazi Cinema* (New York, 1975).

VERNON L. LIDTKE

Songs and Nazis: Political Music and Social Change in Twentieth-Century Germany

Introduction

Almost all modern social and political movements have been accompanied by music and song, but rarely have historians tried to analyze the elusive and fluid relationship between the tonal accompaniment and the social action.[1] This essay is an attempt to probe some of the dimensions of that relationship as exemplified in German National Socialism, a movement saturated with songs and filled with high musical aspirations. It is not the hope here to arrive at conclusions that are valid for the relationship between music and social movements generally, but more modestly to describe and analyze, as far as possible, a pattern that can be discerned in National Socialism. This inquiry is limited moreover to songs specifically related to National Socialism as a political movement and makes no attempt to broach the much larger problem of the relationship between German fascism and music as a whole.[2]

---

[1] Scholars in other disciplines have approached the relationship from a number of perspectives. The structural analysis of modern political songs by Vladimir Karbusicky, *Ideologie im Lied: Lied in der Ideologie* (Cologne, 1973), identifies common denominators by using lyrics from the communist Left and fascist Right. Gert Hagelweide, *Das publizistische Erscheinungsbild des Menschen im kommunistischen Lied* (Bremen, 1968), also provides an extensive textual analysis that can be extremely useful for further work on the interaction of songs and political movements.

[2] This latter theme has been investigated by Donald Wesley Ellis in "Music in the Third Reich: National Socialist Aesthetic Theory as Govermental Policy" (Ph.D. diss., University of Kansas, 1970) and "The Propaganda Ministry and Centralized Regulation of Music in the Third Reich: The 'Biological Aesthetic' as Policy," *Journal of European Studies* 5 (September, 1975): 223–38, and by Michael Meyer in the following articles: "The Nazi Musicologist as Myth Maker in the Third Reich," *Journal of Contemporary History* 10 (October, 1975): 649–65; "Prospects of a New Music Culture in the Third Reich in Light of the Relationships between High and Popular Culture in European Musical Life," *Historical Reflections* 4 (Summer, 1977): 3–26; and "Musicology in the Third Reich: A Gap in Historical Studies," *European Studies Review* 8 (1978): 349–64.

National Socialist values and prejudices from the beginning encouraged the expectation that songs could play a prominent role both
within the movement and throughout German society if the party won
control of the state. Nativist assumptions in the ideology led National
Socialists to rank the assumed creativity of the *Volk* high in their hierarchy of laudable cultural forces. Immanent in the very being of the
German *Volk*, the ideology said, lay a vibrant musicality and creativity
that modern musicians disregard in favor of degenerate modes of musical expression. Hermann Unger hammered away on this point as he
denounced composers and performers who preferred a sophisticated
Publikum to the common people. Musical redemption could be found
only in the spiritual bosom of the *Volk*. Other eminent German musicologists agreed. "In the final analysis," wrote Friedrich Blume, "music, as every cultural activity, is based upon the racial makeup of its
participants." The task, said Karl Hasse, was to win "the German *Volk*
for German Art and German Art for the German *Volk*."[3] It followed for
Nazi ideology that refined aesthetic ideals and virtuosity were less important than the traditional tastes of the *Volk* and its full participation
in German musical life. In practice professional composers and performers did not noticeably alter their commitment to high aesthetic
standards during the Third Reich, but the regime itself especially promoted traditional modes of musical expression that reflected, presumably, the genuine spirit of the German *Volk*.

These ideological preferences meshed neatly with the pragmatic
Nazi realization that music, especially participatory singing, could
serve social and political functions that would be of considerable assistance to the movement. In the early years songs could aid particularly in communicating basic ideas and recruiting new members; once
the party acquired political control music would assist in socializing the
German people into the new system, mobilizing the population for

---

[3] Hermann Unger, "Kunstmusik oder Volksmusik?" *Nationalsozialistische Monatshefte* 5 (July, 1934): 616–19; Friedrich Blume, *Das Rassenproblem in der Musik* (Wol-
fenbüttel and Berlin, 1939), p. 3; Karl Hasse, *Vom deutschen Musikleben* (Regensburg,
[1933]), p. 8. See also the report by Fritz Stege on a questionnaire he sent to leading
German musicians on the question of how to bridge the gap between *Volksmusik* and
Kunstmusik: "Kunstmusik und Volksmusik, Eine Rundfrage," *Nationalsozialistische
Monatshefte* 5 (July, 1934): 620–31; and Otto Brodde, "Politische Musik," *Musik und
Volk* 2 (February/March, 1935): 81–87.

government policies, and creating the aura of sacred legitimacy for the Führer and his movement.[4] To serve these functions a song's aesthetic merits counted far less than its popular appeal. The *Volk's* receptivity to a song could be taken, in Nazi ideology, as proof of its genuine German musical qualities. Political songs fit perfectly into this matrix of shrewd pragmatism and *völkisch* idealism.

Phases of Development: An Overview

The ideological and pragmatic stimuli for the creation of texts and melodies were matched increasingly by the enthusiasm of Nazi poets and musicians. Political songs flourished. They became an integral part of the political struggles of the Weimar years and pliable tools in the hands of the rulers of the Third Reich. The repertory of Nazi songs expanded from a mere handful in the middle 1920s to a vast collection of hundreds, perhaps even thousands, by the late 1930s. In this development, we can detect three broad phases in the formation of the repertory and in the use of music and song by the National Socialists.

The first phase corresponded approximately to what the Nazis called the *Kampfzeit* ("era of struggle"), from the origin of the movement to Hitler's appointment as chancellor in January, 1933. The songs that appeared during the 1920s drew heavily on existing melodies and texts. New lyrics were often written to older melodies, a common practice in all social movements. March melodies were preferred, in part because they were known from the First World War and because Nazis never strolled if they could march. The SA storm troopers constituted the single most important Nazi singing group in the *Kampfzeit*, followed by the Hitler Youth. Commentators noted that Nazi music of the *Kampfzeit* had a "jagged" (*zackig*) quality. Lyrics stressed combat, struggle, revolution, brutality, anti-Semitism, blood, and loyalty to Germany, but always fighting, fighting, fighting. Spontaneity and transmission of word of mouth characterized much of the development

---

[4]There are hints throughout National Socialist commentaries on music about its social and political functions. They were particularly impressed with the communicative function, as in Hans Bajer, "Lieder machen Geschichte," *Die Musik* 31 (June, 1939): 586–87.

during the *Kampfzeit*. As late as 1930 there were only a few books of
Nazi songs. The first one, with about a dozen texts, appeared in 1923,
the first SA songbook in 1931. After that the number increased
gradually.[5]

A second phase began following the accession to power in 1933 and
lasted through the early years of the Second World War. An explosion
took place in the creation of new political songs. The practice of using
older melodies declined; new melodies were composed. The Nazi regime could use music and song for many different occasions and purposes. It required diversity, songs with melodies that would be appropriate for evening relaxation as well as for marching, ceremonial songs
for special festivals and holidays, songs for children and girls as well as
for storm troopers and the Hitler Youth. Songs and songbooks were
needed for the new and expanding organizations of the party and the
Third Reich, for the Hitler Youth, the League of German Girls, the
"Strength-Through-Joy" (Kraft durch Freude), and the Labor Service
(Reichsarbeitsdienst), to mention just a few. Specialization in song
writing went hand in hand with the enlarged organizational and institutional market. Nazi music makers were in their heyday.[6]

The decline came in the third phase, during the years of the Second World War. The output of new Nazi political songs dropped dramatically. On the battlefront soldiers found the old tradition of war
songs about homeland, love, and death more fitting than the optimistic
lyrics of many Nazi political songs. On the home front the ebullient
spirit formerly manifest at celebrations, festivals, and party rallies
faded. The regime resorted to decrees to compel civilians to sing songs
of the movement, but the need for compulsion itself revealed the lack
of enthusiasm below.[7] The collapse of the Third Reich cast nearly the

[5] Ekkehart Pfannenstiel, "Vom Geist und Lied der jungen Nation," *Musik und Volk*
3 (February/March, 1936): 121; see also the brief comments on periodization in Alexander von Bormann, "Das nationalsozialistische Gemeinschaftslied," in *Die deutsche
Literatur im Dritten Reich*, ed. Horst Denkler and Karl Prümm (Stuttgart, 1976), pp.
269–70.

[6] To my knowledge there is no comprehensive bibliography of National Socialist
songbooks. There is nonetheless an extensive list as of 1938 in Wilhelm Ehrmann, *Mu-
sikalische Feiergestaltung: Ein Wegweiser guter Musik für die natürlichen und poli-
tischen Feste des Jahres* (Hamburg, 1938).

[7] In sharp contrast to the situation following the First World War, when researchers
published a number of valuable studies of German war songs, very little has appeared for
the Second World War. My impressions for the Second World War are drawn in part

whole repertory into oblivion, not only because part of it was banned but also because it lost whatever meaningfulness it had only a few years previously.

Sources and Functions: The Kampfzeit

The initial songs of the movement consisted almost entirely of modifications of existing songs or of new lyrics to old melodies. Only a few had original melodies. Because so many were so explicitly derivative, we can identify the most important sources for both melodies and lyrics. According to their origins, Nazi political songs were drawn from one of the following: (1) soldiers' songs (*Kriegslieder*) of the First World War; (2) songs of the Free Corps and veterans' organizations; (3) the repertory of Social Democrats and Communists; (4) well-known German popular songs, commonly referred to as *"Volkslieder"* but more properly called *"volkstümliche Lieder"*; and, finally, (5) in later years, many original lyrics and melodies by Nazi poets and musicians.[8] Until someone compiles a comprehensive catalog of the whole body of National Socialist songs, there is no way of determining precisely what sources were drawn upon most frequently. The exact numbers are perhaps less significant than the fact that during the *Kampfzeit* songs were derived from very diverse sources, reflecting National Socialism's unique place within the complex web of movements and parties in the 1920s. In sharp contrast to the practice of German Social Democrats before the First World War, the Nazis readily and gladly derived texts and melodies from almost any source.

This eclecticism was not entirely accidental. It indicates how well Nazis understood the functions of song for their movement—the wider and more diverse the musical symbolism that they absorbed, the greater the number of people they might touch with their singing. It was entirely natural therefore that members of the SA in the early 1920s often sang soldiers' songs without making any textual alterations. As storm troopers marched to melodies known from the war, it was

---

from Max Mechow, "Der Liedbestand einer Pioniereinheit im 2. Weltkrieg," *Jahrbuch für Volksliedforschung* 14 (1969): 62–84. See also Hannsjost Lixfield, "Soldatenlied," in *Handbuch des Volksliedes*, ed. Rolf Brednich et al. (Munich, 1973), I, 833–62.

[8]This is an expansion of the classification of sources found in Bajer, "Lieder machen Geschichte," p. 589.

equally natural to use the basic text and substitute an occasional word or phrase to infuse Nazi ideological symbolism. The same transformation took place with texts from the Free Corps. For example, where the Free Corps Rossbach had sung "Wir kämpfen unter Roßbachs Fahnen" ("We are fighting under Rossbach's banner"), the SA simply sang "Wir kämpfen unter Hitlers Fahnen" ("We are fighting under Hitler's banner"). Where the Ehrhardt Brigade had sung "Wir tragen am Arme das Wikingerschiff, am Kragen die Gardesterne" ("Our armbands bear the Viking Ship, our neckband the Regiment Star"), the Nazis appropriated an alteration that originated with the ultranationalist Deutschvölkische Freiheitspartei (German-Folkish Freedom Party) and sang "Wir tragen am Arme das Hakenkreuz im schwarzweißroten Bande" ("We wear the swastika on a black-red-white armband"). They took over still other songs from the Deutschvölkische Freiheitspartei, though most of these, as with the songs of the Free Corps, were originally soldiers' songs from the war. Political music thus formed a symbolic link between veterans of the war and the young Nazi movement.[9]

The fact that Nazis also drew on Social Democratic and Communist songs is particularly intriguing and suggestive for the political functions of music. From the beginning the Nazis had exerted considerable effort to attract workers to their ranks as a way of enlarging their cadres and undermining both Social Democrats and Communists. Songs could play a role in this competition in several ways.

The most obvious tactic was for Nazis to use lyrics that expressed sentiments commonly associated with German workers and to claim that National Socialism represented the genuine material and spiritual interests of labor. This was done repeatedly. In one of the movement's earliest songs, Kleo Pleyer proclaimed that National Socialism "wanted to pave the way to freedom for German labor." Karl-Heinz Muschalla declared that National Socialism fought for "freedom, labor, and bread" and that it cleared the way for "labor and justice." Roman Hädelmayr, in a text that gained enormous popularity in the 1920s and 1930s, celebrated the end of the working day in language he thought appropriate to workers. He combined that appeal with anti-Semitic allusions:[10]

[9] Ibid., pp. 589–92.
[10] Texts in Thilo Scheller, ed., *Singend wollen wir marschieren*, 2d ed. (Potsdam,

Es pfeift von allen Dächern
Für heut die Arbeit aus,
Es ruhen die Maschinen,
Wir gehen müd nach Haus.
Daheim ist Not und Elend,
Das ist der Arbeit Lohn.
Geduld verratne Brüder,
Schon wanket Judas Thron.

Whistles blow from every rooftop:
Work is over for today,
The machines are now at rest;
Tired, we are going home.
At home there is need and misery;
This is what our labor earns.
Patience, betrayed brothers,
Judas' throne is already tottering.

In these and many other texts workers were courted and praised, assured that justice, freedom, and bread were guaranteed by National Socialism.

In a second technique Nazis employed melodies fully identified with socialism and communism as a means of attracting the attention of organized workers and political radicals. Shortly before 1930 an unidentified National Socialist wrote lyrics to the melody of the famous workers' "International." At first the text circulated by word of mouth, but it soon was printed and came to be known by several different titles —"The Song of National Socialism," the "Hitlernationale," or simply, "The Revolutionary Song."[11]

Auf, Hitlerleute, schließt die Reihen
Zum Rassenkampf sind wir bereit.
Mit unserem Blut wollen wir das Banner weihen,
Zum Zeichen einer neuen Zeit.
Auf rotem Grund im weißen Felde
Weht unser schwarzes Hakenkreuz.
Schon jubeln Siegessignale,

[1937]), pp. 72, 69; and Hans Bajer, "Ruhmesblätter in der Geschichte des SA.-Liedes," *Die Musik* 29 (December, 1936): 174.

[11] Paul Arendt, ed., *Deutschland erwache! "Das kleine Nazi-Liederbuch"*, Ausgabe B, 5th ed. (Sulzbach-Oberpfalz, [1932]), p. 16.

> Schon bricht der Morgen hell herein
> Der nationale Sozialismus
> Wird Deutschlands Zukunft sein.
>
> Arise, Hitler men, close your ranks,
> We are ready for the racial struggle.
> With our blood we consecrate the banner,
> The symbol of a new era.
> On its red and white background
> Shines our black swastika bright.
> Victory sounds are heard all over,
> As the morning's light breaks through;
> National Socialism
> Is the future of our Land.

Hans Bajer, a Nazi composer and expert on the songs of the movement, recounted gleefully how he and cadres of storm troopers had marched one Sunday afternoon in 1930 through the northern district of Berlin, areas inhabited predominantly by working-class families with Socialist or Communist affiliations. When the storm troopers broke into song, singing the "Hitlernationale," residents threw open their windows, misled momentarily by the familiar tune. Realizing quickly that Nazis were trying to appropriate the melody of their revolutionary anthem, the Socialist residents countered by singing the refrain of the original text—"Völker, hört die Signale! Auf zum letzten Gefecht" ("Comrades, listen to the Signale! Onward to the final battle")—while others pelted the storm troopers with bits of debris. Police promptly moved in to prevent serious trouble.[12]

In a pattern of appropriation found more frequently, Nazis would modify the lyrics of a Socialist or Communist song to fit their own ideology and circumstances. This form of appropriation could be achieved with little difficulty because, regardless of conflicting ideologies, political songs shared numerous structural features.

In two instances Nazis actually appropriated the original Socialist texts as well as modifying verses and adding new ones. This kind of unrestricted appropriation was possible because the original lyrics were lofty and vague and made no specific reference to Socialist ideas. The one song, "Brüder, zur Sonne zur Freiheit" ("Brothers, on to the

---

[12] Bajer, "Ruhmesblätter," pt. 2, *Die Musik* 29 (January, 1937): 264.

sun, on to freedom"), was a Russian workers' song that Hermann Scherchen had learned as a prisoner of war and introduced to the German labor movement. The first stanza of the Socialist text appears in all Nazi versions:[13]

> Brüder, zur Sonne zur Freiheit!
> Brüder, zum Lichte empor!
> Hell aus dem dunklen Vergangnen
> Leuchtet die Zukunft hervor.
>
> Brothers, on to the sun, on to freedom,
> Brothers, on to the light!
> Brightly, out of the dark past
> Hails the future bright.

In at least one Nazi songbook all three of the original Socialist stanzas appeared unaltered.[14] In other publications the second or third stanza was replaced by explicit Nazi language. The following verse embodies a brash attempt to identify National Socialism with a future society dominated by workers:[15]

> Brechet das Joch der Tyrannen!
> Aufgehn muß ihre Saat! [sic]
> Dann hißt die Hakenkreuzfahne
> Über dem Arbeiterstaat!
>
> Break the yoke of the tyrants!
> Their seed must grow. [sic]
> Then raise the swastika banner
> Over the workers' state!

Nazis did not stop there in their adaptations of "Brüder, zur Sonne zur Freiheit." They used the melody for two other texts that they did not derive in any way from the left wing: "Brüder in Zechen und Gruben" ("Brothers in mines and in quarries") and "Brüder, formiert die Kolonnen" ("Brothers, form the columns"). Both were widespread and popular in the Nazi movement, though the first enjoyed special favor. The lyrics are directed to all who labor in factories, fields, and mines. The

---

[13] Arendt, *Deutschland erwache!* p. 8.

[14] *Uns geht die Sonne nicht unter: Lieder der Hitler-Jugend* (Plauen i.V., 1934), p. 17.

[15] Heinz Ameln, ed., *Werkleute singen: Lieder der NS-Gemeinschaft "Kraft durch Freude"* (Kassel, 1936), p. 6.

text is intended to serve as an aid to recruitment, an objective enhanced by the use of a melody originally associated with Socialism.[16]

> Brüder in Zechen und Gruben,
> Brüder ihr hinter dem Pflug,
> Aus den Fabriken und Stuben:
> Folgt unsers Banners Zug!
>
> Brothers in mines and in quarries,
> Brothers behind the plow,
> Brothers in factories and in workrooms:
> Follow the banner's call!

Despite the varied adaptations of the lyrics and melody of "Brüder, zur Sonne zur Freiheit," the song never lost its identity in the popular mind with socialism and communism. The same is true of another Socialist song that Nazis also took over without alterations, "Wann wir schreiten Seit an Seit" ("When we march side by side"). The original lyrics are also lofty and general, looking to the future for a better world, but it never won wide popularity in the Nazi movement.[17]

There is a still more intriguing dimension to the Nazi appropriation of Socialist and Communist songs. In several instances Socialist songs were themselves parodies of soldiers' songs from the First World War. In such cases the lineage can be traced from the soldiers, to the Socialists, and finally to the Nazis. Since there is no need to describe the

---

[16] Scheller, *Singend wollen wir marschieren*, p. 63. The verses "Brüder, formiert die Kolonnen!" are predominantly nationalist, racist, and anti-Semitic and are permeated with images of toughness. The text is in *Uns geht die Sonne nicht unter*, p. 16.

[17] There is significant disagreement about when and under whãt political circumstances the author, Hermann Claudius, wrote the lyrics of "Wann wir schreiten Seit an Seit." Communist tradition holds that Claudius wrote the text in 1915 in conjunction with the struggle of left-wing youth in Hamburg against war and militarism. Hans Bajer, on the other hand, maintains that Claudius had written it in 1913 for the "Rote Falken," a "Wandergruppe der bündischen Jugend." Both accounts agree that Michael Englert composed the melody, but they disagree about the date of the composition. See Inge Lammel, ed., *Lieder der Arbeiter-Jugend* (Leipzig, [1960]), pp. 20–21, and Bajer, "Lieder machen Geschichte," p. 592, for the different accounts. The text is in Scheller, *Singend wollen wir marschieren*, p. 85. Because the original melody of "Wann wir schreiten Seit an Seit" did not catch on in the Nazi movement, Armin Kaub composed a new tune for the same lyrics; it appears in *Liederbuch der Nationalsozialistischen Deutschen Arbeiterpartei*, 51st ed. (Munich, 1941), p. 104. Nonetheless, the original had been sung in the Labor Service, according to Theodor Müller-Pfalz, "Das Liedgut des Arbeitsdienstes," *Nationalsozialistische Monatshefte* 5 (November, 1934): 1061.

process in detail for each song, the songs that belong to this group will be listed according to the first lines in their Communist and Nazi versions,[18] and then one example will be examined more closely.

Communist Original

"Bei Leuna sind viele gefallen"
("At Leuna many have fallen")

"Brüder, ergreift die Gewehre"
("Brothers, take up arms")

"Es zog ein Rotgardist hinaus"
("A Red Guard marched out")

"Auf, auf, zum Kampf, zum Kampf"
("Arise, arise to battle, to battle")

"Von allen unsern Kameraden"
("Of all our comrades")

"Auf, roter Tambour, schlage ein"
("Up, red drummer, beat the drum")

National Socialist Version

"In München sind viele gefallen"
("In Munich many have fallen")

"Brüder, formiert die Reihen"
("Brothers, form the ranks")

"Es zog ein Hitlermann hinaus"
("A Hitler man marched out")

"Auf, auf, zum Kampf, zum Kampf"
("Arise, arise to battle, to battle")

"Von allen unsern Kameraden"
("Of all our comrades")

"Du, kleiner Tambour, schlage ein"
("You little drummer, beat the drum")

To illustrate the process of transmission, without at the same time introducing all the variables for each phase, let us follow the last song through its three textual forms.

[18] Compiled from Wolfgang Steinitz, *Deutsche Volkslieder demokratischen Charakters aus sechs Jahrhunderten* (Berlin [East], 1962), II, 487, 495–512, 515, 535, 545; Martin Wähler, "Das politische Kampflied als Volkslied der Gegenwart," *Mitteldeutsche Blätter für Volkskunde* 8 (October, 1933): 146–48; Bormann, "Das nationalsozialistische Gemeinschaftslied," p. 266.

The first text is the song as it was sung, in one variant at least, during the First World War.[19]

> Ach, kleiner Tambour, schlag doch ein,
> Denn heute gilt es zu marschieren.
> Nach Frankreich müssen wir hinein,
> Der Feind soll unsre Waffen spüren.
> ‖: Am Waldesrand die Rosen blühn,
>   Wo Muskatier zu Felde ziehn. :‖
>
> Und sollten wir nicht siegreich sein,
> So lebt denn wohl, ihr stolzen Eichen;
> Vom Schlachtfeld kehr'n wir nimmer heim,
> In Frankreich sollen unsre Knochen bleichen.
> Auf fremder Erde schlafen wir
> Als tapfre Königsgrenadier.
>
> My little drummer, now beat the drum,
> Today we must start marching.
> On to France we must go;
> Let the enemy feel our arms.
> ‖: On the forest's edge the roses bloom,
>   Where musketeers move on to battle. :‖
>
> And should we not be victorious,
> Then, farewell, proud oaks, to you:
> We will not return from battle;
> Let our bones decay in France.
> We will sleep in foreign soil—
> Heroic royal grenadiers.

This text is but one of several variants sung by soldiers during the war, but it carries the common features. There were also several Communist variations immediately following the war; consider, for example, the first and fourth stanzas from a Communist variant that appeared in numerous books.[20]

> Auf, junger (roter) Tambour, schlage ein, schlage ein,
> Nach München, da wollen wir marschieren.
> Nach München wollen wir hinein, ja hinein,
> die Orgesch soll unsre Waffen spüren.
> ‖: Am Wege rot die Röslein blühn,
>   wenn Rotgardisten nach München ziehn. :‖

[19] Steinitz, *Deutsche Volkslieder*, II, 509.
[20] Ibid., pp. 495–96; and Elfriede Berger and Inge Lammel, eds., *Lieder des Roten Frontkämpferbundes* (Leipzig, [1961]), pp. 111–12.

Und sollten wir nicht siegreich sein, siegreich sein,
Von dem Schlachtfeld, da wollen wir nicht weichen!
Und kehren wir als Sieger heim, Sieger heim,
Dann laßt, Brüder, uns die Hände reichen.
|: Und schießt uns so ein Bluthund tot,
    Wir sterben für die Fahne rot. :|

Up, [red] drummer, beat the drum, beat the drum,
For we must march to Munich.
Into Munich we must now move;
Let Orgesch [Organisation Escherich] feel our arms.
|: On the way little red roses bloom,
    As Red Guards move to Munich. :|

And should we not be victorious,
We'll not leave the battlefield.
But if we come home as victors,
Then, my brothers, shake our hands.
|: And if the bloodhound shoots us dead,
    We shall die for the flag that's red. :|

The Nazi text that follows was written in the late 1920s by Werner
Wessel, the brother of the more famous Horst Wessel.[21] Note in particular how the final lines in the second stanza of the Nazi version imitate
the closing refrain in the Communist text.

Du kleiner Tambour, schlage ein,
Zum Kampfe wollen wir marschieren.
Wir woll'n nicht länger Knechte sein,
Der Feind soll unsre Waffen spüren.
Am Wege wilde Röslein blühen
Wenn Hitlerleut zum Kampfe ziehn.

Und sollten wir nicht siegreich sein,
So lebt denn wohl, ihr deutschen Eichen,
Geschlagen kehren wir nicht heim,
Vorm Feinde wollen wir nicht weichen.
Und schießen uns Marxisten tot,
Für Freiheit kämpfen wir und Brot!

You little drummer, beat the drum,
On to battle we must march.
No more must we be underlings;
Let the enemy feel our arms.

[21] *Liederbuch der Nationalsozialistischen Deutschen Arbeiterpartei*, pp. 17–18.

On the way little wild roses bloom,
As Hitler men go into battle.

And should we not be victorious,
Then, proud German oaks, farewell to you!
We shall not return defeated;
To our foe we shall not yield!
And if Marxists shoot us dead,
We have fought for freedom and for bread.

One needs to see the above process of transmission and appropriation from several perspectives. First, the process included features
common to folkloristic material—that is, adaptation, variability, and
evidence of oral as well as written transmission.[22] For social historians
this folkloristic perspective is particularly suggestive because it em-
phasizes the degree to which the adopted song material was embedded
in the consciousness of certain segments of German society. Most of
these appropriated songs, whether in their military, Communist, or
Nazi versions, belonged to that political culture of physical and ideological conflict which gave Weimar Germany much of its special chaotic atmosphere. Second, we can not overlook the fact that in their appropriation of Socialist and Communist songs Nazis were also using a
calculated and even cynical tactic to manipulate workers into believing
that they would find a genuine defender of their interests in the National Socialist party. There is much to be said for this manipulative
interpretation. It fits well with what we know about the propaganda
techniques of National Socialism and with the fact that opportunism
was a recurrent feature of its policies. Third, there is also the distinct
possibility that some of the left-wing songs were brought into the Nazi
movement by recruits who had been Socialists or Communists. Although no specific documentary evidence has yet been found to prove
that this kind of transmission took place, there is nevertheless circum-
stantial evidence to show that it could have occurred. Historians have
known for a long time that workers constituted a substantial percentage of SA members, and some recent studies conclude that in certain
localities it may have been as high as 70 to 80 percent. It is not unlikely

---

[22] From markedly different political standpoints, both Steinitz (*Deutsche Volkslieder*,
II, 421 ff.) and Wähler ("Das politische Kampflied als Volkslied der Gegenwart") make this
general argument.

that a few of those young working-class recruits had been associated with Socialist or Communist organizations and that they carried familiar songs with them.[23]

Regardless of the imitative and derivative nature of most songs from the *Kampfzeit*, there were also a few new creations, and Nazi commentators were exceedingly proud of the fact that many of these original lyrics grew out of personal experience and were sometimes written in the heat of political battle. Creativity stimulated by struggle—that formula meshed perfectly with their image of Nazism as a dynamic and vibrant movement. Such lyrics embodied, often crudely, the moods and symbolic language of the day-to-day political conflict; they seemed imbued with a natural and spontaneous spirit. Created by amateurs, driven more by political fanaticism than by artistic ability, they could also be sung without difficulty by rank-and-file Nazis.

We seldom get a glimpse of the actual process by which political songs affected individuals. One episode is therefore worth recounting in detail. In 1922, Kleo Pleyer, a student at the German University in Prague, already a two-year member of the Sudeten German affiliate of the NSDAP, led a strike against the university in opposition to the appointment of a Jewish rector. For the occassion he wrote lyrics to be sung to the well-known melody "Stimmt an mit hellem hohen Klang" ("Sing out with bright and noble tone"), composed in 1818 by Albert Methfessel, one of Germany's most successful choral composers of the first half of the nineteenth century. Discarding the original patriotic lyrics written by Matthias Claudius in 1772, Pleyer substituted verses

[23] Wähler ("Das politische Kampflied als Volkslied der Gegenwart," p. 150) and Bajer ("Lieder machen Geschichte," p. 592) assume that former Communists brought songs with them, but they do not cite specific cases. Recent studies on the social composition of the SA that show the high percentages of workers include Lawrence Stokes, "The Social Composition of the Nazi Party in Eutin, 1925–32," *International Review of Social History* 23 (1978): 27–28, and Conan J. Fischer, "The Occupational Background of the SA's Rank and File Membership during the Depression Years, 1929 to mid-1934," in *The Shaping of the Nazi State*, ed. Peter Stachura (London and New York, 1978), pp. 131–59. It should be stressed that these same studies and others point out that the social composition of the NSDAP as a whole was predominantly middle and lower middle class. Peter Stachura believes that in the years before 1933 the Hitler-Jugend had a majority of members from the working class, but he does not find that they came from Social Democratic or Communist backgrounds. See his *Nazi Youth in the Weimar Republic* (Santa Barbara and Oxford, 1975), pp. 57–60, 103–105.

that proclaimed group identity, loyalty to labor, and vicious anti-Semitism—all under the banner of the swastika:[24]

> Wir sind das Heer vom Hakenkreuz,
> Hebt hoch die roten Fahnen!
> Der deutschen Arbeit wollen wir
> Den Weg zur Freiheit bahnen.

> We are the army of the swastika,
> Raise high the red flags!
> For German labor we do seek
> To pave the road to freedom.

Only a year after Pleyer wrote those words, Johann Christ, a teenager of sixteen or seventeen, was sitting one Sunday evening with Communist friends in the Rheinischer Hof, a beer hall–restaurant that served as the meeting place of the Communist party in the vicinity of Wiesbaden. Two strangers entered. Christ related the incident in the following words:

> Without taking a place, each ordered a glass of beer which they left standing on the bar. I was sitting not far from them, and in those times I looked carefully at all strangers who came into our midst. They talked to each other, and it appeared that they wanted to get into a discussion with us. Many of my comrades had good reason to keep quiet. For one thing, some were a thorn in the side of the police, and for another, some among us were being sought by the French [occupation troops]. The two kept on talking to each other . . . [and] one came over to our table and told us about the struggles in the Ruhr. He talked about struggles in the Reich, about the police, burghers, and workers. . . .
>
> I understood little of what the stranger was talking about. I only heard the word "Hitler" and thought about what that meant. Still, I know what I heard at that time. Hitler songs were what the two sang together. And then a song that I myself sang three years later remained in my memory. Then both [strangers] were gone, and with them the thought about Hitler. Only a song remains in my memory from that time:
>
> > Wir sind das Heer vom Hakenkreuz,
> > Hebt hoch die roten Fahnen!
> > Der deutschen Arbeit wollen wir
> > Den Weg zur Freiheit bahnen.
>
> and then,

---

[24] Bajer, "Ruhmesblätter," pp. 171–72. The text is also in numerous Nazi songbooks, including Scheller, *Singend wollen wir marschieren*, p. 72.

Blut, Blut, Blut muß fließen
Knüppelhageldick.
Wir pfeifen auf die Freiheit
Der Judenrepublik.

[Blood, blood, blood must flow
As thick and deep as hailstones.
Fed up we are with all the freedom
Of the Jewish Republic.]

Still on that same night I thought about the two men and wondered who they might be. What was their mission? They were not [Rhenish] separatists, of that I was convinced. They were certainly not enemies of Germany. . . . Days passed. . . . I heard nothing of the two strangers; they did not return. And as I said, only the name "Hitler" and the melodies remained in my memory.[25]

Assuming that Christ's story was not fabricated or seriously distorted after the event, there are several aspects that deserve comment. Pleyer's lyrics had served an elementary communicative function, most discernable because Christ had previously known nothing about Hitler and the Nazi movement. Likewise, the melody helped retain the text in his mind. Perhaps he even forgot most of Pleyer's text, but he associated the melody with the Hitler movement. By serving an elementary communicative function, the song also assisted in recruiting Christ into the Nazi movement. Finally, his citation of the refrain "Blut, Blut, Blut" also illustrates how melodies and verses moved around in the political environment of the time. A genuine folkloristic element is evident. The first version of the refrain appeared in 1848. In that version the second line read, "Es lebe hoch die Freiheit, die deutsche Republik" ("Long live freedom, the German Republic"). At the end of the First World War the verse appeared in the left-wing labor movement, sometimes in the original, but also with "Es lebe hoch die Freiheit, die Räterepublik" ("Long live freedom, the Republic of Workers Soviets").[26] In the version remembered by Christ, the Nazis altered a few words to fit their hatred of Jews and the Weimar Re-

---

[25] Personal memoir by Johann Christ, dated Wiesbaden-Biebrich, December 29, 1936, in Aktenbezeichnungsblatt No. 530, "Kampferlebnisse der alten Garde der N.S.D.A.P.," Microfilm Reel 27, NSDAP Hauptarchiv. I am indebted to Professor Herbert Andrews, Towson State University, for calling this document to my attention and making it available to me.

[26] Steinitz, *Deutsche Volkslieder*, II, 115, 118.

public. A still different variant of this refrain used scatological imagery, and the verses in that version reached the depths of Nazi brutality and vulgarity.[27] Nazi spontaneity, in songs as well as in Julius Streicher's anti-Semitic journal *Der Stürmer*, often elicited vehement expressions of vileness and meanness. Nazi communication was served by appeals to frustration, hatred, and depravity. The songs Christ remembered were permeated with anti-Semitic hatred.

The most popular and therefore probably the most effective songs of the Nazi *Kampfzeit* were drawn from sources familiar and commonplace in the social and political environment of early Weimar. When the SA or other Nazis sang soldiers' songs from the war, one among them might think of new lyrics for the melody. The war song, "Argonnenwald um Mitternacht" ("Argonne Woods at Midnight"), went through such a transformation one night in 1929 as SA troops marched in the vicinity of Berlin. One of those storm troopers, Herbert Hammer, thought up a new text, which itself could be modified easily by changing place names:[28]

> Durch Groß-Berlin marschieren wir.
> Für Adolf Hitler kämpfen wir.
> Die Rote Front, brecht sie entzwei!
> SA marschiert—Achtung—die Straßen frei!

> We march through Greater Berlin
> Fighting for Adolf Hitler.
> Break the Red Front in two!
> The SA is marching—attention—clear the streets!

About the same time, Horst Wessel, the son of a Protestant clergyman, a one-time university student, and a successful SA organizer in Berlin, set words to a melody that appears to have been sung among German sailors. Early in 1930 Horst Wessel was killed—the facts in the case are still in dispute—and in a great propaganda campaign the Nazis raised him to martyrdom and his song soon became the recognized anthem of the whole movement. Although there was no direct link between the original of the song and the fight that led to Horst Wessel's death, Nazis nevertheless took the events as further evidence of how their

---

[27] The full text is printed in Hans-Joachim Gamm, *Der braune Kult* (Hamburg, 1962), p. 137.

[28] Bajer, "Ruhmesblätter," p. 261.

early repertory emerged directly and spontaneously out of the struggles of the party.[29]

There were numerous musicians and composers among the Nazis already during the 1920s, but only a few songs with original melodies caught on. On the occasion of a speech by Hitler in Plauen (Vogtland) in 1925, Bruno Schestak wrote both the melody and the lyrics for "Deutschland erwache aus deinem bösen Traum" ("Germany, awaken from your frightful dream"), which was almost immediately sung throughout the movement and known under the title "Heil Hitler, Dir" ("Hail to you, Hitler").

> Deutschland erwache aus deinem bösen Traum
> Gib fremden Juden in deinem Reich nicht Raum.
> |: Wir wollen kämpfen für dein Auferstehen,
> Arisches Blut darf nicht untergehen. :|
>
> Wir sind die Kämpfer der N.S.D.A.P.
> Kerndeutsch im Herzen, im Kampfe fest und zäh.
> |: Dem Hakenkreuz ergeben sind wir,
> Heil unserm Führer, Heil Hitler, Dir. :|

> Germany, awaken from your frightful dream,
> Keep from the Reich all foreign Jews.
> |: We fight for your resurrection;
> Let Aryan blood not suffer destruction. :|
>
> We are the fighters of the N.S.D.A.P.,
> All-German in our hearts,
> Ever tough and firm in battle,
> |: To the swastika devoted.
> Hail to our Führer, hail to you, Hitler. :|

The text as a whole is an anthology of Nazi slogans and symbols: hatred of Jews as foreigners, yearnings for the resurrection of Germany, praise of Aryan blood, pride in the swastika, and a violent call for the expul-

---

[29] Research on the "Horst Wessel Lied" is still incomplete. In this instance I have relied on Alexander Sydow, *Das Lied: Ursprung, Wesen und Wandel* (Göttingen, 1962), p. 455. National Socialist musicologists developed several theories about the origin of the song, though the subject was treated with such reverence that one must be particularly wary in using the following: Joseph Müller-Blattau, "Das Horst Wessel-Lied," *Die Musik* 26 (February, 1934): 322–28; and Albert Weidemann, "Ein Vorläufer des Horst Wessel-Liedes," *Die Musik* 28 (September, 1936): 911–12. Hans Jürgen Hansen, *Heil Dir im Siegerkranz* (Oldenburg and Hamburg, 1978), p. 75, doubts all explanations hitherto and suspects that Horst Wessel may have used a Socialist song entitled "Die Fahne hoch!" for which, unfortunately, all evidence seems to have vanished.

sion of the Jews from "our German house."[30] No one in Germany could have listened to the words of this and other songs of the *Kampfzeit* and failed to comprehend the basic drives, intentions, and violence of National Socialism. But the violence of the text seemed always ameliorated by the joyous bounce of the march music or the near-religious solemnity of chorales and hymnlike anthems. Music softened the brutal language, disarmed and captivated the unwary.

The Second Phase: Overview

Numerous shifts took place in the creation and singing of Nazi political songs as the party's fortunes improved dramatically in the early 1930s and Hitler became chancellor in January, 1933. The steps taken to establish Nazi control were accompanied by a propaganda campaign to enlist the enthusiastic support of all Germans for an authoritarian and dictatorial system. This called for a greater variety of song and for qualities different from those dominant during the *Kampfzeit*. The early stress on struggle, hatred, and revolution gave way to a greater emphasis on community, the regeneration of Germany, the protective and sacred power of the Führer, qualities that would assist in socializing Germans into the new Reich and in mobilizing support for Hitler's expansionist ambitions. The old songs did not vanish, but remained and were heard frequently. Nonetheless, the new wave of song writing greatly enlarged and diversified the repertory of Nazi political songs. In the creation of songs amateurism and spontaneity began to give way to professionalism and systematic musical production. As new organizations of the party and the Third Reich were established and grew in importance, their members too were expected to participate enthusiastically in small group and mass singing. Writers, poets, and musicians feverishly set to work creating songs for these organizations and for special festive and ceremonial occasions.[31] They could expect to win

---

[30] *Uns geht die Sonne nicht unter*, pp. 17–18.

[31] More information on the many poets and musicians who contributed to this repertory can be found in the essays by Michael Meyer, Hans Bajer, Alexander von Bormann, cited in the preceding notes, and Uwe-K. Ketelson, below. Two works by Hellmuth Langenbucher have biographical data: *Dichtung der jungen Mannschaft* (Hamburg, 1935) and *Volkhafte Dichtung der Zeit*, 6th ed. (Berlin, 1941).

personal recognition and material benefits from the state and party for their productive zeal. Whereas music for disciplined movement, especially marches, dominated in the *Kampfzeit*, there was a new emphasis on melodic phrasing, hymnlike melodies with reverential texts, chorales, and songs for singing during evening leisure hours. Hundreds of new songs were published during the Third Reich, and hundreds more were never printed. Within the Labor Service alone, Thilo Scheller reported a "flood of *Marsch- und Feierlieder*" (marching and festival songs), although only a small percentage of these ever became part of the standard repertory.[32]

The functions of song also shifted. Previously it had been essential to call attention to the party and its slogans and to recruit members. Membership had been voluntary, and leaders could easily arouse a sense of belonging and comradeship in the initiates. Many had joined out of a yearning to merge themselves into a movement that seemed to provide both the ideology and the realities of community. After coming to power, the Nazis sought on the one hand to exclude certain groups completely (especially Jews and Communists) and on the other hand to mold everyone else into one immense, organic *Volksgemeinschaft* (national-racial community). They enlisted music to assist in this task of persuasion and socialization. To enhance the legitimacy of their rule they elaborated the cultist forms that originated in the earlier epoch and initiated new ones—the ritual rededication to the holy cause of the Nazi martyrs who fell on November 9, 1923, the fetishism of the swastika banner, and the deification of the Führer, to mention only a few. Music and song were suited to aid in creating that aura of sanctity in which the Nazi regime attempted to enshroud itself.

The most appropriate musical form for all these tasks was the communal song (*Gemeinschaftslied*). Through singing communal songs individuals would be swept up by the totality, would lose their sense of

[32]Thilo Scheller, "Das Liedgut im Reichsarbeitsdienst," *Musik in Jugend und Volk* 4 (1941): 130. On how to classify the variety of National Socialist songs there are helpful suggestions in Uwe-K. Ketelson, "Nationalsozialismus und Drittes Reich," in *Geschichte der politische Lyrik in Deutschland*, ed. Walter Hinderer (Stuttgart, 1978), p. 300, and Bormann, "Das nationalsozialistische Gemeinschaftslied," pp. 267–72. Contemporary experts in National Socialist songs also suggested various classifications. See Josef Heer, "Das Lied der jungen Generation," *Völkische Musikerziehung* 5 (February, 1939): 53–61.

self-identity and be merged, momentarily at least, with the organic wholeness of the German *Volksgemeinschaft*.[33] These functions of political song in the Third Reich can be perceived in a sampling of the activities of particular organizations, in festivals and celebrations, and in the annual party rallies.

The Functions of Political Song through Organizations

Every Nazi organization perceived the value of communal singing. In 1934 "Strength-Through-Joy" called for special *Abendsingwochen* (evening song weeks) for workers and others. Singing was also sponsored in shops and factories. By August, 1934, reports came in from more than 300 localities—including Zwickau, Leipzig, Glauchau, Chemnitz, Aue (Saxony), Naumburg (near Kassel), Bochum, Dortmund, Dortmund-Hörde, Dortmund-Dorstfeld, and Berlin—of singing sessions in which large numbers of workers had participated. In a corset factory in Döbelin (Saxony) between 60 and 150 female workers were said to be so enthusiastic after the initial singing week that they held open singing hours at the end of the working day. Reports from central Brandenburg (Kurmark) told of women workers at the Maas Company singing "in the workroom amidst whistling boilers," of two shifts of men at the Woeschner firm singing before starting to work, and of men and women at Sänger and Stockwald holding choral sessions after work. Huge numbers were said to have attended evening singing sessions in other towns: 568 *Volksgenossen* in Düsseldorf, 2,005 in Gladbach-Rheydt, 666 in Neuss-Grevenbroich, 1,480 in Viersen-Kempen, and no less than 10,306 in Solingen.[34]

The promoters of singing in shops and factories drew up principles and guidelines on how to involve the maximum number of workers. There was no doubt, as one "Strength-Through-Joy" commentator

[33] These impressions about the intentions of the Nazi use of *Gemeinschaftslieder* are derived from numerous contemporary Nazi writers, including Hans Bajer, "Zur Geschichte des ersten SA.-Liederbuches," *Völkische Musikerziehung* 5 (February, 1939): 38–43, and other essays by Bajer cited in the preceding notes; Otto Brodde, "Politische Musik," *Musik und Volk* 2 (February/March, 1935): 81–87; and Gerhard Pallmann, "Das Lied der Wehrmacht," *Die Musik* 30 (March, 1938): 361–71. I have also drawn on Ketelson, "Nationalsozialismus und Drittes Reich," pp. 296–97.

[34] Bernhard von Peinen, "Der deutsche Arbeiter singt wieder," *Musik und Volk* 1 (August/September 1934): 215–23.

said, that "music education is becoming a political task."[35] Labor Service leaders spelled out the principles. Singing well was welcome, but not essential. "What is at stake in our singing is not only ability, but also conviction." The most important goal was to get all workers involved in music so that "in this way they can make their contribution to the building of the *Gemeinschaft*." Individual distinction in performance could undermine the *Gemeinschaft*. Simplicity should be the practical rule; singing in unison was to be encouraged. They should sing to glorify the fatherland. "In all that we feel, think, and do, we are responsible to Germany. This responsibility is also the reason and goal of our singing."[36]

They also determined what would be sung. In addition to the general party songbooks, every organization had at least one published anthology, carefully edited to advance Nazi ideology and to appeal to a particular constituency. Thilo Scheller organized the songbook for the Labor Service, *Singend wollen wir marschieren* (*Singing, we march*), around the cycle of the working day, including even a small selection of songs to be sung while peeling potatoes!

Such guidance went still further. Leaders selected certain texts as "obligatory songs" (*Pflichtlieder*), which every member of the organization was expected to learn. In the Labor Service ten songs were chosen for this distinction. (See the accompanying table, List of Obligatory Songs [*Pflichtlieder*] in the Labor Service.) They expressed the beliefs, prejudices, and goals that Nazi leaders wanted drilled into the consciousness of rank-and-file Germans. In 1935 the regime made enrollment in the Labor Service compulsory for all young German males, and thus during the latter 1930s a whole generation was exposed systematically to these songs. The young men were gathered into work camps where they participated in the daily routine. Early-morning flag raising was to be accompanied by the four-voice round:

> Grüßet die Fahnen,
> Grüßet die Zeichen,
> Grüßet den Führer,

[35] Anon., "Aus der Musikarbeit der 'Osnabrücker Hitler-Jugend' in Gemeinschaft mit der NSG. 'Kraft durch Freude'," *Musik in Jugend und Volk* 2 (1939): 111.

[36] Anon., "Aufgabe und Wege der Musikarbeit in den Betrieben," *Musik in Jugend und Volk* 3 (1940): 257–59. Advice also in Friedrich-Franz Gerhardt, "Die Musik im Leben der Betriebsgemeinschaft," ibid., pp. 254–56.

Es tönt auf grüner Heide
(The green heath resounds)
Text: Eberhard Hübner. Melody: Max Depolo

Heiliges Feuer brennt in dem Land
(A holy fire sweeps our Land)
Text and melody: Will Decker

Wir tragen das Vaterland
(We carry the Fatherland)
Text and melody: Will Decker

Grüßet die Fahnen
(Salute the flags)
Text and melody: Adolf Seifert

Gott, segne die Arbeit
(God bless our work)
Title: "Feierlied der Arbeit" ("Evening Song of Labor")
Text: Thilo Scheller. Melody: Will Decker and Dietrich Steinbecker

Siehst du im Osten das Morgenrot?
(Do you see the eastern morning glow?)
Title: "Volk, ans Gewehr" ("Folk, Take Arms")
Text and melody: Arno Pardun

Singend wollen wir marschieren
(Singing, we march into the new era)
Text and melody: Will Decker

Unsere Spaten sind Waffen im Frieden
(Spades are our weapons in peacetime)
Text: Thilo Scheller. Melody: Dietrich Steinbecker

Es zittern die morschen Knochen
(The world, its rotten bones are shaking)
Title: "Wir werden weitermarschieren" ("We Shall Keep On Marching")
Text and melody: Hans Baumann (fourth stanza: Thilo Scheller)

Nun ist der Tag entschwunden
(Now the day has passed)
Title: "Abendlied" ("Evening Song")
Text: Thilo Scheller. Melody: Dietrich Steinbecker

SOURCE: Thilo Scheller, ed., *Singend wollen wir marschieren*, 2d ed. (Potsdam, [1937]), which prints all texts and melodies. In most cases, the first line is identical with the title.

der sie schuf,
Grüßet alle,
die für sie starben,
folget getreulich
ihrem Ruf!

Salute the flags,
Salute the emblems,
Salute the Führer
Who created them.
Salute the brave
Who died for them.
Always be faithful
To their call!

Will Decker, author and composer of many Nazi songs, filled his lyrics with notions and symbols of the *völkisch* cult:[37]

Wir tragen das Vaterland in unseren Herzen.
Des Führers Gebot getreu zum Tod
Stehen wir im Kampf für Arbeit und Brot.

We carry the Fatherland in our hearts.
True unto death to the Führer's command,
We go into battle for labor and bread.

Heiliges Feuer brennt in dem Land,
Aufwacht das Volk aus dem Schlafe.
. . . .
Taten braucht unser deutsches Land,
Worte genug sind gefallen.

A holy fire sweeps our Land;
The Folk rises from its sleep.
. . . .
Action is what Germany needs;
Enough words have been said.

Marching to and fro from the barracks to the workplace, members of the Labor Service were expected to sing another of Will Decker's songs:

Singend wollen wir marschieren in die neue Zeit.
Adolf Hitler soll uns führen, wir sind stets bereit.

[37] Although he wrote melodies and lyrics for many National Socialist songs, biographical material on Will Decker has not been available.

Unser Wille soll uns zwingen in die Bruderschaft,
Unser Leben neu durchdringen mit des Glaubens Kraft.

Singing, we march into the new era;
Let Adolf Hitler be our leader—we are always ready.
Let our will make us true brothers,
And fill our life with strength and faith.

They were to express pride in their spades and shovels, to announce that class differences had been overcome in Hitler's Reich:

Unser Spaten sind Waffen im Frieden,
Unser Lager sind Burgen im Land.
Gestern in Stände und Klassen geschieden,
Gestern der eine vom andern gemieden,
Graben wir heute gemeinsam im Sand.
Treu dem Befehl des Führers, Stoßtrupp des Friedens zu sein,
Ziehn wir mit Hacke and Schaufel und Spaten
Stolz in die Zukunft hinein.

Spades are our weapons in peacetime;
Our camps are forts in the Land.
Divided, before, into ranks and classes,
The one shunning the other,
Today we are digging as one.
True to the Führer's command,
To be the shock troops of peace,
We move into the future,
With pickaxe and shovel and spade.

But the yearning for an organic community could never be separated in Nazism from hatred of Jews and appeals to racism:

Wir jungen und Alten, Mann für Mann,
Umklammern das Hakenkreuzbanner.
Ob Bauer, ob Bürger, ob Arbeitsmann,
Sie schwingen das Schwert und den Hammer,
Sie kämpfen für Hitler, für Arbeit und Brot.
Deutschland erwache! und Juda—den Tod. Volk, ans Gewehr!

As one man, we, both young and old,
Embrace the swastika flag.
Farmers and burghers and workers
Are wielding both hammer and sword.
They fight for Hitler, for labor and bread.
Germans, wake up! and death to the Jew!
Folk, take arms!

Hans Baumann, author and composer of hundreds of Nazi songs, expressed the arrogance of Nazi expansionism, the eagerness for war, and the indifference to the possibility of total destruction:[38]

> Es zittern die morschen Knochen der Welt vor dem roten Krieg.
> Wir haben den Schrecken gebrochen, für uns wars ein großer Sieg.
> ‖: Wir werden weiter marschieren, wenn alles in Scherben fällt;
>   Denn heute da hört uns Deutschland, und morgen die ganze Welt. :‖
> Und liege vom Kampfe in Trümmern die ganze Welt zuhauf,
> Das soll uns den Teufel kümmern, wir bauen sie wieder auf.

> The world, its rotten bones are shaking in fear of a war with the Reds.
> But we [Nazis] have crushed that monster, a splendid victory is ours.
> ‖: We shall continue to march on, even if all be destroyed.
>   For today Germany heeds us, tomorrow the whole world. :‖
> And if the world lies in rubble from the battle
> That disturbs us not at all, for we'll just build it up again!

At the end of the day men in the Labor Service were to reflect on duties faithfully fulfilled and once again declare their loyalty to the Führer ("Nun ist der Tag entschwunden"). In their singing they prayed to the Lord to bless their thoughts and deeds, and to give His special blessing to Hitler and the fatherland:

> Gott segne die Arbeit und unser Beginnen,
> Gott segne den Führer und diese Zeit.
> Steh uns zur Seite, Land zu gewinnen,
> Deutschland zu dienen mit all unseren Sinnen,
> Mach uns zu jeder Stunde bereit.

> Gott segne die Arbeit und unser Ringen;
> Gott segne die Spaten mit blankem Schein
> Werk unsrer Hände, laß es gelingen,
> Denn jeder Spatenstich, den wir vollbringen,
> Soll ein Gebet für Deutschland sein.

[38] One of the most prolific songwriters of Nazi Germany, Baumann (born in Amberg, April 22, 1914) had joined the Hitler Youth in 1932 and played several leadership roles in Nazi youth organizations until he joined the Wehrmacht in 1939. During the 1930s he published at least six collections of his own songs. According to Langenbucher (*Volkhafte Dichtung der Zeit*, p. 566), Baumann's poetry "lives much stronger in the *Gemeinschaft* than in book form. [His verses] go from mouth to mouth and are sung in the ranks of the youth who have found in the inner spirituality and political credo [*Bekenntnis*] a reaffirmation of a most beautiful simplicity." Baumann survived six years in the Wehrmacht and then turned to writing children's literature after 1945. In 1956 the city of Brunswick awarded him the Gerstäcker Prize, and in 1958 he won the New York Herald Tribune Prize for his contributions to children's literature. See Stachura, *Nazi Youth in the Weimar Republic*, p. 212.

God bless our work and our new efforts,
God bless the Führer and our times.
Help us to save our country,
To serve our Land with strength,
Ready for its needs.

God bless our work and our struggle;
God bless our shining spades.
Make the work of our hands successful,
For every spade of earth we dig
Is a prayer for Germany.

Men in the Labor Service sang these songs regularly. Their leaders believed that the adoption of "obligatory songs" stimulated popular dissemination, so that these lyrics were becoming the "common property of the people" (*Gemeingut des Volkes*).[39]

What was true for the intended role of music and political song in the Labor Service generally held for other organizations of the Third Reich, though there were differences in emphasis, patterns of activity, and choice of repertory. As an instrument for indoctrination and socialization, songs may have been used even more intensely in the Hitler Youth than in the Labor Service. Baldur von Schirach, "Youth-Führer" of the Reich between 1933 and 1940, was himself the author of numerous poems that were set to music, and he consistently promoted political songs as well as other types of music. He wrote lyrics for the principal "obligatory song" of the Hitler Youth, "Vorwärts, Vorwärts" ("Forward, Forward").[40] Throughout the 1930s musicians and writers composed new songs that meshed with the activities of the Hitler Youth and affirmed the commitment of the young to the cults of the Führer, *Blut und Boden*, and the flag, as well as to values of German nationalism and militarism.[41] Bellicose storm trooper songs from the *Kampfzeit*

---

[39] Anon., "Singend wollen wir marschieren," *Musik in Jugend und Volk* 4 (1940): 134.

[40] Schirach's major collection appeared sometime in the 1930s under the title *Die Fahne der Verfolgten* (Berlin, no date). In addition, he edited *Blut und Ehre* (Berlin, no date), a collection for the Hitler Youth, and an anthology of poems by unnamed members of the Austrian Hitler Youth, *Das Lied der Getreuen 1933–37* (Leipzig, 1938).

[41] Wolfgang Stumme edited three series of music and song for the Hitler Youth: *Musikblätter der Hitler-Jugend* (Wolfenbüttel and Berlin, 1934 ff.), *Liederblätter der Hitlerjugend* (Wolfenbüttel and Berlin, 1935 ff.), and *Junge Gefolgschaft. Neue Lieder der Hitlerjugend* (Wolfenbüttel and Berlin, 1935 ff.). Contemporaries commented extensively on both the new repertory and the musical activities of the Hitler Youth. The most informative are: Walter Kurka, "Die Musikarbeit der HJ in ihren Veröf-

fit well into this program of melodic socialization. By contrast, the most strident combat songs of the *Kampfzeit* had little place in the songbooks of the League of German Girls (Bund deutscher Mädel) and in the National Socialist Women's Organization (NS-Frauenschaft). These omissions reflected the common Nazi assumption that girls and women belonged in traditional and subordinate roles and that it was therefore not important to mobilize them politically to the same degree as men.[42] For most organizations there were special songbooks, always including a substantial selection of Nazi political songs.[43] The Third Reich was flooded with functional political songs.

The Role of Songs at Festivals, Ceremonies, and Party Rallies

Music contributed much to the public image of Nazism as a dynamic movement imbued with a sacred mission and redemptive power. The most dramatic display of the fusion of politics and music can be seen in the public events so masterfully staged by the Nazi movement. The annual cycle of German celebrations, memorial days, and festivals had been transformed to focus upon the personalities and legendary events of National Socialism. Enveloped on these occasions by parades, speeches, and music, individual Germans were to be swept away by

---

fentlichungen," *Musik und Volk: Sonderheft* 4 (October/November, 1936): 13–20; Rudolf Leyk, "Singen im Zeltlager der Hitler-Jugend," ibid., 3 (August/September, 1936): 305–307; Willi Schulze, "Das Liedgut der Hitlerjugend im Aufbau sommerlicher und herbstlicher Feiern," ibid., 2 (August/September, 1935): 206–13; Wolfgang Stumme, "Musik in der deutschen Jugend," *Völkische Musikerziehung* 2 (June, 1936): 263–70; and Walter Kurka, "Hitlerjugend singt und spielt," ibid., pp. 270–74.

[42] See *Wir Mädel singen: Liederbuch des Bundes Deutscher Mädel*, 2d ed. (Wolfenbüttel and Berlin, 1943); and Robert Kothe, ed., *Liederbuch der N.S.-Frauenschaft* (Magdeburg, no date).

[43] In addition to the books cited in the notes above, I have also been able to examine the following: Erich Lauer, ed., *SA-Liederbuch*, 2nd ed. (Munich, 1938); *Wir wandern und singen: Liederbuch der NS-Gemeinschaft "Kraft durch Freude"* (Munich, no date); Hans Buchner, ed., *Horst Wessel-Marschalbum*, 2 pts. (Munich, 1933); Carl Clewing, ed., *Liederbuch der Luftwaffe*, 4th ed. (Berlin-Lichterfelde, 1939); Edmund Heines, ed., *Schlesisches SA-Liederbuch*, 4th ed. (Breslau, 1933); *Liederbuch der Nationalsozialistischen Deutschen Arbeiterpartei* (Munich, 1926); Gerhard Pallmann and Ernst Lothar von Knorr, eds., *Soldaten Kameraden: Liederbuch für Wehrmacht und Volk*, 2d ed. (Hamburg, 1938); and Gerhard Pallmann, ed., *Wohlauf, Kameraden: Ein Liederbuch der jungen Mannschaft von Soldaten, Bauern, Arbeiter und Studenten*, 2d ed. (Kassel, no date).

euphoria into the all-encompassing spirit of the *Volksgemeinschaft*. The senses were bombarded by stimuli to arouse emotional commitment and to inspire a spirit of loyal dedication. To celebrate the Nazi takeover on January 30, participants sang of faith, loyalty, and willingness to die. (They normally sang "Wir tragen das Vaterland in unser'n Herzen" ["We carry the Fatherland in our hearts"].) To commemorate Hitler's birthday (April 20), tones of sacred trust were heard as Nazis sang a hymn by Herbert Böhme and Erich Lauer:[44]

> Führer, wir rufen dich an!
> Führer, trage die Fahne hinan
> Zu Wolken und Sonne
> Zu Freiheit und Ruhm,
> Denn die Fahne is unser Heiligtum,
> Führer, schreite voran!

> Führer, we call to you!
> Führer, take the flag
> To the clouds and the sun,
> To freedom and to glory.
> For the flag is our sacred relic.
> Führer, lead us right on.

May 1, once the holiday of Socialists and Communists, became "Labor Day" (*Tag der Arbeit*), and festival participants and spectators would hear still another *Gemeinschaftslied* by Böhme and Lauer:[45]

> Arbeiter, Bauern, Soldaten,
> Kameraden der Pflicht,
> Haltet die Fahne der Taten,
> Daß euer Werk nicht zerbricht.

> Workers, farmers, and soldiers,
> Comrades all duty-bound,
> Hold up the banner of action,
> So that your work will not fail.

On May 1, and on the festival of the summer solstice, members of the Young Folk (Jungvolk), the Hitler Youth, and the League of German Girls would sing "Vorwärts, Vorwärts" (lyrics by Baldur von Schirach), as they were obligated to do at every youth festival.[46]

---

[44] *Liederbuch der Nationalsozialistischen Deutschen Arbeiterpartei*, pp. 72–73.
[45] Ibid., p. 80.
[46] *Uns geht die Sonne nicht unter*, pp. 4–5; Gamm, *Der Braune Kult*, p. 49.

Unsere Fahne flattert uns voran,
In die Zukunft ziehn wir Mann für Mann.
Wir marschieren für Hitler durch Nacht und durch Not.
Mit der Fahne der Jugend für Freiheit und Brot.
Unsre Fahne flattert uns voran.
Unsre Fahne ist die neue Zeit,
Und die Fahne führt uns in die Ewigkeit.
Ja, die Fahne ist mehr als der Tod!

Our flag flutters before us,
We enter the future man for man.
For Hitler we march through night and need,
With the flag of youth, for freedom, for bread.
Our flag flutters before us.
Our flag is the new era.
It leads us into eternity.
Our flag means more to us than death!

For Nazis, especially the *Alte Kämpfer* (earliest Nazi members), the most hallowed memorial took place on November 9, a day to venerate the "martyrs" who had fallen in the abortive Putsch of 1923. The commemoration became a Nazi holy day as each year Hitler and the *Alte Kämpfer* would march to the Feldherrnhalle bearing the same flag they carried in 1923. Consecrated as the "Blood Flag" (*Blutfahne*), this Nazi relic was taken from its permanent sanctuary only twice each year, on November 9 and for the annual party rallies. Music accompanied the ceremony.[47]

In München sind viele gefallen,
In München warn viele dabei;
‖: Es traf vor der Feldherrnhalle
Deutsche Helden das tödliche Blei. :‖

Sie kämpften für Deutschlands Erwachen
Im Glauben an Hitlers Mission
‖: Marschierten mit Todesverachten
In das Feuer der Reaktion! :‖

In München sind viele gefallen
Für Ehre, für Freiheit und Brot.
‖: Es traf vor der Feldherrnhalle
Sechzehn Helden der Märtyrertod. :‖

Ihr Toten vom neunten November,

[47] *Liederbuch der Nationalsozialistischen Deutschen Arbeiterpartei*, p. 134.

Ihr Toten, wir schwören es euch:
|: Es lebe noch vieltausend Kämpfer
　Für das dritte, das Großdeutsche Reich. :|

Many have fallen in Munich,
In Munich many there'd been.
|: In front of the Feldherrnhalle
　Lead bullets killed brave German men. :|

They fought for German awakening,
With faith in Hitler's call,
|: They went, fearless of dying,
　Into the reactionaries' fire. :|

In Munich many have fallen
For honor, for freedom, for bread.
|: In front of the Feldherrnhalle
　Sixteen martyrs fell dead. :|

You dead of the Ninth of November,
You dead we swear to you:
|: There are still thousands of fighters
　In the Third Reich, the Great German Reich! :|

The ritual of November 9 paralleled, in the suggestive interpretation of Hans-Joachim Gamm, the religious tradition of medieval Passion Plays. One went to relive the experience of those who had sacrificed their lives and to rededicate oneself to the sacred cause symbolized by the Blood Flag.[48]

All ingredients of the Nazi matrix were evident at the annual party rallies (the *Parteitage*)—cultists rituals, Führer adulation, disciplined cadres, political theater, demagogic speechmaking, marching masses, with bands and bugle corps playing endlessly. Everywhere there was singing. Without music the pace would have slowed and the euphoria would have been muted. But the pace did not slacken. Music set the tone. At one rally, fifty thousand men from units of the Labor Service, spades over their shoulders, sang seventy-five different songs as they marched past Hitler's stand at his hotel, the Deutscher Hof. At another, an equal number from the youth organizations would sing "Wir sind nicht Bürger, Bauern, Arbeitsmann" ("We are not burghers, farmers, or working men"), and at a nighttime rally, amid torches and floodlights, thousands and thousands of storm troopers would bellow

---

[48] Gamm, *Der braune Kult*, p. 142.

"Wir halten zusammen, ob lebend, ob tot, mag kommen was immer da wolle" ("We stand together, whether living or dead, come what may"). For the ritual consecration of new regiments, the Führer had directed that at each party rally the very first of the Nazi songs, "Storm, Storm, Storm, Storm, Storm" by Dietrich Eckart, should be played and sung. Throughout the week one heard the familiar strains of the "Horst Wessel Lied." All of this was mixed with bubbling march music and thunderous "*Sieg Heil*"s. Reverential solemnity had its place as Nazis honored the fallen of the First World War by singing "Ich hatt' einen Kameraden" in the manner of a funeral hymn, a rendering they began in the mid-1920s. To claim again a sacred endorsement of all that had happened during a week of Nazi political theater and idolization of Hitler, thousands of men from the Labor Service closed the ceremonies singing,[49]

> Gott, segne die Arbeit und unser Beginnen,
> Gott, segne den Führer und diese Zeit.

The communal song had served its vital function in the ultimate communal experience of German Nazis.

Conclusion

It is not the goal here to try to evaluate how well songs actually fulfilled all the functions discussed above. Even with more evidence one could offer only approximate answers. The lack of direct testimony about how people felt when listening or singing makes firm conclusions about effectiveness nearly impossible. Moreover, National Socialism and the Third Reich lasted a comparatively short time, making it difficult to sort out with confidence the songs of lasting appeal from the less successful. Except for a number of songs from the *Kampfzeit*, the overwhelming percentage was in the repertory for only a few years, a period too short to allow for a natural process of selectivity. In addition, the songs were one part of an authoritarian system that did not hesitate to use violence to compel Germans to comply with the regime's directives. Germans who remained hostile to Hitler's rule were not likely to

---

[49] Scheller, "Das Liedgut im Reichsarbeitsdienst," p. 132; Gamm, *Der braune Kult*, p. 114; Richard Meran Barsam, *Filmguide to Triumph of the Will* (Bloomington, Ind., 1975), pp. 44–46; Bajer, "Lieder machen Geschichte," p. 594.

be drawn in by parades, songs, and speeches if the threat of violence had failed to change their minds. Political songs belonged to the weapons of persuasion. Songs could encourage those already willing to be persuaded. Even then, such persons were probably unaware of the influence of Nazi music on them. The influence could remain undetected below the conscious level, manifest only in patterns of speech and behavior formed over years of exposure. To investigate the unconscious level, we need the assistance of several disciplines, including social psychology and the psychology of music. Until research theories and strategies are developed for taking such an approach, we must be content with describing and analyzing the substance of the songs and the way in which they originated, were disseminated, and were used.

If effectiveness is difficult to judge, other kinds of tentative generalizations are possible. The experience of twentieth-century Germany strongly suggests that political songs fit most readily into movements inclined to emphasize emotionalism and communalism. In these respects, National Socialism outdid all competitors. Among Social Democrats and Communists the emphasis on working-class solidarity provided a communal ingredient, but neither movement could abandon itself to fanatical emotionalism. Socialists and Communists ran a poor second to National Socialists in the exploitation of music to support a political movement. German liberalism was even less well suited to the unrestrained use of song. By the 1920s, liberalism's tradition of political songs had perished. From a different perspective, we can see that for all movements many of the most appealing texts (and sometimes melodies) appear early in the life of a movement. Spontaneity plays its role early. The early songs fulfill various functions from the beginning and can become the basis for a lively tradition. Movements that fail to create songs in their early years are unlikely to create them at any time. What made the Nazi exploitation of music particularly striking was the combination of rank-and-file spontaneity with the eagerness of leaders to employ every possible device to manipulate public sentiment.

DATE DUE
